Matthew

ABOUT THE AUTHORS

General Editor:

Clinton E. Arnold (PhD, University of Aberdeen), professor and chairman, department of New Testament, Talbot School of Theology, Biola University, Los Angeles, California

Gospel of Matthew:

Michael J. Wilkins (PhD, Fuller Theological Seminary), professor of New Testament and dean of the faculty, Talbot School of Theology, Biola University, Los Angeles, California

Zondervan Illustrated Bible Backgrounds Commentary

Matthew

Michael J. Wilkins

Clinton E. Arnold   *general editor*

ZONDERVAN.com/
AUTHOR**TRACKER**
follow your favorite authors

Zondervan Illustrated Bible Backgrounds Commentary: Matthew
Copyright © 2002 by Michael J. Wilkins

Requests for information should be addressed to:

Zondervan, *Grand Rapids, Michigan 49530*

Library of Congress Cataloging-in-Publication Data
Zondervan illustrated Bible backgrounds commentary / Clinton E. Arnold, general editor.
    p.cm.
Includes bibliographical references.
ISBN 978-0-310-27831-3
1. Bible. N.T.—Commentaries.   I. Arnold, Clinton E.
BS2341.52.Z66 2001

225.7—dc21   2001046801

Printed in China

Interior design by Sherri L. Hoffman

---

08 09 10 11 12 13 • 12 11 10 9 8 7 6 5 4 3 2

CONTENTS

INTRODUCTION

All readers of the Bible have a tendency to view what it says it through their own culture and life circumstances. This can happen almost subconsiously as we read the pages of the text.

When most people in the church read about the thief on the cross, for instance, they immediately think of a burglar that held up a store or broke into a home. They may be rather shocked to find out that the guy was actually a Jewish revolutionary figure who was part of a growing movement in Palestine eager to throw off Roman rule.

It also comes as something of a surprise to contemporary Christians that "cursing" in the New Testament era had little or nothing to do with cussing somebody out. It had far more to do with the invocation of spirits to cause someone harm.

No doubt there is a need in the church for learning more about the world of the New Testament to avoid erroneous interpretations of the text of Scripture. But relevant historical and cultural insights also provide an added dimension of perspective to the words of the Bible. This kind of information often functions in the same way as watching a movie in color rather than in black and white. Finding out, for instance, how Paul compared Christ's victory on the cross to a joyous celebration parade in honor of a Roman general after winning an extraordinary battle brings does indeed magnify the profundity and implications of Jesus' work on the cross. Discovering that the factions at Corinth ("I follow Paul . . . I follow Apollos . . .") had plenty of precedent in the local cults ("I follow Aphrodite; I follow Apollo . . .") helps us understand the "why" of a particular problem. Learning about the water supply from the springs of Hierapolis that flowed into Laodicea as "lukewarm" water enables us to appreciate the relevance of the metaphor Jesus used when he addressed the spiritual laxity of this church.

My sense is that most Christians are eager to learn more about the real life setting of the New Testament. In the preaching and teaching of the Bible in the church, congregants are always grateful when they learn something of the background and historical context of the text. It not only helps them understand the text more accurately, but often enables them to identify with the people and circumstances of the Bible. I have been asked on countless occasions by Christians, "Where can I get access to good historical background information about this passage?" Earnest Christians are hungry for information that makes their Bibles come alive.

The stimulus for this commentary came from the church and the aim is to serve the church. The contributors to this series have sought to provide illuminating and interesting historical/cultural background information. The intent was to draw upon relevant papyri, inscriptions, archaeological discoveries, and the numerous studies of Judaism, Roman culture, Hellenism, and other features of the world of the New Testament and to make the results accessible to people in the church. We recognize that some readers of the commentary will want to go further, and so the sources of the information have been carefully documented in endnotes.

The written information has been supplemented with hundreds of photographs, maps, charts, artwork, and other graphics that help the reader better understand the world of the New Testament. Each of the writers was given an opportunity to dream up a "wish list" of illustrations that he thought would help to illustrate the passages in the New Testament book for which he was writing commentary. Although we were not able to obtain everything they were looking for, we came close.

The team of commentators are writing for the benefit of the broad array of Christians who simply want to better understand their Bibles from the vantage point of the historical context. This is an installment in a new genre of "Bible background" commentaries that was kicked off by Craig Keener's fine volume. Consequently, this is not an "exegetical" commentary that provides linguistic insight and background into Greek constructions and verb tenses. Neither is this work an "expository" commentary that provides a verse-by-verse exposition of the text; for in-depth philological or theological insight, readers will need to have other more specialized or comprehensive commentaries available. Nor is this an "historical-critical" commentary, although the contributors are all scholars and have already made substantial academic contributions on the New Testament books they are writing on for this set. The team intentionally does not engage all of the issues that are discussed in the scholarly guild.

Rather, our goal is to offer a reading and interpretation of the text informed by what we regard as the most relevant historical information. For many in the church, this commentary will serve as an important entry point into the interpretation and appreciation of the text. For other more serious students of the Word, these volumes will provide an important supplement to many of the fine exegetical, expository, and critical available.

The contributors represent a group of scholars who embrace the Bible as the Word of God and believe that the message of its pages has life-changing relevance for faith and practice today. Accordingly, we offer "Reflections" on the relevance of the Scripture to life for every chapter of the New Testament.

I pray that this commentary brings you both delight and insight in digging deeper into the Word of God.

Clinton E. Arnold
General Editor

LIST OF SIDEBARS

Matthew

LIST OF CHARTS

INDEX OF PHOTOS AND MAPS

ABBREVIATIONS

1. Books of the Bible and Apocrypha

1 Chron.	1 Chronicles
2 Chron.	2 Chronicles
1 Cor.	1 Corinthians
2 Cor.	2 Corinthians
1 Esd.	1 Esdras
2 Esd.	2 Esdras
1 John	1 John
2 John	2 John
3 John	3 John
1 Kings	1 Kings
2 Kings	2 Kings
1 Macc.	1 Maccabees
2 Macc.	2 Maccabees
1 Peter	1 Peter
2 Peter	2 Peter
1 Sam.	1 Samuel
2 Sam.	2 Samuel
1 Thess.	1 Thessalonians
2 Thess.	2 Thessalonians
1 Tim.	1 Timothy
2 Tim.	2 Timothy
Acts	Acts
Amos	Amos
Bar.	Baruch
Bel	Bel and the Dragon
Col.	Colossians
Dan.	Daniel
Deut.	Deuteronomy
Eccl.	Ecclesiastes
Ep. Jer.	Epistle of Jeremiah
Eph.	Ephesians
Est.	Esther
Ezek.	Ezekiel
Ex.	Exodus
Ezra	Ezra
Gal.	Galatians
Gen.	Genesis
Hab.	Habakkuk
Hag.	Haggai
Heb.	Hebrews
Hos.	Hosea
Isa.	Isaiah
James	James
Jer.	Jeremiah
Job	Job
Joel	Joel
John	John
Jonah	Jonah
Josh.	Joshua
Jude	Jude
Judg.	Judges
Judith	Judith
Lam.	Lamentations
Lev.	Leviticus
Luke	Luke
Mal.	Malachi
Mark	Mark
Matt.	Matthew
Mic.	Micah
Nah.	Nahum
Neh.	Nehemiah
Num.	Numbers
Obad.	Obadiah
Phil.	Philippians
Philem.	Philemon
Pr. Man.	Prayer of Manassah
Prov.	Proverbs
Ps.	Psalm
Rest. of Est.	The Rest of Esther
Rev.	Revelation
Rom.	Romans
Ruth	Ruth
S. of III Ch.	The Song of the Three Holy Children
Sir.	Sirach/Ecclesiasticus
Song	Song of Songs
Sus.	Susanna
Titus	Titus
Tobit	Tobit
Wisd. Sol.	The Wisdom of Solomon
Zech.	Zechariah
Zeph.	Zephaniah

2. Old and New Testament Pseudepigrapha and Rabbinic Literature

Individual tractates of rabbinic literature follow the abbreviations of the *SBL Handbook of Style*, pp. 79–80. Qumran documents follow standard Dead Sea Scroll conventions.

2 Bar.	*2 Baruch*
3 Bar.	*3 Baruch*
4 Bar.	*4 Baruch*
1 En.	*1 Enoch*
2 En.	*2 Enoch*
3 En.	*3 Enoch*
4 Ezra	*4 Ezra*
3 Macc.	*3 Maccabees*
4 Macc.	*4 Maccabees*
5 Macc.	*5 Maccabees*
Acts Phil.	*Acts of Philip*

Acts Pet.	Acts of Peter and the 12 Apostles
Apoc. Elijah	Apocalypse of Elijah
As. Mos.	Assumption of Moses
b.	Babylonian Talmud (+ tractate)
Gos. Thom.	Gospel of Thomas
Jos. Asen.	Joseph and Aseneth
Jub.	Jubilees
Let. Aris.	Letter of Aristeas
m.	Mishnah (+ tractate)
Mek.	Mekilta
Midr.	Midrash I (+ biblical book)
Odes Sol.	Odes of Solomon
Pesiq. Rab.	Pesiqta Rabbati
Pirqe. R. El.	Pirqe Rabbi Eliezer
Pss. Sol.	Psalms of Solomon
Rab.	Rabbah (+biblical book); (e.g., Gen. Rab.=Genesis Rabbah)
S. ʿOlam Rab.	Seder ʿOlam Rabbah
Sem.	Semahot
Sib. Or.	Sibylline Oracles
T. Ab.	Testament of Abraham
T. Adam	Testament of Adam
T. Ash.	Testament of Asher
T. Benj.	Testament of Benjamin
T. Dan	Testament of Dan
T. Gad	Testament of Gad
T. Hez.	Testament of Hezekiah
T. Isaac	Testament of Isaac
T. Iss.	Testament of Issachar
T. Jac.	Testament of Jacob
T. Job	Testament of Job
T. Jos.	Testament of Joseph
T. Jud.	Testament of Judah
T. Levi	Testament of Levi
T. Mos.	Testament of Moses
T. Naph.	Testament of Naphtali
T. Reu.	Testament of Reuben
T. Sim.	Testament of Simeon
T. Sol.	Testament of Solomon
T. Zeb.	Testament of Zebulum
Tanh.	Tanhuma
Tg. Isa.	Targum of Isaiah
Tg. Lam.	Targum of Lamentations
Tg. Neof.	Targum Neofiti
Tg. Onq.	Targum Onqelos
Tg. Ps.-J	Targum Pseudo-Jonathan
y.	Jerusalem Talmud (+ tractate)

3. Classical Historians

For an extended list of classical historians and church fathers, see *SBL Handbook of Style*, pp. 84–87. For many works of classical antiquity, the abbreviations have been subjected to the author's discretion; the names of these works should be obvious upon consulting entries of the classical writers in classical dictionaries or encyclopedias.

Eusebius

Eccl. Hist.	Ecclesiastical History

Josephus

Ag. Ap.	Against Apion
Ant.	Jewish Antiquities
J.W.	Jewish War
Life	The Life

Philo

Abraham	On the Life of Abraham
Agriculture	On Agriculture
Alleg. Interp	Allegorical Interpretation
Animals	Whether Animals Have Reason
Cherubim	On the Cherubim
Confusion	On the Confusion of Thomas
Contempl. Life	On the Contemplative Life
Creation	On the Creation of the World
Curses	On Curses
Decalogue	On the Decalogue
Dreams	On Dreams
Drunkenness	On Drunkenness
Embassy	On the Embassy to Gaius
Eternity	On the Eternity of the World
Flaccus	Against Flaccus
Flight	On Flight and Finding
Giants	On Giants
God	On God
Heir	Who Is the Heir?
Hypothetica	Hypothetica
Joseph	On the Life of Joseph
Migration	On the Migration of Abraham
Moses	On the Life of Moses
Names	On the Change of Names
Person	That Every Good Person Is Free
Planting	On Planting
Posterity	On the Posterity of Cain
Prelim. Studies	On the Preliminary Studies
Providence	On Providence
QE	Questions and Answers on Exodus
QG	Questions and Answers on Genesis
Rewards	On Rewards and Punishments
Sacrifices	On the Sacrifices of Cain and Abel
Sobriety	On Sobriety
Spec. Laws	On the Special Laws
Unchangeable	That God Is Unchangeable
Virtues	On the Virtues
Worse	That the Worse Attacks the Better

Apostolic Fathers

1 Clem.	First Letter of Clement
Barn.	Epistle of Barnabas
Clem. Hom.	Ancient Homily of Clement (also called 2 Clement)

Did.	*Didache*
Herm. Vis.;	*Shepherd of Hermas,*
Sim.	*Visions; Similitudes*
Ignatius	*Epistles of Ignatius* (followed by the letter's name)
Mart. Pol.	*Martyrdom of Polycarp*

4. Modern Abbreviations

AASOR	Annual of the American Schools of Oriental Research
AB	Anchor Bible
ABD	*Anchor Bible Dictionary*
ABRL	Anchor Bible Reference Library
AGJU	Arbeiten zur Geschichte des antiken Judentums und des Urchristentums
AH	*Agricultural History*
ALGHJ	Arbeiten zur Literatur und Geschichte des Hellenistischen Judentums
AnBib	Analecta biblica
ANRW	*Aufstieg und Niedergang der römischen Welt*
ANTC	Abingdon New Testament Commentaries
BAGD	Bauer, W., W. F. Arndt, F. W. Gingrich, and F. W. Danker. *Greek-English Lexicon of the New Testament and Other Early Christina Literature* (2d. ed.)
BA	*Biblical Archaeologist*
BAFCS	Book of Acts in Its First Century Setting
BAR	*Biblical Archaeology Review*
BASOR	*Bulletin of the American Schools of Oriental Research*
BBC	*Bible Background Commentary*
BBR	*Bulletin for Biblical Research*
BDB	Brown, F., S. R. Driver, and C. A. Briggs. *A Hebrew and English Lexicon of the Old Testament*
BDF	Blass, F., A. Debrunner, and R. W. Funk. *A Greek Grammar of the New Testament and Other Early Christian Literature*
BECNT	Baker Exegetical Commentary on the New Testament
BI	*Biblical Illustrator*
Bib	*Biblica*
BibSac	*Bibliotheca Sacra*
BLT	Brethren Life and Thought
BNTC	Black's New Testament Commentary
BRev	*Bible Review*
BSHJ	Baltimore Studies in the History of Judaism
BST	The Bible Speaks Today
BSV	Biblical Social Values
BT	*The Bible Translator*

BTB	*Biblical Theology Bulletin*
BZ	*Biblische Zeitschrift*
CBQ	*Catholic Biblical Quarterly*
CBTJ	*Calvary Baptist Theological Journal*
CGTC	Cambridge Greek Testament Commentary
CH	*Church History*
CIL	*Corpus inscriptionum latinarum*
CPJ	*Corpus papyrorum judaicorum*
CRINT	*Compendia rerum iudaicarum ad Novum Testamentum*
CTJ	*Calvin Theological Journal*
CTM	*Concordia Theological Monthly*
CTT	Contours of Christian Theology
DBI	*Dictionary of Biblical Imagery*
DCM	*Dictionary of Classical Mythology.*
DDD	*Dictionary of Deities and Demons in the Bible*
DJBP	*Dictionary of Judaism in the Biblical Period*
DJG	*Dictionary of Jesus and the Gospels*
DLNT	*Dictionary of the Later New Testament and Its Developments*
DNTB	*Dictionary of New Testament Background*
DPL	*Dictionary of Paul and His Letters*
EBC	*Expositor's Bible Commentary*
EDBT	*Evangelical Dictionary of Biblical Theology*
EDNT	*Exegetical Dictionary of the New Testament*
EJR	*Encyclopedia of the Jewish Religion*
EPRO	Études préliminaires aux religions orientales dans l'empire romain
EvQ	*Evangelical Quarterly*
ExpTim	*Expository Times*
FRLANT	Forsuchungen zur Religion und Literatur des Alten und Neuen Testament
GNC	Good News Commentary
GNS	Good News Studies
HCNT	*Hellenistic Commentary to the New Testament*
HDB	*Hastings Dictionary of the Bible*
HJP	*History of the Jewish People in the Age of Jesus Christ,* by E. Schürer
HTR	*Harvard Theological Review*
HTS	Harvard Theological Studies
HUCA	*Hebrew Union College Annual*
IBD	*Illustrated Bible Dictionary*
IBS	*Irish Biblical Studies*
ICC	International Critical Commentary

IDB	*The Interpreter's Dictionary of the Bible*
IEJ	*Israel Exploration Journal*
IG	*Inscriptiones graecae*
IGRR	*Inscriptiones graecae ad res romanas pertinentes*
ILS	*Inscriptiones Latinae Selectae*
Imm	*Immanuel*
ISBE	*International Standard Bible Encyclopedia*
Int	*Interpretation*
IvE	*Inschriften von Ephesos*
IVPNTC	InterVarsity Press New Testament Commentary
JAC	*Jahrbuch fur Antike und Christentum*
JBL	*Journal of Biblical Literature*
JETS	*Journal of the Evangelical Theological Society*
JHS	*Journal of Hellenic Studies*
JJS	*Journal of Jewish Studies*
JOAIW	*Jahreshefte des Osterreeichischen Archaologischen Instites in Wien*
JSJ	*Journal for the Study of Judaism in the Persian, Hellenistic, and Roman Periods*
JRS	*Journal of Roman Studies*
JSNT	*Journal for the Study of the New Testament*
JSNTSup	Journal for the Study of the New Testament: Supplement Series
JSOT	*Journal for the Study of the Old Testament*
JSOTSup	Journal for the Study of the Old Testament: Supplement Series
JTS	*Journal of Theological Studies*
KTR	*Kings Theological Review*
LCL	Loeb Classical Library
LEC	Library of Early Christianity
LSJ	Liddell, H. G., R. Scott, H. S. Jones. *A Greek-English Lexicon*
MM	Moulton, J. H., and G. Milligan. *The Vocabulary of the Greek Testament*
MNTC	Moffatt New Testament Commentary
NBD	*New Bible Dictionary*
NC	Narrative Commentaries
NCBC	New Century Bible Commentary Eerdmans
NEAE	*New Encyclopedia of Archaeological Excavations in the Holy Land*
NEASB	*Near East Archaeological Society Bulletin*
New Docs	*New Documents Illustrating Early Christianity*
NIBC	New International Biblical Commentary
NICNT	New International Commentary on the New Testament
NIDNTT	*New International Dictionary of New Testament Theology*
NIGTC	New International Greek Testament Commentary
NIVAC	NIV Application Commentary
NorTT	*Norsk Teologisk Tidsskrift*
NoT	*Notes on Translation*
NovT	*Novum Testamentum*
NovTSup	Novum Testamentum Supplements
NTAbh	Neutestamentliche Abhandlungen
NTS	*New Testament Studies*
NTT	New Testament Theology
NTTS	New Testament Tools and Studies
OAG	*Oxford Archaeological Guides*
OCCC	*Oxford Companion to Classical Civilization*
OCD	*Oxford Classical Dictionary*
ODCC	*The Oxford Dictionary of the Christian Church*
OGIS	*Orientis graeci inscriptiones selectae*
OHCW	*The Oxford History of the Classical World*
OHRW	*Oxford History of the Roman World*
OTP	*Old Testament Pseudepigrapha,* ed. by J. H. Charlesworth
PEQ	*Palestine Exploration Quarterly*
PG	*Patrologia graeca*
PGM	*Papyri graecae magicae: Die griechischen Zauberpapyri*
PL	*Patrologia latina*
PNTC	Pelican New Testament Commentaries
Rb	*Revista biblica*
RB	*Revue biblique*
RivB	*Rivista biblica italiana*
RTR	*Reformed Theological Review*
SB	Sources bibliques
SBL	Society of Biblical Literature
SBLDS	Society of Biblical Literature Dissertation Series
SBLMS	Society of Biblical Literature Monograph Series
SBLSP	*Society of Biblical Literature Seminar Papers*
SBS	Stuttgarter Bibelstudien
SBT	Studies in Biblical Theology
SCJ	*Stone-Campbell Journal*
Scr	*Scripture*
SE	*Studia Evangelica*
SEG	*Supplementum epigraphicum graecum*

SJLA	Studies in Judaism in Late Antiquity
SJT	*Scottish Journal of Theology*
SNTSMS	Society for New Testament Studies Monograph Series
SSC	Social Science Commentary
SSCSSG	Social-Science Commentary on the Synoptic Gospels
Str-B	Strack, H. L., and P. Billerbeck. *Kommentar zum Neuen Testament aus Talmud und Midrasch*
TC	Thornapple Commentaries
TDNT	*Theological Dictionary of the New Testament*
TDOT	*Theological Dictionary of the Old Testament*
TLNT	*Theological Lexicon of the New Testament*
TLZ	*Theologische Literaturzeitung*
TNTC	Tyndale New Testament Commentary
TrinJ	*Trinity Journal*
TS	*Theological Studies*
TSAJ	Texte und Studien zum antiken Judentum
TWNT	*Theologische Wörterbuch zum Neuen Testament*
TynBul	*Tyndale Bulletin*
WBC	Word Biblical Commentary Waco: Word, 1982
WMANT	Wissenschaftliche Monographien zum Alten und Neuen Testament
WUNT	Wissenschaftliche Untersuchungen zum Neuen Testament
YJS	Yale Judaica Series
ZNW	*Zeitschrift fur die neutestamentliche Wissenschaft und die Junde der alteren Kirche*
ZPE	*Zeischrift der Papyrolgie und Epigraphkik*
ZPEB	*Zondervan Pictorial Encyclopedia of the Bible*

5. General Abbreviations

ad. loc.	in the place cited
b.	born
c., ca.	circa
cf.	compare
d.	died
ed(s).	editors(s), edited by
e.g.	for example
ET	English translation
frg.	fragment
i.e.	that is
ibid.	in the same place
idem	the same (author)
lit.	literally
l(l)	line(s)
MSS	manuscripts
n.d.	no date
NS	New Series
par.	parallel
passim	here and there
repr.	reprint
ser.	series
s.v.	*sub verbo*, under the word
trans.	translator, translated by; transitive

Zondervan Illustrated Bible Backgrounds Commentary

MATTHEW

by Michael J. Wilkins

Introduction to The Gospel According to Matthew

On the surface of the Mediterranean world lay the famed *pax Romana*, "the peace of Rome," which the Roman historian Tacitus attributes almost solely to the immense powers of Caesar Augustus. But as Tacitus observes, the "peace" that Augustus inaugurated did not bring with it freedom for all of his subjects; many continued to hope for change.[1] Tides of revolution swirled just below the surface and periodically rose to disturb the so-called peace of the Roman empire.

In one of the remote regions of the empire, where a variety of disturbances repeatedly surfaced, the hoped for freedom finally arrived in a most unexpected way. A rival to Augustus was born in Israel. But this rival did not appear with fanfare, nor would he challenge directly the military and political might of Rome. Even many of his own people would become disappointed with

MOUNT OF BEATITUDES

Overlooking the Sea of Galilee

◀

▶ Matthew
IMPORTANT FACTS:

- **AUTHOR:** While technically anonymous, the first book of the New Testament canon was unanimously attributed by the early church to Matthew-Levi, one of the Twelve apostles of Jesus Christ.
- **DATE:** A.D. 60–61 (Paul imprisoned in Rome).
- **OCCASION:** Matthew addresses a church that is representative of the emerging Christian community of faith—it transcends ethnic, economic, and religious barriers to find oneness in its adherence to Jesus Messiah. His Gospel becomes a manual on discipleship to Jesus, as Jew and Gentile alike form a new community in an increasingly hostile world.
- **PORTRAIT OF CHRIST:** Jesus is the true Messiah, Immanuel, God-incarnate with his people.
- **KEY THEMES:**
  1. The bridge between Old and New Testaments.
  2. Salvation-historical "particularism" and "universalism."
  3. The new community of faith.
  4. The church built and maintained by Jesus' continuing presence.
  5. A "great commission" for evangelism and mission.
  6. The structure of five discourses contributes to a manual on discipleship.

the revolution that he would bring, because it was a revolution of the heart, not of swords or chariots.

This is the story of the arrival of Jesus of Nazareth, recorded by the apostle Matthew as a compelling witness that Jesus was the long-anticipated Messiah, the prophesied fulfillment of God's promise of true peace and deliverance for both Jew and Gentile.

Author

All of the four Gospels are technically anonymous, since the names of the authors are not stated explicitly. This is natural since the authors were not writing letters to which are attached the names of the addressees and senders. Rather, the evangelists were compiling stories of Jesus for churches of which they were active participants and leaders. They likely stood among the assembly and first read their Gospel account themselves. To attach their names as authors would have been unnecessary, because their audiences knew their identity, or perhaps even inappropriate, since the primary intention was not to assert their own leadership authority, but to record for their audiences the matchless story of the life and ministry of Jesus.

Therefore we must look to the records of church history to find evidence for the authorship of the Gospels. The earliest church tradition unanimously ascribes the first Gospel to Matthew, the tax-collector who was called to be one of the original twelve disciples of Jesus. The earliest and most important of these traditions come from Papias, bishop of Hierapolis in Asia Minor (c. 135), and from Irenaeus, bishop of Lyons in Gaul (c. 175). These church leaders either knew the apostolic community directly or were taught by those associated with the apostles; thus, they were directly aware of the origins of the Gospels. While the full meaning of their statements is still open to discussion, no competing tradition assigning the first Gospel to any other author has survived, if any ever existed. False ascription to a relatively obscure apostle such as Matthew seems unlikely until a later date, when canonization of apostles was common.

Matthew, the Person

The list of the twelve disciples in Matthew's gospel refers to "Matthew the tax collector" (10:3), which harks back to the incident when Jesus called Matthew

---

▶ **Early Church Testimony to Matthean Authorship**

Papias, bishop of Hierapolis in Asia Minor, lived approximately A.D. 60–130. It is claimed that Papias was a hearer of the apostle John and later was a companion of Polycarp.[A-1] He was quoted and endorsed by the church historian Eusebius (c. A.D. 325) as saying: "Matthew for his part compiled/collected the oracles in the Hebrew [Aramaic] dialect and every person translated/interpreted them as he was able" (Eusebius, *Eccl. Hist.* 3.39.16).

Irenaeus, bishop of Lyons in Gaul, was born in Asia Minor in approximately A.D. 135, studied under Polycarp, bishop of Smyrna, and according to tradition died as a martyr around A.D. 200. In one of his five monumental books against the Gnostic heresies, Irenaeus states, "Matthew also issued a written Gospel among the Hebrews in their own dialect, while Peter and Paul were preaching at Rome, and laying the foundations of the Church."[A-2]

while he was sitting in the tax office (cf. 9:9). When recounting the call, the first Gospel refers to him as "Matthew" (9:9), while Mark's Gospel refers to him as "Levi son of Alphaeus" (Mark 2:14), and Luke's Gospel refers to him as "Levi" (Luke 5:27). Speculation surrounds the reason for the variation, but most scholars suggest that this tax collector had two names, Matthew Levi, either from birth or from the time of his conversion.

The name Levi may be an indication that he was from the tribe of Levi and therefore was familiar with Levitical practices. Mark's record of the calling refers to him as the "son of Alphaeus" (Mark 2:14), which some have understood to mean that he was the brother of the apostle "James son of Alphaeus" (cf. Mark 3:18). But since the other pairs of brothers are specified as such and linked together, it is unlikely that Matthew-Levi and James were brothers.

Matthew-Levi was called to follow Jesus while he was sitting in the tax collector's booth. This booth was probably located on one of the main trade highways near Capernaum, collecting tolls for Herod Antipas from the commercial traffic traveling through this area. Matthew immediately followed Jesus and arranged a banquet for Jesus at his home, to which were invited a large crowd of tax collectors and sinners (9:10–11; Luke 5:29–30). Since tax collectors generally were fairly wealthy and were despised by the local populace (cf. Zacchaeus, Luke 19:1–10), Matthew's calling and response were completely out of the ordinary and required nothing short of a miraculous turn-around in this tax collector's life.

Little else is known of Matthew-Levi, except for the widely attested tradition that he is the author of this Gospel that now bears his name. As a tax collector he would have been trained in secular scribal techniques, and as a Galilean Jewish Christian he would have been able to interpret the life of Jesus from the perspective of the Old Testament expectations. Eusebius said that Matthew first preached to "Hebrews" and then to "others," including places such as Persia, Parthia, and Syria (Eusebius, *Eccl. Hist.* 3.24.6). The traditions are mixed regarding Matthew's death, with some saying that he died a martyr's death, while others saying that he died a natural death.

Date and Destination

No precise date for the writing of Matthew is known, although Jesus' prophecy of the overthrow of Jerusalem (24:1–28), has recently been used to indicate that this Gospel must have been written after A.D. 70. However, such a conclusion is necessary only if one denies Jesus the

PAPYRUS MANUSCRIPT OF MATTHEW 26:19–52

This is a third-century A.D. fragment known as *p³⁷* now housed at the University of Michigan.

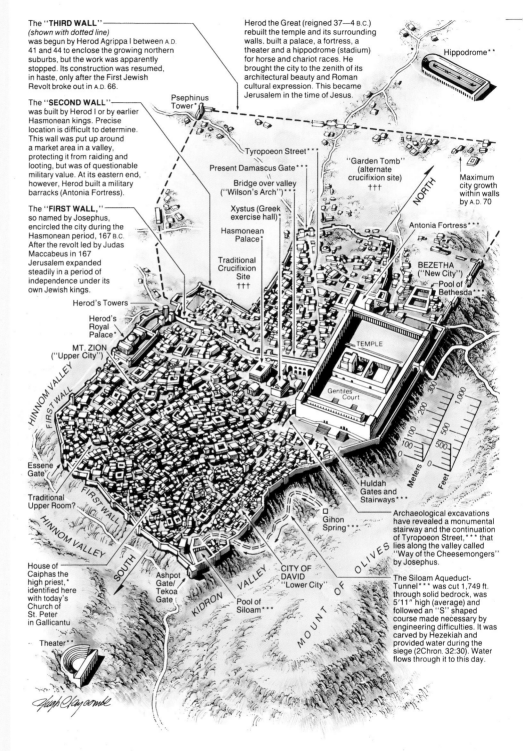

The **"THIRD WALL"** ———
(shown with dotted line)
was begun by Herod Agrippa I between A.D. 41 and 44 to enclose the growing northern suburbs, but the work was apparently stopped. Its construction was resumed, in haste, only after the First Jewish Revolt broke out in A.D. 66.

The **"SECOND WALL"** ———
was built by Herod I or by earlier Hasmonean kings. Precise location is difficult to determine. This wall was put up around a market area in a valley, protecting it from raiding and looting, but was of questionable military value. At its eastern end, however, Herod built a military barracks (Antonia Fortress).

The **"FIRST WALL,"**
so named by Josephus, encircled the city during the Hasmonean period, 167 B.C. After the revolt led by Judas Maccabeus in 167 Jerusalem expanded steadily in a period of independence under its own Jewish kings.

Herod the Great (reigned 37—4 B.C.) rebuilt the temple and its surrounding walls, built a palace, a fortress, a theater and a hippodrome (stadium) for horse and chariot races. He brought the city to the zenith of its architectural beauty and Roman cultural expression. This became Jerusalem in the time of Jesus.

Hippodrome**

Psephinus Tower*

Tyropoeon Street***

Present Damascus Gate***

Bridge over valley ("Wilson's Arch")***

Xystus (Greek exercise hall)*

Hasmonean Palace*

Traditional Crucifixion Site †††

"Garden Tomb" (alternate crucifixion site) †††

NORTH

Maximum city growth within walls by A.D. 70

Antonia Fortress***

BEZETHA ("New City")

Pool of Bethesda***

Herod's Towers

Herod's Royal Palace*

MT. ZION ("Upper City")

HINNOM VALLEY

FIRST WALL

TEMPLE

Gentiles Court

Essene Gate*

Traditional Upper Room?

FIRST WALL

HINNOM VALLEY

SOUTH

Ashpot Gate/ Tekoa Gate

House of Caiphas the high priest,* identified here with today's Church of St. Peter in Gallicantu

Theater**

KIDRON VALLEY

Pool of Siloam***

CITY OF DAVID "Lower City"

Gihon Spring***

Huldah Gates and Stairways***

MOUNT OF OLIVES

Meters / Feet scale: 0 100 200 300 / 0 500 1,000

Archaeological excavations have revealed a monumental stairway and the continuation of Tyropoeon Street,*** that lies along the valley called "Way of the Cheesemongers" by Josephus.

The Siloam Aqueduct-Tunnel*** was cut 1,749 ft. through solid bedrock, was 5'11" high (average) and followed an "S" shaped course made necessary by engineering difficulties. It was carved by Hezekiah and provided water during the siege (2Chron. 32:30). Water flows through it to this day.

* Location generally known, but style of architecture is unknown; artist's concept only, and Roman architecture is assumed.

** Location and architecture unknown, but referred to in written history; shown here for illustrative purposes.

*** Ancient feature has remained, or appearance has been determined from evidence.

Buildings, streets and roads shown here are artist's concept only unless otherwise named and located. Wall heights remain generally unknown, except for those surrounding the Temple Mount.

ability to predict the future. Since the early church father Irenaeus (c. A.D. 175) indicates that Matthew wrote his Gospel while Paul and Peter were still alive,[2] the traditional dating has usually settled on the late 50s or early 60s.

The highly influential church at Antioch in Syria, with its large Jewish-Christian and Gentile contingents (cf. Acts 11:19–26; 13:1–3), has often been recognized as the original recipients of this Gospel. This is confirmed in part because of its influence on Ignatius, the bishop of Antioch, and on the *Didache*. But Matthew's message was equally relevant for the fledgling church throughout the ancient world, and appears to have been disseminated fairly quickly.

Purpose in Writing

Matthew's first verse gives the direction to his purpose for writing: It is a book that establishes Jesus' identity as the Messiah, the heir to the promises of Israel's throne through King David and to the promises of blessing to all the nations through the patriarch Abraham. Against the backdrop of a world increasingly hostile to Christianity, Matthew solidifies his church's identity as God's true people, who transcend ethnic, economic, and religious barriers to find oneness in their adherence to Jesus Messiah. His gospel becomes a manual on discipleship, as Jew and Gentile become disciples of Jesus who learn to obey all he commanded his original disciples.

Matthew's Story of Jesus Messiah

Matthew's Gospel, according to citations found in early Christian writers, was the most widely used and influential of any of the Gospels.[3] It has retained its appeal throughout the centuries and has exerted a powerful influence on the church. Its popularity is explained at least in part because of the following distinctives that are found throughout this gospel.

(1) The bridge between Old and New Testaments. From the opening lines of his story, Matthew provides a natural bridge between the Old Testament and New Testament. He demonstrates repeatedly that Old Testament hopes, prophecies, and promises have now been fulfilled in the person and ministry of Jesus, beginning with the "fulfillment" of the messianic genealogy (1:1), the fulfillment of various Old Testament prophecies and themes, and the fulfillment of the Old Testament law.[4] The early church likely placed Matthew first in the New Testament canon precisely because of its value as a bridge between the Testaments.

(2) Salvation-historical "particularism" and "universalism." These terms emphasize that Matthew's Gospel lays striking emphasis on both the fulfillment of the promises of salvation to a particular people, Israel, and also the fulfillment of the universal promise of salvation to all the peoples of the earth. Matthew's Gospel alone points explicitly to Jesus' intention to go first to the lost sheep of the house of Israel (10:5–6; 15:24), showing historically how God's promise of salvation to Israel was indeed fulfilled. Yet the promises made to Abraham that he would be a blessing to all the nations are also fulfilled as Jesus extends salvation to the Gentiles (cf. 21:44; 28:19). The church throughout the ages has found assurance in Matthew's Gospel that God truly keeps his promises to his people.

(3) The new community of faith. Facing the threat of gathering Roman persecution within a pagan world, Matthew addresses a church that is representative of the emerging community of faith. The community apparently has a large membership of Jewish Christians, familiar with temple activities and the Jewish religious system. But it also has a large contingent of Gentile Christians, who are discovering their heritage of faith in God's universal promise of salvation. The church has consistently found in Matthew's Gospel a call to a new community that transcends ethnic and religious barriers to find oneness in its adherence to Jesus Messiah.

(4) The church is built and maintained by Jesus' continuing presence. Matthew alone among the evangelists uses the term *ekklēsia*, which later became the common term to designate the church. He emphasizes explicitly that God's program of salvation-history will find its continuation in the present age as Jesus builds his church and maintains his presence within its assembly.[5] Whoever responds to his invitation (22:10)—whether Jew or Gentile, male or female, rich or poor, slave or free—are brought within the church to enjoy his fellowship and demonstrate the true community of faith.

(5) A "great commission" for evangelism and mission. The form of Jesus' commission to "make disciples of all the nations" (28:19) is unique to Matthew's Gospel, providing continuity between Jesus' ministry of making disciples in his earthly ministry and the ongoing ministry of making disciples to which the church has been called. This "great commission" has been at the heart of evangelistic and missionary endeavor throughout church history.

(6) The structure of five discourses contributes to a manual on discipleship. The concluding element of the commission, in which Jesus states that new disciples are to be taught "to obey everything I have commanded you" (28:20), gives a hint to one overall purpose for Matthew's Gospel. The presentation of five of Jesus' major discourses, all of which are addressed at least in part to Jesus' disciples (chs. 5–7, 10, 13, 18, 24–25), forms the most comprehensive collection of Jesus' earthly instructional ministry found in the Gospels. They provide a wholistic presentation on the kind of discipleship that was to be taught to disciples as the basis for full-orbed obedience to Christ and became the basis for Christian catechesis within the church throughout its history.

The Geneaology of Jesus Messiah (1:1–17)

This is the story of the arrival of Jesus of Nazareth, recorded as a compelling witness that Jesus was the long-anticipated Messiah, the prophesied fulfillment of

THE COURT OF THE PRIESTS IN HEROD'S TEMPLE

This model shows the altar and the bronze laver.

▼

God's promise of deliverance for both Jew and Gentile.

A record of the genealogy of Jesus Christ (1:1). The Greek word translated "genealogy" in 1:1 is *genesis*, "beginning," which is the title of the Greek translation (LXX) of Genesis, where it implies that it is a book of beginnings. Genesis gave the story of one beginning—God's creation and covenant relations with Israel—while Matthew gives the story of a new beginning—the arrival of Jesus the Messiah and the kingdom of God.

Jesus Christ the son of David, the son of Abraham (1:1). Matthew's opening had special importance to a Jewish audience, which traced their ancestry through the covenants God made with Israel. "Jesus" (*Iēsous*) was the name normally used in the Gospels,[6] derived from the Hebrew *Yeshua*, "Yahweh saves" (Neh. 7:7), which is a shortened form of Joshua, "Yahweh is salvation" (Ex. 24:13). "Christ" is a title, the transliteration of the Greek *Christos*,[7] which harks back to David as the anointed king of Israel. The term came to be associated with the promise of a Messiah or "anointed one" who would be the hope for the people of Israel. God had promised David through Nathan the prophet that the house and throne of David would be established forever (2 Sam. 7:11b–16), a promise now fulfilled in Jesus as the "son of David." But Jesus is also the "son of Abraham." The covenant God made with Abraham established Israel as a chosen people, but it was also a promise that his line would be a blessing to all the nations (Gen. 12:1–3; 22:18).

Abraham the father of Isaac (1:2). The Jews kept extensive genealogies, which served generally as a record of a family's descendants, but which were also used for practical and legal purposes to establish a person's heritage, inheritance, legitimacy, and rights.[8]

Matthew most likely draws on some of the genealogies found in the Old Testament[9] and uses similar wording (cf. 1:2 with 2 Chron. 1:34). For the listing of the individuals after Zerubbabel, when the Old Testament ceases, he probably uses records that have since been lost. Other sources indicate that extensive genealogical records were extant during the first century,[10] with some of the more important political and priestly families' records kept in the temple.[11] The official extrabiblical genealogies were lost with the destruction of the temple and

REFLECTIONS

THE GENUINENESS, AND UN-likeliness, of this genealogy must have stunned Matthew's readers. Jesus' ancestors were humans with all of the foibles, yet potentials, of everyday people. God worked through them to bring about his salvation. There is no pattern of righteousness in the lineage of Jesus. We find adulterers, harlots, heroes, and Gentiles. Wicked Rehoboam was the father of wicked Abijah, who was the father of good King Asa. Asa was the father of the good King Jehoshaphat (v. 8), who was the father of wicked King Joram. God was working throughout the generations, both good and evil, to bring about his purposes. Matthew shows that God can use anyone—however marginalized or despised—to bring about his purposes. These are the very types of people Jesus came to save.

Jerusalem in A.D. 70, yet private genealogies were retained elsewhere.

Matthew gives a descending genealogy of Jesus in the order of succession, with the earliest ancestor placed at the head and later generations placed in lines of descent. This is the more common form of genealogy in the Old Testament (e.g., Gen. 5:1–32). Luke gives an ascending form of genealogy that reverses the order, starting with Jesus and tracing it to Adam (Luke 3:23–38; cf. Ezra 7:1–5). This reverse order is found more commonly in Greco-Roman genealogies.

Jesse [was] the father of King David. David was the father of Solomon (1:6). David is not simply the son of Jesse (Luke 3:31–32), but "King" (Matt. 1:6). Matthew traces Jesus' genealogy through David's son Solomon, who had succeeded his father as king of Israel, while Luke traces the line through David's son Nathan, who had not actually reigned as king.[12] David's greater Son, the anticipated Davidic messianic king, has arrived with the birth of Jesus.[13]

Tamar ... Rahab ... Ruth ... whose mother had been Uriah's wife ... Mary (1:3, 5, 6, 16). Women were not always included in Old Testament genealogies since descent was traced through men as the head of the family. When women were included, there was usually some particular reason.[14] Matthew seems to emphasize that these women, some of whom were Gentiles, others disreputable, and others wrongfully treated because of their gender, each had a role to play in the line of Messiah. By including them in this genealogy Matthew shows that God is reversing the gender marginalization of women found in some circles in Judaism to bring about his purposes.

Jacob the father of Joseph, the husband of Mary, of whom was born Jesus, who is called Christ (1:16). While the genealogy establishes that Joseph is the legal father of Jesus, Matthew emphasizes that Mary is the biological parent "of whom" Jesus was born, preparing for the virgin birth by shifting attention from Joseph to Mary.

Thus there were fourteen generations (1:17). Matthew skips some generations in Jesus' family tree so that the structure can be made uniform for memorization, while other members are given prominence to make a particular point. The number fourteen may be a subtle reference to David, because the numerical value of the Hebrew consonants of his name is fourteen (d w d = 4+6+4). The Jewish practice of counting the numerical value for letters is called *gematria*. Some forms of Jewish mysticism took the practice to extremes,[15] but its most basic form helped in memorization and for encoding theological meaning.

The Angelic Announcement of the Conception of Jesus Messiah (1:18–25)

Joseph her husband was a righteous man (1:19). Joseph first learns of Mary's condition without knowing of the concep-

tion's supernatural origin, and therefore, as a righteous man, it is appropriate to obtain a certificate of divorce because he thinks that she has committed adultery. Once Joseph discovers that Mary is pregnant, he experiences a personal dilemma. Divorce for adultery was not optional, but mandatory, among many groups in ancient Judaism, because adultery produced a state of impurity that, as a matter of legal fact, dissolved the marriage.

He had in mind to divorce her quietly (1:19). Joseph cannot follow through and marry her, because that would condone what he thinks is her sin of adultery. Therefore Joseph has only two options open to him. He can make Mary's condition known publicly—but then she will be subject to widespread disgrace as an adulteress, and it can make her liable to be stoned as an adulteress according to the demands of the law.[16] Or he can divorce her quietly—the only option that allows him to retain his righteousness and yet save Mary from public disgrace and possible death. Since the law did not require the deed to be made public, it

---

▶ Jewish Marriage Customs: Betrothal and Wedding

The marriage customs of Jewish culture at that time usually included two basic stages of the relationship, the betrothal and the wedding.[A-3]

(1) Betrothal (or engagement). The first stage of betrothal[A-4] was the choosing of a spouse. The family in ancient Near Eastern culture usually initiated the arrangements. Although we find in the Old Testament examples of young men and women making their preferences known (Ruth 2–4), customarily the parents of a young man chose a young woman to be engaged to their son (e.g., Gen. 21:21; 38:6). Young men and women were often pledged between twelve and thirteen years of age, although later rabbinic texts suggest that men in Jesus' day often married around the age of eighteen.[A-5]

The second stage of betrothal involved the official arrangements. In a formal prenuptial agreement before witnesses, the young man and woman entered into the state of betrothal or engagement. This was a legally binding contract, giving the man legal rights over the woman. It could only be broken by a formal process of divorce.[A-6] The terminology "husband" and "wife" were now used to refer to the betrothed partners (see 1:16, 19, 20, 24). While there is some evidence in Judea of the betrothed couple being alone during this interval at the man's father's home,[A-7] in Galilee sexual relations between the betrothed partners were not tolerated, and the girl did not leave her own family to live with the man. Sexual unfaithfulness during this stage was considered adultery, the penalty for which was death by stoning (cf. Lev. 20:10; Deut. 22:23–24), although by New Testament times stoning was rare. If one of the partners died during the betrothal period, the one remaining alive was a "widow" or "widower."[A-8]

(2) Wedding. In a formal ceremony about a year after the betrothal, the marriage proper was initiated.[A-9] Dressed in special wedding garments, the bridegroom and companions went in procession to the bride's home and escorted the bride and bridesmaids back to the groom's home, where a wedding supper was held (Matt. 22:1–14; Ps. 45:14–15). Parents and friends blessed the couple (Gen. 24:60; Tobit 7:13), and the father of the bride drew up a written marriage contract.[A-10] Soon afterward in a specially prepared nuptial chamber[A-11] the couple prayed and consummated sexually the marriage, after which a bloodstained cloth was exhibited as proof of the bride's virginity (Deut. 22:13–21). The wedding festivities continued sometimes for a week or more (Gen. 29:27; Tobit 8:20). Afterward the couple established their own household, although they usually lived with the extended family.

made allowance for a relatively private divorce (two to three witnesses).

An angel of the Lord appeared to him (1:20). Sometimes in the Old Testament God himself is represented by the phrase "angel of the Lord,"[17] but here the angel is one of God's created spirit beings.[18] The word "angel" (Gk. *angelos*; "messenger") speaks of one of an angel's primary roles as a messenger from God to humanity. Nothing is said of this angel's appearance, but they sometimes took the form of humans (Gen. 18). Gabriel appears in the book of Daniel as an agent of eschatological revelation (Dan. 8:15–26; 9:20–27), and in Luke's Gospel he is "the angel of the Lord," who announces both the birth of John the Baptist to Zechariah and the birth of Jesus to Mary (Luke 1:11, 19, 26ff.). The unnamed "angel of the Lord" who announced the birth of Jesus to the shepherds (Luke 2:9) and here the conception of Jesus to Joseph may also be

Gabriel, who seems to have a special role in announcements.[19]

In a dream (1:20). Dreams were commonly believed in the Greco-Roman world not only to be of natural origin, but also to be a medium of divine communication.[20] In the Old Testament, dreams were believed to derive from natural, divine, and evil sources,[21] but primarily point to a message from God about present activities or future events.[22] The expression "in a dream" is more restricted in its New Testament use, found only in Matthew's Gospel. In each case the dream is related to Jesus,[23] providing supernatural guidance.

What is conceived in her is from the Holy Spirit (1:20). The Old Testament writers repeatedly refer to the Spirit of God as the agency of God's power (e.g., Gen. 1:2; Judg. 3:10), but it is not until here in the incarnation that the Spirit is clearly understood as a person distinct from the Father and Son.

Give him the name Jesus, because he will save his people from their sins (1:21). The name "Jesus" was popular in Judaism of the first century (see comments on 1:1), being given to sons as a symbolic hope for Yahweh's anticipated sending of salvation. A highly popular expression of this salvation was the expectation of a Messiah who would save Israel from Roman oppression and purify his people (e.g., *Pss. Sol.* 17). But the angel draws on a less popular, although perhaps more important theme: Salvation from sin is the basic need of Israel.[24]

All this took place to fulfill what the Lord had said through the prophet (1:22). The events surrounding the conception of Jesus fulfill Isaiah's prophecy

R E F L E C T I O N S

MATTHEW COMBINES THE REMARKABLE FACTS OF Jesus' human nature in the genealogy and his divine nature in the conception narrative. Without giving details, the angelic announcement makes clear that the conception is not of ordinary human means, but by a totally unparalleled action of the Holy Spirit. Matthew does not theorize how such a conception can take place but merely presents it as historically authentic.

There is something both natural and supernatural about Jesus in his conception, birth, and development. Matthew presents the virgin conception and birth of Jesus as an accepted reality, thus accounting for the astounding truth that God has taken on human nature and is now with his people. It is only this God-man who can atone for the sin of humanity, which should cause us to pause in unending gratitude and worship him as Jesus, "God saves," and Immanuel, "God with us."

made during the dark days of national threat under Ahaz, king of Judah. Isaiah declared that God would not allow an invasion to happen, reassuring the king that God would maintain his promise that a descendent of David would sit on his throne forever (2 Sam. 7:11–17).

The virgin will be with child (1:23). There are two primary words for "virgin" in Hebrew. The term ʿalmah, which occurs in the prophecy of Isaiah 7:14, means "maiden, young girl" and never refers to a married woman.[25] The other primary term is bᵉṭulah, which can indicate a "virgin" (Gen. 24:16; Lev. 21:3), but also "old widow" (Joel 1:8). The Jewish translators of Isaiah 7:14 (LXX) rendered the Hebrew term ʿalmah with the Greek term parthenos, which almost without exception specifies a sexually mature, unmarried woman who is a virgin.

"They will call him Immanuel"—which means, "God with us" (1:23). Earlier the angel instructs Joseph to name the child Jesus (1:21)—the name by which he was called through his earthly life and by the early church. We have no record of Jesus being called "Immanuel" by his family or followers. Instead, as Matthew translates it, the name indicates Jesus' identity— "God with us." The name *Jesus* specifies *what he does* ("God saves"), while the name *Immanuel* specifies *who he is* ("God with us").

But he had no union with her until she gave birth to a son (1:25). Matthew's phrase (lit., "he was not knowing her") is a delicate way in both Hebrew and Greek to refer to sexual intercourse. Sexual abstinence during pregnancy was widely observed in Judaism of the first century; e.g., "Do not lay your hand upon your wife when she is pregnant."[26] Josephus writes, "For the same reason none who has intercourse with a woman who is with child can be considered pure."[27] Abstinence maintains Joseph and Mary's ritual

---

▶The Fulfillment of "The Virgin Will Be with Child. . ."

Isaiah prophesied that a woman who was a virgin at the time of Ahaz (734 B.C.) would bear a son named Immanuel. Since neither the queen nor Isaiah's wife was a virgin, this most likely was some unmarried young woman within the royal house with whom Ahaz was familiar. The woman would soon marry and conceive a child, and when it was born give it the name Immanuel—perhaps as a symbolic hope of God's presence in these dark times of national difficulty. Before the child was old enough to know the difference between right and wrong, Judah would be delivered from the threat of invasion from King Pekah of Israel and King Rezin of Aram (Isa. 7:14–17). The northern alliance was broken in 732 B.C., when Tiglath-Pileser III of Assyria destroyed Damascus, conquered Aram, and put Rezin to death. All this was within the time-frame miraculously predicted as the sign to Ahaz, plenty of time for the virgin to be married and to carry the child for the nine months of pregnancy, and for the approximately two years it would take until the boy knew the difference between good and evil. Thus there was immediate fulfillment of a miraculous prediction.

The sign given to Ahaz and the house of Judah was also a prediction of a future messianic figure who would provide spiritual salvation from sin. A future messianic age would honor Galilee of the Gentiles (Isa. 9:1–2), with a child born who would be called " Wonderful Counselor, Mighty God, Everlasting Father, Prince of Peace" (9:6). Of this one to whom Isaiah points, only Jesus can be the fulfillment.

purification during the pregnancy as well as ensures that Jesus is virgin born. But this is not a hint of continued celibacy after Jesus' birth. The expression "until" most naturally means that Mary and Joseph have normal marital sexual relations after Jesus' birth (cf. 12:46; 13:55).

The Magi Visit the Infant Jesus (2:1–12)

After Jesus was born in Bethlehem in Judea (2:1). As chapter 2 opens, the time frame has jumped ahead upwards of two years (see comments on 2:16). The baby is now a "child" (2:8, 10), and the family lives in a house "in Bethlehem in Judea" (2:1), six miles south/southwest of Jerusalem.

Magi (2:1). The term "Magi" (*magoi*) was originally used in early records to refer to a priestly caste in ancient Persia, perhaps followers of Zoroaster, the Persian teacher and prophet. Babylonian elements were also introduced. These Magi were leading figures in the religious court

life of their country of origin, employing a variety of scientific (astrology), diplomatic (wisdom), and religious (magical incantations) means to try to understand present and future life. This is in distinction from a more common type of "magician" (e.g., Acts 13:6, 8).

Magi from the east came to Jerusalem (2:1). Since a large colony of Jews remained in the east after the Exile, especially in Babylon, Parthia, and Arabia, these Magi apparently had been exposed to Judaism from those Jewish colonies. Pagan leaders, both political and religious, were well aware of Jewish religious distinctives, such as the Sabbath observance and marital restrictions.[28] If the Magi came from the environs of Babylon, they would have traveled approximately nine hundred miles. Since they would have had to make arrangements for the journey and gather a traveling party, it could have taken several months from the time they first saw the star until they arrived in Jerusalem (cf. Ezra and the returning exiles in Ezra 7:9).

Where is the one who has been born king of the Jews? (2:2). In the world of the first century an expectation circulated that a ruler would arise from Judea. Suetonius writes, "Throughout the whole of the East there had spread an old and persistent belief: destiny had decreed that at that time men coming forth from Judea would seize power [and rule the world]."[29] Israel's prophets had long spoken of a period of world peace and prosperity that was to be instituted by a future Davidic deliverer (e.g., Ezek. 34:23–31).[30]

We saw his star in the east (2:2). Through the Jewish community in their homeland,

the Magi may have become familiar with Balaam's prophecy, "A star will come out of Jacob; a scepter will rise out of Israel" (Num. 24:17). In many quarters within Judaism this prophecy was understood to point to a messianic deliverer.[31] In the book of Revelation Jesus refers to himself in similar language: "I am the Root and the Offspring of David, and the bright Morning Star."[32]

Have come to worship him (2:2). Suetonius describes the homage that the princely *magos* Tiridates of Armenia paid to Emperor Nero: "As Tiridates approached along a sloping platform, the emperor first let him fall at his feet, but raised him with his right hand and kissed him."[33] Tiridates even addressed Nero as "god." Similarly, the Magi in Matthew's infancy narrative worship Jesus, but with their mixture of influence from paganism, astrology, and the Jewish Scriptures, it is doubtful that the Magi knowingly worshiped Jesus in recognition of his incarnate nature as God-man.

When King Herod heard this he was disturbed (2:3). Herod had developed a profound fear of attack from the east, especially because of prior invasions of Parthinians and Trachonites. So he built a series of fortress/palaces all along the eastern border, including Masada, Hyrcanium, Machaerus, and the Herodium, to ensure safety from invading forces.[34] Since the Magi most likely travel with servants and possibly guards or a military escort to protect themselves and the gifts they are to present to the child, this sizeable company prompts Herod to think that invading forces from the east are joining forces within Israel to oust him.

The people's chief priests and teachers of the law (2:4). The chief priests were members of the Sanhedrin (cf. 26:57), joining the high priest in giving oversight to the temple activities, treasury, and priestly orders. The term "teacher of the law" (*grammateus*, "scribe") was once most closely associated with reading, writing, and making copies of the Scriptures. But by New Testament times it came to signify an expert in interpreting the Law and was used interchangeably with the term "lawyer" or "expert in the law."[35]

In Bethlehem in Judea (2:5). The prophet Micah had referred to Bethlehem as the birthplace of the future Messiah (Mic. 5:2), which had become a fairly widespread expectation (cf. John 7:42). Although a small and seemingly insignificant village, Bethlehem was noted as the home of Ruth and Boaz, the ancestors of King David, and the birthplace of David himself.[36]

On coming to the house (2:11). Houses built on level ground often formed a series of rooms built around a courtyard. Included in these rooms were living spaces, which doubled as sleeping quarters, cooking area, stables, and storage rooms. Houses built in hilly areas might find two-story homes. The lower floor had a courtyard surrounded by stables, while the upper floor had the living/sleeping rooms. In rocky cavernous areas, the lower floor might incorporate caves or grottos into the structure as underground stables.[37]

They opened their treasures and presented him with gifts of gold and of incense and of myrrh (2:11). When approaching royalty or persons of high

▶ The Christmas Star

Several possibilities have been proposed as to the nature of the star.

(1) Many suggest that it was a natural phenomenon that can be traced back to some known periodically occurring astronomical event, whether a comet (e.g., Halley's Comet was visible in 12 and 11 B.C.), a supernova, or a conjunction of planets. One widely discussed possibility is an unusual conjunction of planets that occurred on May 27, 7 B.C.[A-12] According to this theory, Jupiter represented the primary deity in the Babylonian astrology. When Jupiter came close to Saturn (representing the Jews) in the constellation Pisces (representing Palestine), the Magi referred to Jupiter as the star of the king they were seeking, and the association with Saturn and Pisces showed them among which nation (the Jews) and where (Palestine) to look for him. Jupiter rose on March 11, 7 B.C., so this would have been the date when his star rose. A related suggestion draws on this conjunction, but links the specific star to a supernova that Chinese and Korean astronomers recorded in March-April 5 B.C. One astronomer concludes that the conjunction alerted the Magi to some supernatural appearance, but the supernova triggered their journey to Jerusalem.[A-13]

(2) Others suggest that the "star" was a super-natural astral phenomenon that God used to herald Jesus' birth. Note how it appears and reappears as well as moves to direct the Magi to the house Jesus and his family are occupying (2:9), not the normal activity of stars. Some conclude that this was a star-like phenomenon that may have only been seen by the Magi.

(3) Another plausible suggestion is that the supernatural phenomenon was an angel sent to the Magi to announce the birth of Messiah and to guide them to Jesus so they would be a witness to his birth through their worship. Good angels are commonly referred to as stars,[A-14] as are fallen angels and Satan.[A-15] Angels were used to guide and protect Israel to the Promised Land (Ex. 14:19; 23:20), and often appear in Jewish and Christian literature as guides.[A-16] The apocryphal Arabic *Gospel of the Infancy* (ch. 7) relates Matthew's account of the Magi but expands it to say, "In the same hour there appeared to them an angel in the form of that star which had before guided them on their journey; and they went away, following the guidance of its light, until they arrived in their own country." One scholar concludes, "This, I believe, only makes explicit what is implicit in Matthew, namely, that the guiding star was a guiding angel."[A-17]

religious, political, or social status, gifts were often brought to demonstrate obeisance.[38] "Gold" was valued throughout the ancient world as a medium of exchange as well as a precious metal for making jewelry, ornaments, and dining instruments for royalty. "Incense" or frankincense[39] is derived from an amber resin, which produced a sweet odor when burned. It was used as a perfume (Song 3:6; 4:6, 14), but in Israel it was used ceremonially for the only incense permitted on the altar (Ex. 30:9, 34–38).[40] "Myrrh" consists of a mixture of resin, gum, and the oil myrrhol and was used in incense (Ex. 30:23), as a perfume for garments or for a lover's couch,[41] as a stimulant (cf. Mark 15:23), and to pack in the wrappings of the clothing of a deceased person to stifle the smell of the body decaying (cf. John 19:39).[42]

They returned to their country by another route (2:12). The Magi may have gone south around the lower extremity of the Dead Sea to link up with the trade route north through Nabatea and Philadelphia in the Decapolis east of the Jordan River to Damascus and then east. Or they may have traveled south to Hebron and then west to the Mediterranean coast to link up with the trade route traveling north on the coastal plain, then through Sepphoris and Capernaum to Damascus and then east.

The Escape to Egypt and the Bethlehem Massacre (2:13–18)

Take the child and his mother and escape to Egypt (2:13). During the turn of the first century, Egypt was a Roman province outside of Herod's jurisdiction, so Joseph and his family would have found a natural hiding place there among their fellow dispersed Jews. As far back as

Abraham, Egypt had become a haven of refuge for the people of Israel when they faced difficulties or danger.[43] Perhaps the largest, most significant, and culturally creative center of the Jewish Diaspora ("dispersion") in the first century flourished in Alexandria. According to the Jewish philosopher Philo (15 B.C.-A.D. 50), who lived there, its population included about a million Jews.

So he got up, took the child and his mother during the night and left for Egypt (2:14). The border lies approximately eighty miles from Bethlehem. If they took the primary route, Joseph and the family would have traveled south to Hebron, west to the coast at Gaza, and then south again to the Nabatean border. From there, it is about fifty miles to the Egyptian border and over two hundred miles to the main Jewish community in Egypt at Alexandria.

"Out of Egypt I called my son" (2:15). The nation of Israel was consistently reminded by Old Testament authors to

◀
—————
COINS

These were minted in Israel during the reign of Herod the Great.

▶ Herod, King of the Jews

Birth to kingship (73–39 B.C.). Herod (c. 73–4 B.C.) was born of noble stock from Idumean and Nabatean heritage.[A-18] His grandfather on his father's side, Antipas, converted to Judaism during the reign of Hyrcanus I. His father, Antipater II, was appointed adviser to Hyrcanus II. After the Roman general Pompey invaded Judea and deposed the Hasmonaean dynasty (63 B.C.), Antipater was made procurator of Judea by Julius Caesar (47 B.C.).[A-19] Antipater appointed his son Herod governor of Galilee when he was twenty-five years old (c. 47 B.C.). After his father's death by poisoning, Herod was appointed king of Judea by Emperor Augustus and the Roman Senate (39 B.C.).[A-20]

Solidification (38–25 B.C.). Herod's rule was troubled in the early years by lingering bitterness from surviving members of the Hasmonaean house, and he sought to solidify his position by marrying Mariamne I, a princess of the Hasmonaean line. He later had her executed, thinking that she would rouse popular opposition to him. This had a profound effect on Herod; he became seriously ill, almost to the point of death, and it instilled in him a paranoia that lasted throughout his lifetime.

Prosperity (25–14 B.C.). Herod is regarded as one of the greatest builders in antiquity. These projects often benefited his Jewish subjects, such as the rebuilding of the temple in Jerusalem. The rabbinic saying, "whoever has not beheld Herod's building [i.e., the temple] has not seen anything beautiful in his life,"[A-21] attests to the magnificence of this undertaking. Herod built or restored a chain of fortress/palaces all along the eastern border, which later aided the Jews in their rebellion against Rome. But Herod also alienated the Jews by some of his projects. He built a new city on the ancient site of hated Samaria, naming it Sebaste in honor of Emperor Augustus, and he built a temple dedicated to his worship. The creation of the port city of Caesarea Maritima is considered one of the marvels of antiquity, but it had many Gentile reminders. In Jerusalem, Jericho, and Caesarea, Herod built theaters, amphitheaters, and hippodromes for the Greek games inaugurated in honor of Augustus.

Intrigue and decline (14–4 B.C.). Herod's ten wives produced offspring who contended against each other for his throne.[A-22] As Herod became older he grew increasingly paranoid, and he had a number of his own relatives imprisoned and executed, including two of his favorite sons, Alexander and Aristobulus, his sons by Miramne I, whom he had executed earlier.[A-23] He had his eldest son, Antipater III, by his first wife Doris, executed just five days before his own death.[A-24] After several incidents of this sort, Caesar Augustus supposedly made the famous pun that he would rather be Herod's pig (*hus*) than his son (*huios*).[A-25]

Herod died at his palace in Jericho in March, 4 B.C.[A-26] Deathly ill with a painful terminal disease,[A-27] Herod commanded that many influential Jews should be executed when he died so that the people would mourn at the time of his death instead of rejoicing. But the order was countermanded after he died by his sister Salome.[A-28] An extensive burial procession of national dignitaries and military units marched with Herod's body on a golden bier studded with precious stones with a purple cover to where he was buried at or near the Herodium.[A-29]

Although he had been raised with the beliefs and practices of the Jews, and despite his attempts to win their favor, the Jewish people hated Herod as a foreigner and a friend of the Romans. Even the solicitous Josephus says of him, "He was a man who was cruel to all alike and one who easily gave in to anger and was contemptuous of justice."[A-30]

look back to the way in which God redeemed Israel by bringing them out of Egypt.[44] The yearly Passover was a reminder, but also a promise, that God had provided a sacrificial lamb for his people Israel. Jesus' infancy corresponds analogically to Israel's history (cf. Hos. 11:1).

He gave orders to kill all the boys in Bethlehem (2:16). Only 123 men returned to Bethlehem from the Babylonian deportation (Ezra 2:21), and it appears not to have grown beyond a small village of perhaps a thousand people at the birth of Jesus. Herod's forces kill all the infant boys under the age of two years, which would calculate to between ten to thirty boys. Although this number of infant boys massacred would be a huge loss for the village of Bethlehem, it is not an incident that stands out significantly when seen in the light of other horrific events in Herod's infamous career, and historians would have easily bypassed it.

"A voice is heard in Ramah, weeping and great mourning" (2:18). Centuries earlier, Nebuchadnezzar's army had gathered the captives from Judah in the town of Ramah before they were taken into exile to Babylon (Jer. 40:1–2). Jeremiah depicts Rachel, who is the personification of the mothers of Israel, mourning for her children as they are being carried away. However, there was hope for their future because God would restore Rachel's children to their own land (31:16–17), and messianic joy would come in the future establishment of the new covenant with Israel (31:31–34).

The Return to Nazareth (2:19–23)

After Herod died (2:19). The family stays in Egypt until after Herod's death (March/April 4 B.C.), when the angel tells them to return to Israel (2:20). They probably stay in Egypt no more than a year.

Archelaus was reigning in Judea in place of his father Herod (2:22). After remaking his will at least seven times, Herod finally settled on dividing the kingdom between three of his remaining sons, Archelaus, Herod Antipas (14:1ff.), and Herod Philip (16:13).[45] Archelaus, a nineteen-year-old son by Malthace, was appointed successor to Herod's throne with power over Judea (including Samaria and Idumaea). Archelaus quickly displayed the same kind of cruelty that marked his father's reign. He overreacted to an uprising in the temple at Passover after his father's death, sending in troops and a cavalry who killed about three thousand pilgrims.[46] He was notorious for his cruel treatment of both Jews and Samaritans,[47] continually using oppressive measures to quell uprisings of the people. Augustus feared a revolution from the people, so he deposed Archelaus from

EGYPT AND JUDEA

The map traces the possible route Joseph took on the flight to Egypt.

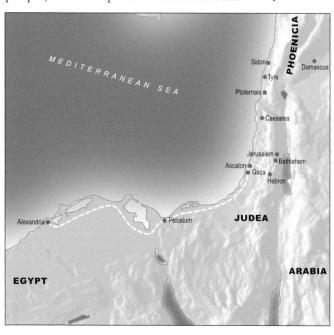

office and banished him to Gaul in A.D. 6. The rule over Judea was thereafter passed to Roman prefects.

Having been warned in a dream, he withdrew to the district of Galilee (2:22). Joseph led the family to the region of Galilee, which was not under the jurisdiction of Archelaus. Galilee was governed by another of Herod the Great's sons, Herod Antipas, who did not yet have the same bloodthirsty reputation as did his older brother.

He went and lived in a town called Nazareth (2:23). Nazareth was occupied early in Israel's history, but was apparently deserted in 733 B.C. during the Assyrian invasion of the northern kingdom and appears to have been uninhabited from the eighth to third centuries B.C. Modern archaeological excavations have uncovered the remains of houses and a tomb from the Herodian period, indicating that Nazareth was reestablished as a small agricultural village around the third century B.C., perhaps founded and named by exiles returning from the Babylonian captivity. The town

COIN OF HEROD ARCHELAUS, SON OF HEROD THE GREAT

▶Modern Calendars and the Date of Jesus' Birth

Modern calendars begin the present era, often called the "Christian era," with Jesus' birth. Dates after his birth are designated A.D. (Latin *anno domini*, "in the year of our Lord"). The birth of Jesus marks the beginning point of modern chronologies. The first person to develop this system was the Christian monk Dionysius Exiguus, in A.D. 525. Prior to him the Romans had developed the dating system used throughout the Western world. They commenced all dating with the establishment of the city of Rome, using the designation "AUC" (*ab urbe condita*—"from the foundation of the city [of Rome]"—or *anno urbis conditae*—"in the year of the foundation of the city").

Dionysius believed that it would be more reverent for calendrical dating to begin with Jesus' birth rather than the foundation of Rome. So with the historical records available to him, he reckoned the birth of Jesus to have occurred on December 25, 753 AUC. That placed the commencement of the Christian era at January 1, AUC (allowing for lunar adjustment), or under the new reckoning, January 1,

A.D. 1. However, Dionysius did not have all of the historical data now available to scholars to make a more precise dating. We now know that Herod died in March/April 750 AUC. Since Jesus was born while Herod was still alive, he was actually born according to the Roman calendar between 748–750 AUC, four to six years earlier than Dionysius's calculations. Dionysius's dating was questioned by the English saint Bede in the eighth century and rejected outright by the German monk Regino of Prüm at the end of the ninth century. But Gregory XIII, pope from 1572 to 1585, using largely the dating of Dionysius, produced the system currently in use throughout the Western world and in parts of Asia (the Gregorian calendar).

Therefore, more accurate dating of the birth of Jesus places it before the start of the Christian Era, in 4–6 B.C. This has nothing to do with the accuracy of the biblical records, only the historical accuracy of the well-intentioned, but misguided Dionysius Exiguus.

is located in the hills in lower Galilee, twenty miles from the Mediterranean Sea to the west and fifteen miles from the Sea of Galilee to the east. Nazareth was not a strategic town politically, militarily, or religiously in Jesus' day, so it is largely left out of documents of the first century.[48] However, it was not isolated. A ten minute walk up to the ridge north of Nazareth provided villagers with a magnificent view of the trade routes a thousand feet below on the valley floor and of Herod Antipas's capital city, Sepphoris. In Jesus' day, this humble agricultural village probably had a relatively small population of around five hundred people.[49]

So was fulfilled what was said through the prophets: "He will be called a Nazarene" (2:23). The term "Nazarene" (Gk. *Nazōraios*) derives from "Nazareth" (Gk. *Nazaret*) to indicate a person from that town.[50] The returning founders of the village were apparently from the line of David and gave the settlement a con-sciously messianic name. They connected the establishment of the town with the hope of the coming messianic *neṣer*, "branch" (Isa. 11:1), and the believing remnant of Israel (Isa. 60:21; NIV "shoot"). The "Branch" or "Shoot" had became an important designation of the Messiah in Jewish literature.[51] One text from Qumran says, "This refers to the 'branch of David,' who will arise with the Interpreter of the law who will rise up in Zion in the last days."[52] Matthew also points to "Nazarene" as a slang term for an individual from a remote, despised area. He draws a connection between the divinely arranged association of Jesus with Nazareth and various Old Testament prophets who foretold that the Messiah would be despised.[53]

John the Baptist Prepares the Way (3:1–6)

Matthew now jumps from Jesus' infancy to his adulthood. More than twenty-five

HEROD'S FORTRESS

The remains of the Herodium, Herod's citadel built near Bethlehem.

▼

years elapse from the time Joseph takes his family to Nazareth to the time that John the Baptist appears in the Judean desert.

In those days John the Baptist came, preaching in the Desert of Judea (3:1). John probably appears in the barren desert area in the lower Jordan River valley and hills to the west of the Dead Sea. The desert wilderness was an important place in Israel's history for the giving of the Law, revelation of the prophets, Maccabean guerilla warfare, and expected messianic deliverance.[54] Although there are several points of similarity between John the Baptist and the Qumran community near the Dead Sea, the significant dissimilarities lead most scholars to the conclusion that John had not been a member of the Qumran community.[55] Most notably, John's message calls the entire nation to repentance, not isolationism, which makes him more like the Old Testament prophets than Qumran. While it is a matter of conjecture as to whether John may have ever been connected with Qumran, the Gospels' portrait of John makes it doubtful.

Repent (3:2). "Repentance" in the Old Testament prophets called for a change in a person's attitude toward God, which

▶

NAZARETH

The church of the Annunciation. The cave underneath the church contains the remains of a fourth-century church and possibly an earlier synagogue.

would impact one's actions and one's overall direction in life. External signs of repentance regularly included confession of sin, prayers of remorse, and abandonment of sin.

The kingdom of heaven is near (3:2). "Kingdom of heaven" is interchangeable with the expression "kingdom of God."[56] "Kingdom of heaven" reflects the Hebrew expression *malkut šamayim*, found abundantly in Jewish literature.[57] A feeling of reverence and not wishing inadvertently to blaspheme the name of God (Ex. 20:7) led the Jews at an early date to avoid as far as possible all mention of the name of God. "Heaven" is one of the usual substitutions.[58]

John's clothes were made of camel's hair, and he had a leather belt around his waist (3:4). John's description is strikingly similar to the prophet Elijah (2 Kings 1:8). Goat or camel hair was often woven into a thick, rough, dark cloth, which was used as an outer garment or cloak, particularly by nomadic desert dwellers. It was so dense that it was waterproof. It was proverbially the garb of poorer people, in distinction from the finery worn by those in the royal court.[59] Since sackcloth symbolized distress or self-affliction,[60] John the Baptist's garment of camel hair visualizes the repentance to which he calls the people.[61]

His food was locusts and wild honey (3:4). Locusts and wild honey were not an unusual diet for people living in the desert.[62] The locust is the migratory phase of the grasshopper and was allowable food for the people of Israel to eat, as opposed to other kinds of crawling and flying insects (Lev. 11:20–23). They are an important food source in many areas of the world, especially as a source of protein, because even in the most desolate areas they are abundant. They are often collected, dried, and ground into flour. Protein and fat were derived from locusts, while sugar came from the honey of wild bees.[63]

The Impact of the Kingdom of Heaven (3:7–12)

He saw many of the Pharisees and Sadducees coming (3:7). The Pharisees and Sadducees were distinct and often opposed to each other. John recognizes immediately that they are not coming to validate his ministry; they come with

bottom left

JUDEAN WILDERNESS

The rugged terrain where John the Baptist spent much time.

bottom right

LOCUST

A food source for John the Baptist.

▼

▶Baptism in the Ancient World

Various kinds of "washings" were commonly known and practiced throughout much of Israel's history, always as a symbol of some deeper meaning.

- The Old Testament prescribed various forms of water rituals for different types of symbolic purification.[A-31] These cleansings were understood to be ongoing symbols of God's inner cleansing (e.g., Ps. 51:2, 7) and were practiced into the New Testament era.
- Widespread voluntary forms of water rituals were primarily symbolic of purification, such as the table fellowship of the Pharisees[A-32] or commitment to the community at Qumran.[A-33] Ceremonial *mikveh* ("immersion pool") baths have been discovered by archaeologists throughout Israel, indicating regular washings by immersion and by pouring flowing water over oneself. Ritual water purifications were repeated, sometimes more than once a day.
- By the time of John it was possible that Gentile proselytes were required to undergo baptism as an act of initiation into Judaism. This was a one-time baptism signifying the conversion of adults from a Gentile background to Judaism.
- John's baptism was also symbolic of purification, but it was a one-time baptism, whereas groups such as those at Qumran and the Pharisees had highly structured regulations for regular, repeated washings. John's baptism had some similarity to proselyte one-time baptism, but it was far different since John was baptizing Jews, not Gentiles. Those responding were heeding the call to the presence of the kingdom and the "Coming One" whom John announced.

JORDAN RIVER

Near the outlet at the Sea of Galilee.

▼

ulterior motives. Matthew notes two other occasions when the Pharisees and Sadducees are listed together in their opposition to Jesus (16:1–4; 16:5–12).

You brood of vipers (3:7). "Brood of vipers" (cf. 12:34; 23:33) is a reference to the dozen or more small, dangerous snakes that can emerge at birth from a mother snake. Vipers are proverbial for their subtle approach and attack, as was the original serpent (Gen. 3).

I baptize you. . . . He will baptize you (3:11). The Coming One will baptize the repentant with the blessing of the Holy Spirit. But the unrepentant, those who are not receptive to the Coming One, will be baptized with the judgment of eternal fire (cf. Joel 2:28–29).

▶ Pharisees and Sadducees

Josephus refers to the Pharisees, Sadducees, and Essenes as "schools of thought,"[A-34] something of a mix between a religious faction and a political affiliation.

1. The name *Pharisee* is probably derived from the Hebrew/Aramaic *perušim*, the separated ones, alluding to both their origin and their characteristic practices. They tended to be politically conservative and religiously liberal and held the minority membership on the Sanhedrin:[A-35]

- They held to the supreme place of Torah, with a rigorous scribal interpretation of it.
- Their most pronounced characteristic was their adherence to the oral tradition, which they obeyed rigorously as an attempt to make the written law relevant to daily life.
- They had a well-developed belief in angelic beings.
- They had concrete messianic hopes, as they looked for the coming Davidic messianic kingdom. The Messiah would overthrow the Gentiles and restore the fortunes of Israel with Jerusalem as capital.
- They believed in the resurrection of the righteous when the messianic kingdom arrived, with the accompanying punishment of the wicked.
- They viewed Rome as an illegitimate force that was preventing Israel from experiencing its divinely ordained role in the outworking of the covenants.

- They held strongly to divine providence, yet viewed humans as having freedom of choice, which ensures their responsibility.
- As a lay fellowship or brotherhood connected with local synagogues, the Pharisees were popular with the common people.

2. The *Sadducees* were a small group with aristocratic and priestly influence, who derived their authority from the activities of the temple. They tended to be politically liberal and religiously conservative and held the majority membership on the Sanhedrin:

- They held a conservative attitude toward the Scriptures, accepting nothing as authoritative except the written word, literally interpreted.
- They accepted only Torah (the five books of Moses) as authoritative, rejecting any beliefs not found there.
- For that reason they denied the resurrection from the dead, the reality of angels, and spirit life.
- They produced no literature of which we are aware.
- They had no expressed messianic expectation, which tended to make them satisfied with their wealth and political power.
- They were open to aspects of Hellenism and often collaborated with the Romans.
- They tended to be removed from the common people by economic and political status.

right ▶

DOVE

A symbol of the coming of the Spirit upon Jesus

His winnowing fork is in his hand (3:12). At the end of the season the farmer brought the harvested wheat into the threshing floor, a stone or hard-packed dirt surface, often with a short wall around the perimeter. He then took a large pitchfork and tossed the wheat into the air, where the wind blew the lighter chaff away, leaving only the good wheat heads in the threshing floor. The wheat would be stored in the granary for later grinding into flour to make bread, but the chaff would be raked into piles and burned.[64]

▶

WINNOWING GRAIN

A modern winnowing fork.

John Baptizes Jesus (3:13–17)

Heaven was opened (3:16). As Jesus comes up from the water, the heavens are opened, not an uncommon expression in Scripture to refer to significant times of God's revealing something important to his people.[65]

The Spirit of God descending like a dove (3:16). The descent of the Spirit alludes to the anointing of the Servant of the Lord by the Spirit (Isa. 42:1) and the anointing of the Davidic Branch by the Spirit (Isa. 11:2). Jesus' anointing by the Spirit is both the coronation of Israel's Messiah and the commissioning of God's righteous Servant for the work that he will now carry out in the power and presence of the Spirit.

This is my Son, whom I love (3:17). The phrase calls to mind the well-known messianic image of Father and Son in Psalm 2:7. The title "Son of God" had clear messianic significance prior to Jesus' ministry.[66]

With him I am well pleased (3:17). Jesus, the divine Son, is the triumphant messianic King (Ps. 2) and the humble, suffering Servant (Isa. 43), a pronouncement repeated by the voice in the Transfiguration (Matt. 17:5). Through the anointing of the Spirit, the Father has placed into the hands of his beloved Son the mission of the Servant to bring salvation to the nations (Isa. 42:1, 4; cf. *Tg. Isa.* 42:1).

Temptations of the Messiah (4:1–11)

Then Jesus was led by the Spirit into the desert (4:1). Jesus' ministry, like John the Baptist's, begins in the desert. Early Christian tradition placed Jesus' forty-day-and-night fast on the mountain site of Jebel Quarantal in the Jericho area. Emperor Justinian in the sixth century erected a church on the summit to commemorate Jesus' vigil. While it is possible that this is the actual site, one cannot be certain. The desert stretches west for a dozen miles as it rises from the Jordan River valley to the heights of Jerusalem, a virtual no-man's-land.

To be tempted by the devil (4:1). Entering for the first time on the scene of Matthew's story is "the devil," or, as he will be called later, Satan (4:10; 12:26; 16:23). The devil leads a host of other powerful spiritual beings that assist him in trying to thwart God's purposes. Paul calls him "the ruler of the kingdom of the air" (Eph. 2:2). The word "tempted" is the verb *peirazō*, which can mean either "I tempt" or "I test."[67] A *temptation* is an enticement to get a person to go contrary to the will of God, as Satan will try to do to Jesus. A *test* tries to get a person to prove oneself faithful to God's will, with the good intention that the person pass the test.

After fasting forty days and forty nights, he was hungry (4:2). Fasting was often used as a means of focusing one's attention in prayer, disciplining oneself to unite body and soul. Jesus has been readying himself for his public ministry. Forty days of hardship often indicated preparation for a particularly significant involvement in God's activities, such as Moses, Elijah, Ezekiel, and here, Jesus.[68]

If you are the Son of God (4:3, 6). Satan does not doubt Jesus' identity as the Son of God, nor is he trying to get Jesus to

MASADA AREA

In the wilderness of Judea.

REFLECTIONS

JOHN AND JESUS GIVE US A POWER-ful example of humility as they carry out their roles as the prophet and the Savior. Neither got carried away with appearances. They demonstrated strength in carrying out their roles in the plan of salvation, yet that strength also included diminishing the appearance of their own importance. The key word here is humility, a term that does not get much good press in our day, since we hear much more of rights. But the picture John and Jesus give to every age is the incongruity of their humility relative to the significance of their roles.

We don't like to give up our appearance of importance. But knowing God's purposes for our lives and not allowing our self-promotion to get in the way will enable us to accomplish God's calling for our lives as well.

doubt it; rather, he is trying to get Jesus to misuse his prerogatives as the Son of God.

The highest point of the temple (4:5). The identification of this "highest point" is debated, but it may refer either to the southeast corner of the temple area, where it looms some 450 feet high over the Kidron Valley,[69] or to a high gate of the temple.

Throw yourself down (4:6). Satan quotes from Psalm 91, where the psalmist asserts God's protecting care for the faithful in

Israel (vv. 11–12). This is a blatant misuse of Scripture to try to manipulate Jesus.

Do not put the Lord your God to the test (4:7). In the first century many believed that the Messiah would descend the Mount of Olives, enter the holy city through the Shushan gate, which was left ajar in this expectation, and then triumphantly enter the temple. This is a very devilish temptation for Jesus to gain the following of the nation Israel by a spectacular display at the central place of Israel's religion, the temple.

If you will bow down and worship me (4:9). The pictures of the king of Tyre (Ezek. 28:2, 11–19) and the king of Babylon (Isa. 14:12–14) epitomize this obsession and have often been understood as pointing beyond those earthly diabolical rulers to Satan.

Jesus Messiah Begins His Galilean Ministry (4:12–17)

When Jesus heard that John had been put in prison (4:12). Josephus tells us that John was imprisoned by Herod Antipas for political reasons; that is, Herod Antipas feared that John's popularity with the people and his preaching and baptism might lead the people to some form of sedition.[70] Matthew will fill in later that there was an additional moral reason behind John's arrest (see on 14:1–12).

He went and lived in Capernaum (4:13). Jesus makes Capernaum in Galilee his base of operations and his new hometown for the length of his ministry in Galilee. Capernaum is the Greek form of the Hebrew *Kefar Nahum*, which means the "village of Nahum." Josephus gives one of the earliest Greek renderings as

---

REFLECTIONS

THREE IMPORTANT IMPLICATIONS

surface in reflecting on Jesus' temptations:

(1) Satan's power. Satan does have significant influence over the people and powers of this world,[A-36] but his influence is limited.

(2) The Scripture's power. Temptations involve the twisting of reality, so the antidote comes from the truth of Scripture.

(3) The Spirit's power. Jesus was guided and empowered by the Spirit in his temptations. He was never alone in his struggle, even at the most difficult moments. Jesus relied on the power of the Spirit to enable him to resist the devil's temptations.

Throughout his life Jesus gives the ultimate example of how Christians today can also overcome the temptations that will come our way: Resist the devil in the power of the Spirit through the guidance of the Word to accomplish the will of God.

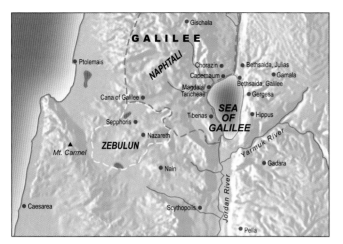

"Land of Zebulun and land of Naphtali, the way to the sea, along the Jordan" (4:15). Zebulun and Naphtali were the two tribes of Israel that settled in the northernmost region near the Sea of Galilee. Nazareth was in the territory of Zebulun in the lower Galilee region, while Capernaum was in Naphtali in the upper Galilee region. The trade route that ran through this region to the Mediterranean Sea was called the "Via Maris" or "way to the sea." Jesus' ministry will extend far beyond the physical confines of Jewish Galilee, influencing those traveling through the region.

◀ *left*

GALILEE

The land of Zebulun and Naphtali.

Kapharnaoum,[71] for what is most likely the site today called by Arabs Tell-Hum on the northwest shore of the Sea of Galilee. Capernaum was a Galilean frontier town, with around a thousand inhabitants.[72] What may have been a 2,500-foot promenade with several piers extending out into the water made for a bustling fishing trade and transportation center at Capernaum for crossing the Sea of Galilee.[73] Capernaum, Chorazin, and Bethsaida are the cities in which most of Jesus' miracles are performed, an area of gospel operation referred to as the "Evangelical Triangle."[74]

"Galilee of the Gentiles" (4:15). The tribes of Israel in the north were surrounded on three sides by non-Jewish populations. Ever since the Assyrian campaign that reduced it to a province under an Assyrian governor in 732 B.C. (2 Kings 15:29), this region had long experienced

CAPERNAUM

Remains of the synagogue at Capernaum.

▼

turmoil and forced infiltration of Gentile influence.

"The people living in darkness" (4:16)
The term "people" (*laos*) in Matthew regularly refers to Israel (cf. 1:21), so this is a description of Jewish people awaiting deliverance while living among the hopelessness of the Gentiles.

Jesus Calls Fishers of Men (4:18–22)

They were casting a net into the lake (4:18). The fishing industry was an important contributor to Capernaum's prosperity. "Casting a net" describes a customary form of fishing on the lake, even up to recent times. The "cast net" (*amphiblēstron*) was used by a single fisherman, either while standing in a boat or in shallow water. It was circular, about 20–25 feet in diameter, with lead sinkers attached to the outer edge. The net was pulled down by the sinkers on the outer ring (like a parachute), finally sinking to the bottom with fish trapped inside. The

fisherman would dive to the bottom and pull the trapped fish through the net one by one, placing them in a pouch, or he would carefully pull together the edges of the net and carry it to the surface with the catch inside.[75]

Come, follow me (4:19). The normal pattern in Israel was for a prospective disciple to approach a rabbi and ask to study with him (e.g., 8:19). Joshua b. Perahyah said, "Provide thyself with a teacher and get thee a fellow disciple," which Rabban Gamaliel echoed, "Provide thyself with a teacher and remove thyself from doubt."[76] At the inauguration of his kingdom mission Jesus establishes a new pattern, because he is the one who takes the initiative to seek out and give a call for these brothers to enter into a permanent relationship with him.[77]

They were in a boat (4:21). Fishing boats were a common sight on the Sea of Galilee. Josephus indicates that they were so plentiful that on one occasion he ordered 230 available boats to be assem-

▶ The Sea of Galilee

The "Sea of Galilee," located about sixty miles north of Jerusalem, is a 12.5 by 7 mile lake. In the Old Testament it is called "Sea of Kinnereth,"[A-37] the name by which it is known today in Israel. It is also called the "Sea of Tiberias,"[A-38] because Herod Antipas's capital city Tiberias lay on the west shore. Luke calls it the "Lake of Gennesaret or Gennesar," derived from a town and plain by that name situated above the west/northwest shore.[A-39] Josephus implies that this was the oldest and most common name used by the local people.[A-40]

The lake is located in the great Jordan rift valley, at least 636 feet (212 meters) below sea level. The Jordan River enters the lake in the north and exits

to the south, where it finally terminates in the Dead Sea about 65 miles to the south. Ancient writers all acclaim the Sea of Galilee for its fresh waters and pleasant temperatures, unlike the Dead Sea. It had clear sandy beaches rather than swampy marshes along the seashore, and all remarked that it was well stocked with fish.[A-41] The lake's low elevation provides it with relatively mild year-round temperatures, permitting sleeping outdoors in the surrounding areas as a common practice.[A-42] However, encompassed as it is with mountain ranges to the east and west that rise over 2,650 feet from the level of the lake, the low-lying setting results in sudden violent downdrafts and storms.[A-43]

bled to form a naval armada.[78] The recent (1986) extraordinary discovery of an ancient fishing boat at Galilee from the time of Jesus gives us an idea of the kind of boat the Zebedees may have owned. The wooden vessel, called the "Kinneret boat," is approximately 26.5 feet long, 7.5 feet wide, and 4.5 feet high, and equipped for both sailing and rowing. A crew of at least five was needed to handle the boat (four rowers and one rudder man), but it was able to carry as many as eight to sixteen.[79] It was equipped for cooking during nightlong commercial fishing expeditions on the lake.[80]

Preparing their nets (4:21). These nets may have been the larger *seine* or "drag-net,"[81] but more likely the *trammel* net, the only net used in ancient times that is still widely used commercially on the lake today. It is a compound net of three layers, five units each over a hundred feet long, used by at least two crews of boats throughout the night when the fish cannot see the entangling nets.[82] Probably after a long night of fishing with their father and others of their hired crew (cf. Mark 1:20), James and John are mending or preparing their nets for the next commercial excursion on the lake.

left

KINNERET BOAT

A first-century fishing boat recently discovered in the Sea of Galilee.

◀

MODERN FISHERMEN ON THE SEA OF GALILEE

Jesus Unfolds the Gospel of the Kingdom (4:23–25)

Jesus went throughout Galilee (4:23). Approximately forty-five miles from north to south and twenty-five miles from east to west, Galilee must have been intensively cultivated and extensively populated in Jesus' day. Conservative estimates place the population at around 300,000 people in the two hundred or more villages and towns in Galilee, which make for a large citizenry to whom Jesus presents the message of the kingdom.[83]

Teaching in their synagogues (4:23). Teaching (*didaskōn*) is often related to explanation of truth to those already familiar with the content (see comments

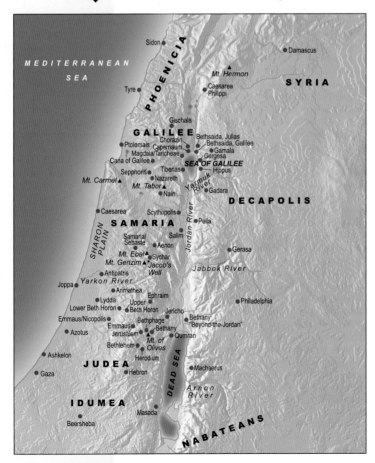

on 5:1–2). In the Jewish synagogues Jesus clarifies the nature of his message from the Old Testament Scriptures, demonstrating that he is the expected messianic deliverer (cf. Luke 4:16–30).

Preaching (4:23). "Preaching" (*kēryssōn*) is generally related to the proclamation of truth to those unfamiliar with the content (cf. 24:14). When he is in the countryside, where many are most likely not proficient in the Old Testament Scriptures, Jesus gives a straightforward proclamation of the message.

The good news of the kingdom (4:23). Matthew uses the noun "gospel" (*euangelion*) only four times, three of which occur in the phrase, "gospel of the kingdom," found only in Matthew.[84] The real "good news" is that the age of the kingdom of God has finally dawned in the ministry of Jesus.

Healing every disease and sickness among the people (4:23). This good news is also demonstrated as Jesus is "healing" every disease and sickness among the people. Healing signals that Jesus has authority over the powers of this world and confirms the reality of the arrival of the kingdom of God (11:4–6).

Those suffering severe pain, the demon-possessed, those having seizures, and the paralyzed, and he healed them (4:24). As news of Jesus' ministry spreads outside the borders of Galilee, even to the Gentile region of Syria in the north (4:24), people bring those suffering "severe pain" or "torment" (cf. Luke 16:23, 28). The "demon-possessed" are also brought, indicating Jesus' continuing power over the devil's realm. Jesus also heals "epileptics" (lit., "moonstruck"), an illness associated with demon-possession (17:14–21), and "paralytics," a distressing affliction at a time when foot-travel is the most common.

Large crowds from Galilee, the Decapolis, Jerusalem, Judea and the region across the Jordan followed him (4:25). The Decapolis ("ten cities") is the generally Gentile district to the south and east of the Sea of Galilee. The region known as "across the Jordan" is a common expression to designate the area of Perea,[85] presupposing a typical Jewish point of view west of the Jordan River. Those coming to Jesus are still primarily Jews, but they come from all of the surrounding regions.

The Beatitudes of the Kingdom of Heaven (5:1–12)

He went up on a mountainside (5:1). This first major discourse gets its name from the geographical setting, "on a mountain" somewhere in Galilee. The traditional site, as well as the most recent consensus, identifies it above Tabghah, near Capernaum. The local mountain of Capernaum is actually a ridge of hills just to the west of the town. Ancient tradition named this hillcrest "Eremos," a transliteration of the Greek word for "lonely" or "solitary" (*erēmos*). At the foot of Eremos lies the area of "seven springs," *Heptapegon*, later roughly transliterated into Arabic as *et-Tabgha*.[86]

He . . . sat down. His disciples came to him, and he began to teach them (5:1–2). Sitting down is the typical position from which a teacher in Judaism taught (cf. 23:2), a position Jesus takes regularly.[87] Since Jesus' teaching in this setting is directed primarily to the disciples, not the crowds, it can be designated in large part as training in discipleship. Yet the response at the conclusion of the message indicates that the crowds are being offered an invitation to discipleship in the kingdom (7:28–29).

HILL OF THE BEATITUDES

Marking the traditional site of the Sermon on the Mount. The Sea of Galilee is in the background.

▼

Blessed are . . . (5:3). The name "beatitude" is derived from the Latin noun *beatitudo*, because the first word of each statement in the Latin *Vulgate* is *beati* (adj. related to the noun), which translates the Greek word *makarios* (traditionally rendered in English as "blessed").

Theirs is . . . they will be . . . (cf. 5:3, 10 with 5:4–9). In the first and last beatitude, an identical phrase in the present tense gives the reason for the blessing: "for theirs *is* the kingdom of heaven" (5:3, 10). This creates "bookends" to the beatitudes—an example of the common literary device called an *inclusio*, indicating that kingdom life is a present possession of Jesus' disciples. The third through seventh beatitudes (5:4–9) have a future tense (e.g., "for they *will be* comforted," 5:4), indicating that the blessings will not be experienced completely until the future when the kingdom is established completely on the earth.

Blessed are the poor in spirit (5:3). The poor are not only those who have encountered unfortunate circumstances from an economic point of view (19:21; 26:11), but also those who are spiritually and emotionally oppressed and disillusioned and in need of God's help.

R E F L E C T I O N S

MAKARIOS **IS A STATE OF EXISTENCE IN RELATIONSHIP** to God in which a person is "blessed" from God's perspective even when he or she doesn't feel happy or isn't presently experiencing good fortune. This does not mean a conferral of blessing or an exhortation to live a life worthy of blessing, but rather is an acknowledgment that the ones indicated are blessed. Negative feelings, absence of feelings, or adverse conditions cannot take away the blessedness of the one who exists in relationship with God.

For theirs is the kingdom of heaven (5:3). The kingdom of God belongs to those who see themselves, and are seen by others, as having no resources, material or spiritual, to help them before God. These are the "poor" to whom Jesus has come to announce "good news" (11:5), and to whom the kingdom of heaven belongs.

Blessed are those who mourn (5:4). The loss of anything that a person counts valuable will produce mourning, whether it is one's financial support, loved ones, status in society, or even one's spiritual standing before God (Ps. 119:136).

For they will be comforted (5:4). The arrival of the kingdom in Jesus' ministry brings the first taste of God's comforting blessing on those in Israel who have realized their loss and who mourn over it (cf. Isa. 40:1; 61:1–3), but they will receive final comforting in the presence of the heavenly Lamb (Rev. 7:17).

Blessed are the meek (5:5). The "meek" (or better, "gentle") are those who do not assert themselves over others in order to advance their own causes. That this does not imply weakness becomes plain when we see this same term applied to Jesus (11:29; 21:5).

For they will inherit the earth (5:5). This perhaps recalls the lowly position before others found in the reference in Isaiah 61:1, 3. Ultimately this points to the reign of Christ on this earth (25:35), but even now Jesus' disciples have entered into their spiritual inheritance.[88]

Blessed are those who hunger and thirst for righteousness (5:6). Those who "hunger and thirst" are in dire need. In the context of the preceding beatitudes, righteousness here includes several facets: (1) "justice" for those who have been downtrodden or who have experienced injustice; (2) personal ethical righteousness for those who desire a deeper purity in their own lives; (3) God's promised salvation come to the earth.

For they will be filled (5:6). The ultimate source of this righteousness is found only in God himself (cf. Ps. 42:1–2; 63:1). His gift of kingdom life is the only true satisfaction for those who long to see and experience true justice, personal righteousness, and salvation. God's enablement is the only satisfaction for those who long for his standard of righteousness written in his law (e.g., Ps. 119:10–11, 20).

Blessed are the merciful (5:7). In God's great mercy he does not give humans what they deserve; rather, he gives to them what they do not deserve (cf. Ps. 25:6–7; Prov. 14:21). In like manner, the merciful are those who demonstrate forgiveness toward the guilty and kindness for the hurting and needy.

Blessed are the pure in heart (5:8). The rabbis were developing a complex system of laws for maintaining ceremonial purification, which later comprised *Tohoroth* ("Cleannesses"), one of the divisions of the Mishnah. But all of those laws could bypass the most important purity of all, purity of the heart. A pure heart produces external purity, not vice versa (e.g., 15:1–19). A pure heart describes a person whose single-minded loyalty to God has affected every area of life.[89]

For they will see God (5:8). While no human can look fully at the glorious face of God (Ex. 33:20), the hope that culminates this age is that "they will see his face, and his name will be on their foreheads" (Rev. 22:4).

Blessed are the peacemakers (5:9). The theme of "peace," known by the grand Hebrew term *šâlôm* and the Greek term *eirēnē*, permeates the biblical record. It indicates completeness and wholeness in every area of life, including one's relationship with God, neighbors, and nations.[90] Making peace has messianic overtones (cf. "Prince of Peace" in Isa. 9:6–7), and true peacemakers are those who wait and work for God, who makes whole the division created by humans.

For they will be called sons of God (5:9). Those who have waited for God's messianic peace can now respond to Jesus' invitation and will receive the ultimate reward: They will be called "sons of God," fulfilling the role Israel assumed but takes for granted (Deut. 14:1; Hos. 1:10).

Salt and Light: True Disciples Witness to the Kingdom of Heaven (5:13–16)

You are the salt of the earth (5:13). The variety of important uses for salt as a preservative, as an important element of one's diet, and as a fertilizer leads to different interpretations of what Jesus means to communicate with the analogy.[91] Jesus may not be pointing to one specific application but using it in a broad, inclusive sense to refer to something that is vitally necessary for everyday life. One ancient Jewish writer listed salt as one of the basic necessities of life (Sir. 39:26), and an ancient Roman official commented, "There is nothing more useful than salt and sunshine."[92] Taken in this way, the metaphor indicates that by their very presence Jesus' disciples are necessary for the welfare of the world.

OIL LAMPS

Two of these Roman-era lamps depict the Jewish menorah (candelabrum).

A city on a hill cannot be hidden (5:14). The city may be Jerusalem, which sits on Mount Zion, since Israel with Jerusalem as the holy city were considered the light to the world (Isa. 2:2–5; 42:6; 49:6). Or Jesus may have used a local Galilean city for an illustration, such as Hippos, one of the Greek cities of the Decapolis. It was situated on a rounded hill above the southeastern shore and detached from its background, so it was clearly visible from the Capernaum area, especially when it was lit up at night.[93]

Light a lamp (5:15). The lamp (*lychnos*) that was used in a typical Palestinian home was usually a partially closed reservoir made of clay. It had a hole on top in which

▶If the Salt Loses Its Saltiness

Strictly speaking, salt cannot lose its saltiness, because sodium chloride is a stable compound. What then does Jesus mean in 5:13?

- Jesus may be alluding to rock formations that contained deposits of sodium chloride. Meat and fish were packed in these rocks to preserve them. After a period of time the salt leached out of the rocks, so the rocks were not good for anything and so thrown out.
- Jesus may be referring to the salt collected from the Dead Sea by evaporation, which often includes crystals of another mineral, gypsum, formed by the precipitation of calcium sulfate from seawater. Salt and gypsum were often mixed in various saline deposits. This impure mixture of salt and gypsum could easily be mistaken for pure salt, but the mixture was not usable for either preservation or seasoning and so was regarded as having lost its taste.
- Jesus may be alluding to salt blocks used by Arab bakers to line the floor of their ovens. After some time the intense heat eventually caused the blocks to crystallize and undergo a

change in chemical composition, finally being thrown out as unserviceable.

- Jesus may be citing a well-known proverbial saying. When rebuffing a trick question, Rabbi Joshua ben Haniniah (c. A.D. 90) apparently alludes to a proverbial saying when he asks, "Can salt lose its flavor?" The context of the saying implies that it is impossible for salt to lose its flavor, because he parallels the saying by asking, "Does the mule (being sterile) bear young?" (*b. Bek.* 8b). Sterile mules can no more bear young than can salt lose its flavor.

Thus, Jesus may be using this expression to describe an equally impossible characteristic of his disciples. As they go out into the world as salt, the proof of the reality of their profession is in the nature of their lives. True disciples cannot lose what makes them disciples because they have become changed persons, made new by the life of the kingdom of heaven. However, imposter disciples have only an external flavoring. They cannot be made salty again, because they never had that kingdom life in the first place.

to pour oil, and a spout on one end into which a wick of flax or cotton was set. It was a fairly small lamp, giving off only a modest light, so it was placed on a lampstand to give maximum illumination. Since Jewish homes were often humble one-room structures, such an elevated lamp could give light to everyone in the house.

Put it under a bowl (5:15). The word for "bowl" (*modios*)[94] comes from the Latin *modius*, the basic unit of measure for dry goods, equaling 16 sextarii, or about 2 gallons (7.5 liters). Lamps were essential for finding one's way in enclosed areas during the night and would be placed under a measuring bowl only to extinguish the light.[95]

Jesus and the Kingdom as Fulfillment of the Law (5:17–20)

Do not think that I have come to abolish the Law or the Prophets (5:17). The "Law" or "Torah" refers to the first five books of the Old Testament, called the books of Moses or the Pentateuch. The "Prophets" includes the major and minor prophets of the Old Testament as well as the historical books from Joshua to 2 Kings. The expression "the Law and the Prophets" is a way of referring to the entire Hebrew Scriptures.[96]

I have not come to abolish them but to fulfill them (5:17). The term "fulfill" (*plē-roō*) is more than obedience. Jesus not only fulfills certain anticipated roles, but his interpretation and application of the Old Testament Scriptures completes and clarifies God's intent and meaning through it. All that the Old Testament intended to communicate about God's will and hopes for humanity find their full meaning and accomplishment in Jesus' teaching and ministry.

Anyone who breaks one of the least of these commandments (5:19). The rabbis recognized a distinction between "light" and "weighty" Old Testament commandments and advocated obedience to both.[97] Light commandments are those such as the requirement to tithe on produce (cf. Lev. 27:30; Deut. 14:22), while weighty commandments are those such as profaning the name of God or the Sabbath or matters of social justice (Ex. 20:2–8; Mic. 6:8). Rabbi Simlai stated that "613 commandments were revealed to Moses at Sinai, 365 being prohibitions equal in number to the solar days of the year, and 248 being commands corresponding in number to the parts of the human body."[98]

Unless your righteousness surpasses that of the Pharisees (5:20). This may have been Jesus' most shocking statement, because the Pharisees and teachers of the law were the epitome of righteousness

(*dikaiosynē*). The Pharisees (see "Pharisees and Sadducees" at 3:7) were members of the sect that was committed to fulfilling the demands of the Old Testament through their elaborate oral tradition. Their scrupulous adherence to the written and oral law was legendary in Israel; yet Jesus says it did not gain them entrance to the kingdom of heaven.

You will certainly not enter the kingdom of heaven (5:20). Kingdom righteousness operates from the inside-out, not the outside-in, a principle fully in line with Old Testament understandings of righteousness and purification (e.g., Ps. 51:2, 7, 10, 16–17). Jesus' disciples are called to a different *kind* and *quality* of righteousness than that of the current religious leaders.

Jesus Fulfills the Law (5:21–48)

Do not murder (5:21). Although Hebrew possesses seven words for killing, the verb used in Exodus 20:13 (*rāṣaḥ*) carries the idea of murder with premeditation and deliberateness: self-murder (i.e., suicide), accessory to murder (2 Sam. 12:9), or those who have responsibility to punish known murderers but fail to do so (1 Kings 21:19). Penalty for murder, as against manslaughter (Num. 35:22ff.), was death; it was not reducible to a lesser sentence (Num. 35:31).

Anyone who says to his brother, "Raca" (5:22). "Raca" ("empty-headed") was a term of contempt used as a personal, public affront. Name-calling was highly insulting in Jewish culture, because the significance attached to one's name was thereby stripped from him or her.

Is answerable to the Sanhedrin (5:22). The Sanhedrin was the official adjudicating body of the Jews (similar to a supreme court), which was allowed by the Roman authorities to handle Jewish cases unless they impinged on Roman rule.

Anyone who says, "You fool" (5:22). Calling a person *mōre* ("fool") likewise was highly insulting, because moral connotations were attached to the term (e.g., Prov. 10:23). The Hebrew word *mōreh* means "rebel," indicating a person who was a persistent rebel against God. More likely, however, this expression comes from the Greek term *mōros* (the origin of the English word "moron"), indicating a person who consistently acted moronically.

▶ Not the Smallest Letter, Not the Least Stroke of a Pen (5:18)

Jesus confirms the full authority of the Old Testament as Scripture for all ages (2 Tim. 3:15-16), even down to the smallest components of the written text. (1) The "smallest letter" (Gk. *iōta*; KJV "jot") of the Hebrew alphabet is the *yôd*. (2) "The least stroke of a pen" (Gk. *keraia*; KJV "tittle") most likely refers to a *serif*, a small hook or projection that differentiates one Hebrew letter from a similar one (such as the letters ב bêt/ כ kap, the letters ד dalet/ ר rêš, and the letters ה he/ ח–hêt).

ב – bêt	ד – dalet	ה – he	י – yôd
כ – kap	ר – rêš	ח – hêt	

According to this statement, Jesus indicates that the inspiration and authority of the Old Testament Scripture extends to the actual words, even to the smallest of letters and the least parts of words. Scripture does not simply contain the Word of God; the words of Scripture are the very words of God.

◀

VALLEY OF HINNOM

"Gehenna" was located along the west and south

Will be in danger of the fire of hell (5:22). "Fire of hell" comes from the term *geenna*, "Gehenna." It referred to the "valley of the son of Hinnom," an area west and southwest of Jerusalem. Here Ahaz and Manasseh sacrificed their sons to Molech,[99] which caused Josiah to defile the place (2 Kings 23:10). Later the valley was used to burn refuse from Jerusalem, so the constant burning made the valley an appropriate reference to fires of punishment. Jewish apocalyptic writers began to call the Valley of Hinnom the entrance to hell, later hell itself (*4 Ezra* 7:36).

Your adversary who is taking you to court (5:25). This probably assumes a Gentile legal setting, since there is no record in Jewish law of imprisonment for debt. Before the legal process is put into action, Jesus' disciples are to "settle matters quickly," that is, to "make friends quickly" with their adversaries.

Until you have paid the last penny (5:26). The "penny" (*kodrantēs*) is the Roman bronze/copper coin *quadrans*, the smallest of the Roman coins at approximately 18 mm. A *quadrans* was the least in value of Roman coins, equal to approximately 1/64 of a *denarius* (the *denarius* was equal to approximately a day's wage; cf. 18:28; 20:1–16).[100]

◀ *left*

ALTAR OF BURNT SACRIFICE

A model of the altar in the Court of Priests in the Jerusalem Temple.

◀

QUADRANS

A Roman "penny."

You have heard that it was said, "Do not commit adultery" (5:27). Adultery (Ex. 20:14) involved sexual intercourse with mutual consent between a man, married or unmarried, and the wife of another man. The term and the penalty (death) applied equally to both man and woman, and a betrothed woman was counted as a wife.[101] Joseph recognized that adultery not only would have been an offense to Potiphar, but is especially a "sin against God" (Gen. 39:9; cf. Ps. 51:4).

But I tell you that anyone who looks at a woman lustfully (5:28). God graphically condemns the people of Israel for spiritual adultery not just when they actually worship pagan idols, but when Israel's heart and eyes desired other gods (Ezek. 6:9).

If your right eye causes you to sin, gouge it out (5:29). Jesus uses hyperbole (deliberate exaggeration) for the sake of emphasizing the seriousness of single-minded, single-eyed, single-handed spouse commitment.

"Anyone who divorces his wife must give her a certificate of divorce" (5:31). See comments on 19:3–12.

But I tell you that anyone who divorces his wife (5:32). Jesus states categorically that divorce creates adultery, the despicable nature of which he has just declared (5:27–30), because an illicit divorce turns the woman into an adulteress when she remarries.

Except for marital unfaithfulness (5:32). See comments on 19:3–12.

"Do not break your oath" (5:33). In the Old Testament, God often guarantees the fulfillment of his promises with an oath.

In the same way, the Old Testament permitted a person to swear by the name of God to substantiate an important affirmation or promise. The Pharisees developed a complicated series of rulings regarding *Shebuoth* ("oaths"), which were of two kinds: a positive oath was a promise to do something, while a negative oath was a promise not to do something (*m. Šeb*, 1:1, passim). There was a tendency among some interpreters to make this permission mean that only oaths made by invoking the name of the Lord were binding. If they weren't really serious about their oath they would say, "I swear by heaven," and since they didn't invoke the literal name of God, it wasn't binding. The increasing tendency to try to find loopholes in one's oath included swearing by "less sacred" things (e.g., "earth," "Jerusalem," etc.; cf. Matt. 23:16–22), which in turn led to the devaluation of vows. This caused some Jewish groups to warn against using any kind of oath too often.[102]

Let your "Yes" be "Yes," and your "No," "No" (5:37). A simple "yes" or "no" is enough for a trustworthy person (cf. 2 Cor. 1:15–24), a saying of Jesus that James seemingly reproduces and passes on (James 5:12). A disciple's word should be considered as trustworthy as a signed document or contract. When Jesus goes further to suggest that "anything beyond this is evil," he indicates that swearing by something with the intent to deceive can only have one source, the evil one, Satan (cf. 6:13; 13:19, 38).

"Eye for eye, and tooth for tooth" (5:38). Among some ancient societies punishment was handed out without real regard for individual cases, and often the penalty greatly exceeded the crime. The law of revenge (*lex talionis*) was originally intended as a means of providing justice and of purging evil from among God's people (Deut. 19:20–21). It was established as a check to inappropriate punishment and was not to be administered by individuals, but only by civil authorities and civil courts to protect the public, to punish offenders, and to deter crime.[103]

But I tell you, Do not resist an evil person (5:39). It is not the disciple's personal responsibility to "resist [the] evil." That is the responsibility of society's governing authorities. On the personal level, the disciple's first responsibility is to reverse the dynamic of the situation from taking to giving. Jesus uses four illustrations from the everyday affairs of a people under oppression (cf. Deut. 19:16–21).

If someone strikes you on the right cheek (5:39). To strike a person on the right cheek implied giving someone the back of the hand from a right-handed person. It is not so much the hurt as the *insult* that is here in mind, because it was a symbolic way of insulting a person's honor.[104]

If someone wants to sue you and take your tunic, let him have your cloak as well (5:40). The tunic was the basic garment, a long-sleeved inner robe similar to a nightshirt that a person wore next to the skin. It was often worn short by men and ankle length by the women. The "cloak" was the outer robe (cf. 27:35; John 19:23–24), which was an indispensable piece of clothing. When it was given as a pledge, it had to be returned before sunset, because it was used by the poor as a sleeping cover.[105]

CLOAK

Representation of a Roman woman wearing a cloak *(top)*; an Egyptian (Coptic) tunic.

If someone forces you to go one mile, go with him two miles (5:41). Persian royal post officers could force a civilian to carry official correspondence, and Roman military personnel could organize bands of unpaid laborers from the common people to construct roads, fortifications, and public buildings. The most familiar New Testament scene is when Simon of Cyrene was forced into service by the Roman guards to carry Jesus' cross (27:32; Mark 15:21). The Greek term *milion* means a "thousand paces," which measures approximately 4,854 feet (just under the distance of a modern U.S. "mile").[106]

Give to the one who asks you (5:42). Giving alms and loaning to the poor was a central exercise of Jewish piety (Deut. 15:7–11). However, Jesus widens the obligation by admonishing his disciples generally not to turn away the one who wants to borrow. This is a powerful image of generosity, because the one seeking a loan could be unscrupulous, even one's enemy, who might not repay the loan (cf. Luke 6:34–35). The Old Testament gives a low status to people who consistently seek loans and do not repay them (Ps. 37:21),[107] but to give freely to whoever seeks assistance, especially to those from whom there is little chance of repayment, is the height of generosity.

"Love your neighbor" (5:43). Love for one's neighbor was commanded by God through Moses (Lev. 19:18) and was one of the central truths of the Old Testament. When answering the legal test of a Pharisaic legal expert about the greatest commandment in the law, Jesus replied with love for God and love for one's neighbor (Matt. 22:36–40).

"Hate your enemy" (5:43). This command is not found in the Old Testament.

In fact, Moses directed the people to assist an enemy in need (Ex. 23:4–5). But God's hatred of evil is a central theme that runs through the Old Testament.[108] Those who desired to be righteous learned to adopt God's hatred of evil, so that the Psalmist could say in another place, "Do I not hate those who hate you, O LORD, and abhor those who rise up against you? I have nothing but hatred for them; I count them my enemies" (Ps. 139:21–22; cf. 26:4–5). Later groups within Israel took this further. The starkest extreme may be found at Qumran, which gave in the *Rule of the Community* explicit directions to "hate" those against God: "that they may love all the sons of light, each according to his lot in God's design, and hate all the sons of darkness, each according to his guilt in God's vengeance" (1QS 1.9–11).[109]

That you may be sons of your Father in heaven (5:45). The children of Israel were God's sons by his calling, and that calling included the obligation to carry out God's will. Now anyone who does the will of the Father is a "son" or "daughter" (cf. 12:48–50). If a person responds to God's will in the ministry of Jesus, he or she has God as heavenly Father. That includes the obligation to act like a son or daughter, which means loving as the Father loves.

Be perfect, therefore, as your heavenly Father is perfect (5:48). Jesus' disciples are to pursue the perfection of God himself: "Be holy because I, the LORD your God, am holy" (Lev. 19:2). The word "perfect" (*teleios*) reflects the Hebrew *tâmîm*, which is used for the complete commitment of a person to God, involving ethical blamelessness.[110] *Teleios* is used in the LXX in Deuteronomy 18:13: "You shall be perfect before the LORD your God." It can be used to indicate a person who has attained spiritual "maturity,"[111] but in Matthew 5:48, with the Father as the goal, disciples are to pursue the Father's perfection as the goal of their lives.

The Giving of Alms (6:1–4)

Be careful not to do your "acts of righteousness" before men (6:1). "Acts of righteousness" are the public demonstration of one's piety, which in Judaism often centered on giving alms, praying, and fasting, three issues that Jesus now addresses (6:2–4, 5–15, 16–18). A statement in the apocryphal book of Tobit highlights their interdependence within Judaism:

> Prayer with fasting is good, but better than both is almsgiving with righteousness. A little with righteousness is better than wealth with wrongdoing. It is better to give alms than to lay up gold. For almsgiving saves from death and purges away every sin. Those who give alms will enjoy a full life, but those who commit sin and do wrong are their own worst enemies. (Tobit 12:8–10)

If you do, you will have no reward from your Father in heaven (6:1). The two-ways texts of the Qumran *Rule of the Community* present lists of virtues and vices with their corresponding present world and future life rewards and punishments (1QS 4:2–14). The reward for walking in obedience to the covenant was a profound visitation of God's blessing:

> And the visitation of those who walk in it will be for healing, plentiful peace in a long life, fruitful offspring with all everlasting blessings, eternal enjoyment with endless life, and a crown of glory with majestic raiment in eternal light. (1QS 4:6–8)

Similar notions permeated much of Judaism at the time of Jesus. But Jesus shows here that legalistic obedience does not guarantee reward from God since motive is more important than simple activity.

So when you give to the needy (6:2). Performing deeds of mercy or lovingkindness was one of the pillars of religious life in Israel. Simeon the Just said, "By three things is the world sustained: by the Law, by the [temple-]service, and by deeds of loving-kindness" (*m. ʾAbot* 1.2). Poverty was widespread in ancient agrarian societies, and the people of Israel took seriously the obligation to provide for the poor (cf. Deut. 15:11). By the time of Jesus the phrase "to do mercy" had become a technical expression for doing mercy to the poor by giving alms.[112]

Do not announce it with trumpets (6:2). Some suggest a literal trumpet is in mind, either to call the people to fasts with accompanying almsgiving or to signal an especially large gift being given. Perhaps what is called to mind is the sound of

◄

SHOFAR WITH MENORAH

The ram's horn and candelabrum engraved on a basalt stone at Gamla in Galilee.

coins being tossed into the trumpet-shaped money chests ("shofar-chests") in the temple used for collecting alms.[113] But more likely Jesus is drawing on a vivid piece of typical irony. In our day the same metaphor is well known as a person who wants to "toot his/her own horn."

As the hypocrites do in the synagogues and on the streets, to be honored by men (6:2). The term "hypocrite" (*hypokritēs*) originally was used for actors on a Greek stage who put on various masks to play different roles.[114] Modern usage normally designates a hypocrite to be a person who says one thing and lives a different way. But the religious leaders are indicted by Jesus for a particular form of hypocrisy: They were carrying out external acts of righteousness that masked, even from themselves, their own inner corruption. Their hypocrisy, especially here, means doing *right things* for the *wrong reasons*.

Model Prayer: "The Lord's Prayer" (6:5–13)

When you pray (6:5). Although individual prayer was appropriate at any time, pious Jews prayed publicly at set times: morning, afternoon, and evening (Ps. 55:17; Dan. 6:10; Acts 3:1). Josephus indicates that sacrifices, including prayers,

were offered "twice a day, in the early morning and at the ninth hour."[115]

For they love to pray standing in the synagogues and on the street corners to be seen by men (6:5). When the set time of prayer arrived, pious Jews would stop what they were doing and pray. This could be done discreetly or with a great deal of display.

But when you pray, go into your room (6:6). Since common people did not often have separate, private quarters in their homes, the meaning is intended metaphorically to emphasize privacy, or it may refer to a storeroom for grain and foodstuffs. Jesus does not condemn public prayer, because he prayed publicly himself (14:19; 15:36).

Do not keep on babbling like pagans (6:7). The priests of Baal continued from morning until noon to cry, "O Baal, answer us" (1 Kings 18:26), and the multitude in the theater at Ephesus shouted for two hours "Great is Artemis of the Ephesians" (Acts 19:34).

This, then, is how you should pray (6:9). Jesus doesn't necessitate verbatim repetition of these words, because frequent repetitive use may lead to the sin of formalism condemned here. However, following Jewish custom, some Christians recited the Lord's Prayer three times a day toward the end of the first century (e.g., *Did.* 8.2–3).

Our Father in heaven (6:9). The term for "Father" is *ʾabba*, a term used by children for their earthly fathers to express the warmth and intimacy a child experiences when in the security of a loving father's care. The motif of the "heavenly Father" occurs throughout the Old Testament,[116] growing increasingly popular during the Second Temple period in prayers for protection and forgiveness.[117] The Jewish *Ahabah Rabbah* begins, "Our Father, merciful Father," and the first-century *Eighteen Benedictions* includes the petitions, "Graciously favor us, our Father, with understanding from you," and "Forgive us, our Father, for we have sinned against you."[118] The way Jesus uses "heavenly Father" to address God is unique because Jesus is the unique Son (cf. 3:17), but by calling his disciples to share in the kingdom of heaven, they now have entered into a relationship with his Father as well.[119]

Hallowed be your name (6:9). The first petition is directed toward God's name. The purpose of hallowing that name (the name signifies the person) is that God will be "sanctified" or set apart as holy among all people and in all actions. The Jewish *Qaddish* ("holy") prayer of the synagogue, which likely goes back to Jesus' time, begins similarly: "Exalted and hallowed be his great name in the world which He created according to his will."[120] This affirms the typical Jewish expectation that God is to be treated with the highest honor.

Your kingdom come (6:10). The *Qaddish* continues similarly: "May he establish his kingdom in your lifetime and in your days, and in the lifetime of the whole household of Israel, speedily and at a near time." The Old Testament looked for God to send his anointed one to rule the earth. Now that Jesus has inaugurated that kingdom, his disciples live with the anticipation of the completion of that program. This petition is reflected in a prayer expressed in the early church in *marana tha*, "Come, O Lord!"[121]

Your will be done on earth as it is in heaven (6:10). God reigns in heaven absolutely, which means that all of heaven experiences his perfect will. Jesus prays that earth will experience that same rule of God.

Give us today our daily bread (6:11). "Bread" is an example of synecdoche, a part-whole figure of speech for "food" (4:4), but especially referring to all of the believer's needs, physical and spiritual.[122] The word translated "daily" (*epiousios*) in connection with "bread" has been broadly debated, but the wording seems to recall Israel's daily reliance on God for manna in the desert (Ex. 16). In the same way as manna was only given one day at a time, disciples are to rely on daily provision for life from God, helping them to develop a continuing, conscious dependence on him (cf. Matt. 6:34; Phil. 4:6).

Forgive us our debts, as we also have forgiven our debtors (6:12). Sin creates an obligation or "debt" to God that humans cannot possibly repay. The evidence that a person has truly been forgiven of his or her debt of sin is the willingness to forgive others (cf. 18:21–35), a sentiment found commonly in Judaism: "Forgive your neighbor the wrong he has done, and then your sins will be pardoned when you pray" (Sir. 28:2).

Lead us not into temptation, but deliver us from the evil one (6:13). Since God is not one who tempts his people to do evil (James 1:13) and the word rendered "temptation" can be used for either temptation or test (cf. 1:12–13; see comments on Matt. 4:1), this petition indicates that the disciples should pray either that God removes tests of their faith, such as when manna was given to test Israel,[123] or else they should pray that their testing will not become an occasion for temptation. This is similar to a standardized Jewish morning and evening prayer:

> Bring me not into the power of sin,
> And not into the power of guilt,
> And not into the power of temptation,
> And not into the power of anything
> shameful.[124]

Satan's influence is behind every attempt to turn a testing into a temptation to evil, so Jesus teaches his disciples that they need to rely on God, not only for physical sustenance, but also for moral triumph and spiritual victory.[125]

Fasting (6:16–18)

When you fast (6:16). The law required only one fast a year—on the Day of Atonement.[126] The expression used there is "deny yourselves" (NIV) or "humble your souls" (NASB), indicating that in addition to fasting, the people were to demonstrate a humbling of their souls by wearing sackcloth, mourning, and praying on the Day of Atonement (cf. Ps. 35:13; Isa. 58:3).[127] As time passed, fasts multiplied for legitimate purposes, such as a sign of repentance and seeking God's mercy (e.g., Ezra 8:21–23), and certain days of the year became regular days of fasting (Neh. 9:1; Zech. 8:19).

Do not look somber as the hypocrites do (6:16). Fasting also became legalized among some sectarians to twice a week (cf. Luke 18:12), usually on Monday and Thursday, because Moses is said to have gone up on Sinai on those days. Jesus condemns the practice of hypocritical fasting by the religious leaders, since they were fasting with the intention of getting recognition from the people.

But when you fast, put oil on your head and wash your face (6:17). This kind of anointing and washing is not religious, but is to signify preparation to enjoy life, similar to the expression in Ecclesiastes, "Go, eat your food with gladness, and drink your wine with a joyful heart, for it is now that God favors what you do. Always be clothed in white, and always anoint your head with oil" (Eccl. 9:7–8).

Choose Your Master: God or Wealth (6:19–24)

Do not store up for yourselves treasures on earth (6:19). Material wealth was important to the people of Israel, because wealth was often seen as a sign of God's blessing and the reward for obedience to him (see comments on 6:1). One ancient rabbi said:

> A man should always teach his son a cleanly [or easy] craft, and let him pray to him to whom riches and possessions belong, for there is no craft

wherein there is not both poverty and wealth; for poverty comes not from a man's craft, nor riches from a man's craft, but all is according to his merit. (*m. Qidd.* 4.14)

But the accumulation of wealth for its own sake was deceptive, because one could find a false sense of security or an inaccurate assessment of one's spirituality in material treasure.

Where moth and rust destroy, and where thieves break in and steal (6:19). Jewish writers regularly warned the people that wealth is not the final determination of one's spiritual standing before God. Wealth could be acquired illegitimately, and it also was subject to the destructive effects of life in a fallen world.[128]

But store up for yourselves treasures in heaven (6:20). The idea of storing up good works before God was prominent in Israel's history. Sirach 29:10–11 exhorts, "Lose your silver for the sake of a brother or a friend, and do not let it rust under a stone and be lost. Lay up your treasure according to the commandments of the Most High, and it will profit you more than gold."

The eye is the lamp of the body. If your eyes are good, your whole body will be full of light (6:22). Some Greek and Jewish writers spoke of the eye as a lamp that contained its own source of light that shone outward to illuminate objects, which was the indication of the vitality of life in a person.[129] But here Jesus seems to use the eye in a different metaphorical sense, as a lamp that will illumine a person's inner life. The "evil eye" in the ancient world is an eye that enviously covets what belongs to another. It is a greedy or avaricious eye.[130] A "good

eye" speaks of singleness of purpose, undivided loyalty. It will let into the body that which its sight is fixed upon. If the eye is good, it is fixed on good treasure, the things of God; then the heart will be filled with the light of God's treasure (e.g., *T. Iss.* 4.4–6).

Either he will hate the one and love the other, or he will be devoted to the one and despise the other (6:24). The biblical notion of "hate" and "love" understands them to be patterns of life, not simply emotional reactions. "Do I not hate those who hate you, O LORD, and abhor those who rise up against you? I have nothing but hatred for them; I count them my enemies" (Ps. 139:21–22; cf. Matt. 5:43; 1QS 1.9–11).

You cannot serve both God and Money (6:24). Jesus personifies wealth or possessions of all kinds as a rival god, "Money" (Gk. *mamōnas*). The temptation to worship the god of materialism was well known in Judaism. A heart-rending confession from the second-century B.C. *Testament of Judah* 19:1–2 states: "My children, love of money leads to idolatry, because once they are led astray by money, they designate as gods

MAMMON

First-century bronze coins found in an oil lamp at En Gedi.

▼

A WELL-KNOWN BUMPER STICKER expresses the idolatry of the modern world: "He who dies with the most toys wins." That is, life and the afterlife have no real meaning, so make it your ambition to play hard and find your worth in the materialism and pleasure of this world. One primary way to avoid this form of idolatry is to put God at the center of our lives and love him with all that we have. Money, wealth, and possessions have three primary purposes in Scripture:

- to give appropriate care for one's own family and prevent them from becoming a burden to others.[A-44]
- to help those who are in need, especially the church.[A-45]
- to encourage and support the work of the gospel both at home and around the world.[A-46]

those who are not gods. It makes anyone who has it go out of his mind. On account of money I utterly lost my children." The writer goes on to say, "The prince of error blinded me" (19:4), pointing to Satan's activity in using material idolatry to lead astray the children of God.

Provider of the Disciples' Needs (6:25–34)

Do not worry about your life (6:25). Worry is inappropriate when it is misdirected or in wrong proportion, or when it indicates lack of trust in God. Appropriate concern and work are connected with trusting God and working within the pattern of his creation.

What you will eat or drink; or about your body, what you will wear (6:25). Jesus is speaking to people familiar with life's daily struggle. Much of their daily routine was spent trying to get enough supplies for day-to-day existence. The poor especially did not have extensive supplies, so the question of what one would eat tomorrow was very real, especially with the vagaries of seasonal famine, fire, or flood.

Look at the birds of the air; they do not sow or reap or store away in barns, and yet your heavenly Father feeds them (6:26). Birds expend energy in doing what is their natural way, such as building nests and collecting food for their young, yet it is actually God who feeds and clothes them. A first-century Jewish text states, "For if I am hungry, I will cry out to you, O God, and you will give me (something). You feed the birds and the fish, as you send rain to the wilderness that the grass may sprout to provide pasture in the wilderness for every living thing, and if they are hungry, they will lift up their face to you" (*Pss. Sol.* 5.8–10).

Are you not much more valuable than they? (6:26). This is a typical rabbinic style of arguing "from the lesser to the greater." The point is that when disciples are properly responsible to carry out the ways of life as ordained by God, God is faithful to carry out his responsible care of the order. Humans are the crown and ruler of God's creation (Ps. 8:3–8), and their needs will receive appropriate attention from God.

Who of you by worrying can add a single hour to his life? (6:27). The NIV translation is a good rendering of a curious expression in Greek, which reads, "add one forearm length (*pēchys*) to his age/stature (*hēlikia*)." The term *pēchys* is a standardized unit of measure, the typical length of a forearm, or about eighteen inches, called a "cubit."[131] The term *hēlikia* usually designates a measure of age or maturity (e.g., Heb. 11:11), but occasionally is used for physical stature (e.g., Luke 2:52; 19:3). The present context instead indicates a measure of duration of life. Worrying can't extend one's life.

See how the lilies of the field grow (6:28). "Lilies [*krina*] of the field" draw to mind God's provision in nature for flowers growing wild, which probably surround Jesus, the disciples, and the crowd. Even today, red and purple anemone (*anemone coronaria*) crowning ten-inch stalks, along with blue iris, grow wild on the hillside above the Sea of Galilee.[132]

Not even Solomon in all his splendor was dressed like one of these (6:29). The beautiful flowers growing wild on the Galilean hillside surrounding Jesus elicit a striking contrast to Solomon's royal robes, whose wealth prompted a visit from the Queen of Sheba and whose life became a proverbial success story.[133]

▲

GRASS OF THE FIELD

Grass is being carried by women to feed animals in Samaria.

The grass of the field, which is here today and tomorrow is thrown into the fire (6:30). The green grass of spring when cut, dried, and bundled was a natural source of fuel for fire ovens (6:28) and a common biblical metaphor for dramatic changes of fortune as well as for human frailty and transience.[134]

For the pagans run after all these things, and your heavenly Father knows that you need them (6:32). "Pagans" (*ta ethnē*), rendered elsewhere in Matthew as "the nations" (12:21; 25:32; 28:19), commonly designates non-Jews or Gentiles. Here the emphasis is on those who operate outside of God's values. Those with faith in God's provision will not worry and will reject the pursuits and values of unbelievers.

But seek first his kingdom and his righteousness (6:33). This climactic admonition draws the listeners back to the key verse of the sermon, where Jesus declared,

◀ *left*

"NOT EVEN SOLOMON IN ALL HIS SPLENDOR"

Spring wildflowers in the Middle East

"Unless your righteousness surpasses that of the Pharisees and the teachers of the law, you will certainly not enter the kingdom of heaven" (5:20).

Each day has enough trouble of its own (6:34). Since no exact parallel to this maxim exists,[135] Jesus' saying apparently became proverbial, because James gives an admonition that apparently draws on this truth (James 4:13–15).

The Kingdom Life in Relation to Others (7:1–6)

Do not judge, or you too will be judged (7:1). A similar sentiment is found in an earlier Jewish writing, "Before judgment comes, examine yourself; and at the time of scrutiny you will find forgiveness" (Sir. 18:20).

With the measure you use, it will be measured to you (7:2). A similar warning is found in a rabbinic ruling on adultery: "With what measure a man metes it shall be measured to him again" (*m. Soṭah* 1.7). The "measure" could be a scale, or a vessel or rod used for calculating weight or distance, but was often used figuratively, as here (cf. 23:32).

Why do you look at the speck of sawdust in your brother's eye and pay no attention to the plank in your own eye? (7:3). Jesus now uses hyperbole (intentional exaggeration) as an illustration to make his point. The "speck" refers to a small twig or stalk, in contrast to a "plank" or large beam. The contrast may reflect Jesus' own background as a carpenter's son (13:55). The extreme that Jesus condemns is passing judgment on another person while having a similar problem oneself.

Do not give dogs what is sacred (7:6). "Dog" came to be a derogatory label for a person who was apart from, or an enemy of, Israel's covenant community (see "Dogs and Pigs in the Ancient World"). "What is sacred" in this context most likely refers to the message of the gospel of the kingdom, indicating that this holy message must not be defiled by those who are unreceptive to, or have rejected, Jesus' invitation.

Do not throw your pearls to pigs (7:6). The image of the dog is reinforced by the

▶

ROMAN SCALES

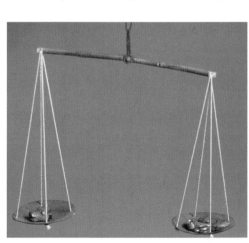

▶ Dogs and Pigs in the Ancient World

Dogs. To modern readers the mention of "dogs" conjures up images of well-groomed household pets, but in the ancient world dogs lived in squalor, running the streets and scavenging for food (Ps. 59:14–15). To refer to a person as a dog was a grave insult, reducing the person's status to among the lowest on the social scale (2 Sam. 16:9). Jews had a particular revulsion for dogs because they alone among domesticated animals were willing to eat human corpses (1 Kings 21:19, 24; 22:38). As a metaphor, "dog" was a humiliating label for those apart from, or enemies of, Israel's covenant community.[A-47] Although dogs were often trained for guarding flocks (Job 30:1) and humans (Isa. 56:10; Tobit 6:2; 11:4), they were not normally brought into the home (see comments on 15:26–28). Jesus' statement means that his disciples are not to treat the gospel message as discarded food thrown to scavengers who are outside the kingdom.

Pigs. Although pork was a highly prized food among many people in the ancient Mediterranean world, it was rejected by Jews (and perhaps some ancient priestly Egyptians), perhaps because pigs, like dogs, were scavenging animals. Their omnivorous habits occasionally led pigs to feed on decaying flesh, a practice deplorable to Jews. The rejection of pork came to symbolize the Jews' separation from the unclean Gentile world. When the martyr Eleazar was forced to eat pork, he refused and was executed by the Greek tyrant Antiochus IV Epiphanes (2 Macc. 6:18–20; *4 Macc.* 5:1–6:30). Pigs were often dangerous because they ravaged fields (Ps. 80:13) and, while running wild in city streets, were sometimes responsible for the death of little children.[A-48]

parallel image of a pig, because pigs, like dogs, were usually wild, scavenging animals. "Pearls" symbolize the value of the message of the kingdom of heaven (see comments on 13:45–46). Something so valuable should not be given to those who have no appreciation for such precious truths, whose nature is demonstrated by their rejection of the message of the gospel.

If you do, they may trample them under their feet, and then turn and tear you to pieces (7:6). Dogs and pigs are linked elsewhere in Scripture (Isa. 66:3; 2 Peter 2:22) as dangerously wild and ritually unclean animals. The bizarre behavior of wild animals produced fear because their often-intense hunger could cause them to attack humans (cf. Ps. 22:16–17). Pigs and dogs were symbols of filth and paganism (cf. Isa. 65:4; 66:3, 17), and the image warns disciples about the danger of those who have rejected the message of the kingdom of heaven.

Prayer and the Disciples' Kingdom Life (7:7–12)

Ask . . . seek . . . knock and the door will be opened to you (7:7). "Ask" means to pray with humility and consciousness of need. "Seek" means to pray and to be active in pursuing God's will. "Knock" seems to point toward persistence. Jesus uses "knocking" here as a metaphor for prayer; in the apostle John's vision the risen Jesus "knocks" so that the church will hear and open themselves to the intimacy of his fellowship (Rev. 3:20).[136]

Bread ... stone ... fish ... snake (7:9–10). Staple food in a Jewish daily diet included bread and fish. A responsible father would not be mean and trick his children with stones that resembled bread (cf. Jesus' first temptation, 4:1–4), now would he trick them with snakes that resembled fish? Jews were prohibited from eating fish that lacked fins and scales (Lev. 11), perhaps because of their resemblance to snakes (e.g., eel, catfish).[137]

True Discipleship: With Jesus or Against Him? (7:13–29)

Enter through the narrow gate (7:13). The image of two roads in life is fairly common, whether speaking of separate roads that lead either to paradise or to Gehenna (*b. Ber.* 28b), or of a narrow road of life's hardships that ultimately

leads to a broad path of eternal blessing (e.g., 2 Esd. 7:3–9).

Watch out for false prophets (7:15). Jesus warns against revolutionary leaders who can lead the people astray with their false form of prophecy, a common Old Testament warning.[138] These are general warnings against those who attempt to

▶The Golden Rule

The moral maxim that has come to be known as the "Golden Rule" is one of the commonly accepted bases of human civilization. It occurs in both positive and negative forms. The ancient Roman philosopher and statesman Seneca (4 B.C.–A.D. 65) expressed the principle positively, "Let us show our generosity in the same manner that we would wish to have it bestowed on us" (*De Beneficiis* 2.1.1), while the Chinese philosopher Confucius (551–479 B.C.) stated it negatively, "Do not do unto others what you would not want others to do unto you!" (*Analects* 15:23).[A-49]

The precept appears to have been a common theme in Judaism of the time of Jesus. Tobit gives a negative form of the principle, "Watch yourself, my son, in everything you do, and discipline yourself in all your conduct. And what you hate, do not do to anyone" (Tobit 4:14b–15). Hillel the Elder (c. 70 B.C.–A.D. 10) supposedly had as his motto, "What is hateful to you, do not do to your neighbor." In the only text in the whole of rabbinic literature that attributes the saying to Hillel, the Elder goes on to say, "That is the whole Torah. The rest is commentary. Go and learn!" (*b. Šabb.* 31a).[A-50]

For Jesus, the kingdom life that he is inaugurating fulfills the deepest inclination of humans, who are created in the image of God. Kingdom life now enables his disciples to live life the way God intends it to be lived. As such it "sums up the Law and the Prophets" (cf. 5:17–20).

lead the people of Israel by falsely speaking for God. Josephus tells of a variety of popular prophets who led the people to insurrection: "Deceivers and imposters, under the pretense of divine inspiration fostering revolutionary changes, they persuaded the multitude to act like madmen, and led them out into the desert under the belief that God would there give them tokens of deliverance."[139] Among the more popular of these leaders of movements were Theudas (c. A.D. 45), the prophet from Egypt (c. A.D. 56), and Jesus son of Hananiah (c. A.D. 62–69).[140]

They come to you in sheep's clothing (7:15). This proverbial expression draws on the natural enmity of sheep and wolves (e.g., Isa. 11:6; 65:25) and will be the basis of Paul's later warning to the Ephesian elders (Acts 20:29) and the early church father Ignatius's warning to the church at Philadelphia (Ign. *Phil.* 2:1–2).

Thus, by their fruit you will recognize them (7:20). False prophets will produce bad fruit, which from an Old Testament perspective includes leading the people away from God to follow false gods (Deut. 13:1–18) or whose prophecies are not fulfilled (18:21–22).

Therefore everyone who hears these words of mine and puts them into practice (7:24). This is typical Jewish figurative language, as is reflected in the Qumran literature (1QH 6:26 [14:26]; 7:8–9 [15:8–9]) and in an early second century Tannaitic saying: "A man of good deeds who has studied much Torah, to what may he be likened? To someone who first lays stones and then bricks. Even when much water rises and lies

against them, it does not dislodge them."[141] But Jesus' saying reflects a more specific reference to his surroundings and the object of his criticism.

Like a wise man who built his house on the rock . . . like a foolish man who built his house on sand (7:24, 26). Jesus demonstrates familiarity with building techniques in this parable, perhaps a reflection of his own training in his father's trade as a carpenter (*tektōn*; see comments on 13:54). The alluvial sand ringing the seashore on the Sea of Galilee was hard on the surface during the hot summer months. But a wise builder would not be fooled by such surface conditions. He would dig down sometimes ten feet below the surface sand to the bedrock below, and there establish the foundation for his house. When the winter rains came, overflowing the banks of the Jordan River flowing into the sea,

REFLECTIONS

THE RELIGIOUS ESTABLISHMENT OF JESUS' DAY advocated a form of surface righteousness that masked an unstable foundation of religious hypocrisy. Jesus gives the bedrock invitation to true life in the kingdom of heaven, but it will be the unpopular way, the hard way, because those who follow him will leave behind the way of comfort found in identifying with the popular religious establishment.

As always, the wise person shows he or she has carefully viewed the shifting sands of life's teachings and understands that Jesus is the only secure truth in life. The wise person thinks ahead to when there will be storms, and he sacrifices the enjoyment of the present good weather for the sake of building his or her life on the rock of Jesus' words about reality. The foolish man thinks only of the present convenient situation and does not plan for storms of life or eternity. The choice is no less stark in our own day. Wise men and women build their lives on Jesus, regardless of cultural weather.

houses built on the alluvial sand surface would have an unstable foundation layer; but houses built on bedrock would be able to withstand the floods. Excavations in the late 1970s in the region uncovered basalt stone bedrock that was apparently used for the foundation of buildings in antiquity.[142]

Cleansing the Leper (8:1–4)

Large crowds followed him (8:1). The people will see that Jesus is not only Messiah in word (chs. 5–7) but is also Messiah in deed (chs. 8–9). Jesus' miracles may be divided into three general classes: healings, exorcisms, and nature miracles, with raisings of the dead as a subcategory of the last. Matthew will focus on each of these types of miracles here as a demonstration that the kingdom of God truly has arrived (cf. 12:28).

A man with leprosy came and knelt before him (8:2). The word "leprosy" is a transliteration of the Greek word *lepros*. In the ancient world leprosy was associated with a variety of skin diseases and suspicious skin disorders. The Old Testa-

ment provided specific guidelines for the examination and treatment of those with skin diseases (see Lev. 13–14), since many of the disorders were considered highly contagious. The line between medical and spiritual impurity was often blurred, however, because of the uncertainty of diagnosis.

All those with leprosy were required to be examined by the priest, who after examination could pronounce a person clean or unclean (Lev. 13:2ff.). If found leprous, the diseased individual was to be isolated from the rest of the community, required to wear torn clothes, cover the lower part of his or her face, and cry out "Unclean! Unclean!" (Lev. 13:45–46; Num. 5:2–4). The rabbinic tractate *Negaʿim* distinguishes two categories of two types each of leprosy: the Bright Spot, which is bright-white like snow, the second shade of which is the white like the lime of the temple; the Rising, which is white like the skin in an egg, the second shade of which is the white like white wool (*m. Neg.* 1:1). The modern conception of leprosy brings to mind the dreaded and debilitating illness known as Hansen's disease, caused by the *Mycobac-*

▶ Military Units of the Roman Army

In the Roman army at the time of Jesus there were twenty-five legions spread throughout the empire—eight on the Rhine, six in the Danube provinces, three in Spain, two in Africa, two in Egypt, and four in Syria (Tacitus, *Ann.* 4.5). The tactical strength called for the following numbers, but each unit often operated with fewer.

- *Legion* = normally 6,000 men (5,300 infantry and 700 cavalry).
- *Cohort* = Each legion was divided into 10 cohorts.

- *Centuria* = Each cohort had 6 *centuria* (century), 100 men, the smallest unit of the Roman legion. Each *centuria* was commanded by a centurion.
- *Centurion* = The centurion was the principal professional officer in the armies of ancient Rome. Most centurions were of plebeian origin and were promoted from the ranks of the common soldiers. They formed the backbone of the legion and were responsible for enforcing discipline. They received much higher pay and a greater share of the spoils than did common soldiers (as much as fifteen times more).[A-51]

terium leprae bacillus. It is most prevalent in low, humid, tropical or subtropical areas of the world, most cases being found in Asia, Africa, South America, and the Pacific Islands.

See that you don't tell anyone. But go, show yourself to the priest (8:4). Lepers had to be reexamined by the priest and declared "clean," and then had to offer a sacrifice on his behalf (Lev. 14:1–32). The sacrifice offered by the cleansed leper was in the category of ᵓašam offering, offered as payment for either purification or reparation.

Healing the Centurion's Servant (8:5–13)

When Jesus had entered Capernaum, a centurion came to him (8:5). The centurion was a Roman military officer. Although there is little tangible evidence of a centurion being stationed in Galilee until A.D. 44,[143] recent excavations reveal a military garrison at Capernaum with quarters to the east of the Jewish village. The troops lived in better houses than the local population. To the surprise of archaeologists, the excavations reveal that these soldiers had a typical Roman bath at their disposal.

My servant lies at home paralyzed and in terrible suffering (8:6). The descriptions have led some to suggest that the cause was poliomyelitis (i.e., polio), a scourge of many ancient societies.

Lord, I do not deserve to have you come under my roof (8:8). The centurion displays a sensitivity for the Jewish populace when he considers himself unworthy to receive the Jewish teacher Jesus into his Gentile home, because entering the home of a Gentile rendered a Jew ceremonially unclean (see Acts 10:28). A rabbinic saying states, "The dwelling places of gentiles are unclean" (*m. ᵓOhal.* 18:7).

▶ Rabbi Hanina Ben Dosa and Healing from a Distance

Much-discussed accounts of healing over distance appear in the rabbinic literature, among them a story of Rabbi Hanina ben Dosa that occurs in the Babylonian Talmud (*b. Ber.* 34b). It reads:

> It happened that when Rabban Gamaliel's son fell ill, he sent two of his pupils to R. Hanina ben Dosa that he might pray for him. When he saw them, he went to the upper room and prayed. When he came down, he said to them, "Go, for the fever has left him." They said to him, "Are you a prophet?" He said to them, "I am no prophet, neither am I a prophet's son, but this is how I am blessed: if my prayer is fluent in my mouth, I know that the sick man is favored; if not, I know that the disease is fatal." They sat down, and wrote and noted the hour. When they came to Rabban Gamaliel, he said to them, "By heaven! You have neither detracted from it, nor added to it, but this is how it happened. It was at that hour that the fever left him and he asked us for water to drink."

Such accounts within Judaism are rare and were considered extraordinary, so Jesus' healing in this manner would have been regarded as astonishing. Rabbi Hanina ben Dosa knew that he was only a prayer intermediary and that he did not have even the stature of a prophet. In striking contrast, Jesus knew that he was himself the source of the healing (8:7, "I will go and heal him"), which the centurion knew as well (8:8, "But just say the word, and my servant will be healed"), a prerogative that only a divine Messiah could claim and validate.

Many will come from the east and the west and will take their places at the feast (8:11). "East and west" points to the breadth of peoples who will come from the ends of the earth. The Old Testament anticipated the inclusion of all the peoples of the earth in the eschatological banquet (Isa. 25:6–9; 56:3–8).

But the subjects of the kingdom will be thrown outside (8:12). The expression "subjects of the kingdom" (lit., "sons of the kingdom") is a Semitism pointing to national Israel,[144] whose leaders have taken exclusive claim to God's kingdom through their Abrahamic heritage (3:8–9). Jesus paints a woeful picture of the future of unrepentant Israel with terms common to descriptions of hell, or Gehenna.[145] These themes are not much different from the Old Testament prophets, who consistently called Israel back to God.

And his servant was healed at that very hour (8:13). Different from other stories of healing that circulated in Judaism, this account of Jesus' authority as the one who himself heals, not as an intermediary, sets him apart from all others (see "Rabbi Hanina Ben Dosa and Healing from a Distance").

Healing Peter's Mother-In-Law (8:14–17)

Jesus came into Peter's house (8:14). In 1968 excavations were undertaken that have convinced most archaeologists that they have found the actual site of Peter's house in Capernaum. Sifting down through the remains of centuries-old

▶ Excavating the House of Simon Peter

Much of church history has venerated a location that is said to be the actual site of Peter's house. The majority of scholars now believe that excavations undertaken in 1968 have basically confirmed the authenticity of the claim.[A-52]

The building was used as a typical home for an extended family from approximately 63 B.C. until A.D. 50. Peter and Andrew apparently moved the family fishing business from Bethsaida to Capernaum and established their residence in this house, large enough for an extended family. Mark tells us it was the home of both Peter and Andrew (cf. Mark 1:29).

During the second half of the first century A.D. the use of the house changed. Domestic pottery ceased to be used and the walls of the large center room were plastered—quite unusual for the region except for where groups of people gathered. Graffiti that mention Jesus as "Lord" and "Christ" in Greek are found. These pieces of evidence indicate that during this time the house became a center of Christian worship.

The house-church continued in existence for nearly three hundred years, as is evidenced from over a hundred Greek, Aramaic, Syriac, Latin, and Hebrew graffiti scratched on the plastered walls, along with numerous forms of crosses, a boat, and other letters. Among the graffiti are at least two possible occurrences of Peter's name.

In the fifth century an octagonal church was built precisely over the original plastered house-church, with the same area and dimensions, a type of architecture used to venerate earlier sacred sites.

Princeton Seminary New Testament scholar James Charlesworth exclaims, "Since there are no rival options for Peter's house, and since it was clearly where the house has been discovered or somewhere close to it, it seems valid to conclude that Peter's house may have been excavated and identified. The discovery is virtually unbelievable and sensational. Despite the sensational nature of the find, learned archaeologists and historians have slowly come to the same conclusion."[A-53]

◀

"HOUSE OF PETER" EXCAVATIONS

The remains of this first-century home are located adjacent to the synagogue.

▼

churches, excavators came to what was originally a house, built in approximately 63 B.C. The house was originally one story, with the walls of black basalt stones and an original roof made from beams and branches of trees covered with a mixture of earth and straw. Pottery shards, oil lamps, and coins discovered in the ruins date back to the first century, along with artifacts that included several fishhooks in the earliest layers of the floor. The house was organized as several rooms built around two interior courtyards. The dimensions were fairly large by ancient standards, but it was similar to other houses in the area.

He saw Peter's mother-in-law (8:14). Mark informs us that this is both Peter and Andrew's house (Mark 1:29). Perhaps it had been a home of Peter and Andrew's parents, but was now occupied by the sons and their larger extended families, including on Peter's side at least his wife and her parent(s). Paul also alludes to Peter's marriage (cf. 1 Cor. 9:5).

Lying in bed with a fever (8:14). Matthew's expression (*beblēmenos*; lit., "having been thrown on a bed") indicates that Peter's mother-in-law is in the throes of severe feverish illness, perhaps malarial. Fever was considered by the populace to be a disease, not a symptom (cf. John 4:52; Acts 28:8).

This was to fulfill what was spoken through the prophet Isaiah: "He took up our infirmities and carried our diseases" (8:17). This is another allusion by Matthew to the Servant of Isaiah's prophecy (Isa. 53:4),[146] here focusing on the Servant's role of bringing healing. The Servant bears the sicknesses of others through his suffering and death. Many modern scholars doubt that first-century Jews would have interpreted Isaiah 53:4 messianically,[147] but some later rabbinic texts knew a messianic interpretation of the passage.[148]

Expected Discipleship Disappointed (8:18–22)

Then a teacher of the law came to him (8:19). Although the Jews had a high percentage of the population trained in the rudiments of reading and writing, only a small segment of people regularly worked with writing materials, and even fewer had access to books or Scriptures. Therefore, the skills of writing and reading were highly valued. Throughout the ancient world a class of people arose called "scribes" (Gk. *grammateus*), people trained in reading, writing, and transcribing. Because of the importance of that trade, their role often went far beyond simple secretarial skills to include teaching, interpretation, and regulation of laws found in official documents. In Judaism a class of scribes had developed who were experts in interpreting and teaching Scripture (hence the NIV "teacher of the law").

Teacher, I will follow you wherever you go (8:19). This teacher of the law has in mind the kind of master-disciple relationship in which the would-be disciple examines various masters and then enlists himself in following the most popular or the best-equipped teacher.[149]

Foxes have holes and birds of the air have nests, but the Son of Man has no place to lay his head (8:20). Jesus draws on a familiar metaphor to explain the uniqueness of his form of master-disciple relationship.

The Son of Man has no place to lay his head (8:20). Jesus' stern reply checks this enthusiastic recruit, because his form of discipleship is a different sort from what he has experienced in his prior training. Teachers of the law enjoyed a relatively high status within Judaism, but Jesus has no school or synagogue or prestigious place of honor among the religious establishment. Jesus apparently stayed at the home of friends, relatives, and disciples through most of his ministry, such as the home of Peter and Andrew while in Capernaum. The expression "no place to lay his head" does not indicate he is a homeless Cynic-type philosopher, but rather that his ministry will not result in an institutional establishment with comfortable benefits.

▶Jesus as the "Son of Man"

The expression "Son of Man" would strike a relatively ambiguous chord with the scribal teacher of the law. In Ezekiel, God refers to the prophet with the expression "son of man" over ninety times,[A-54] pointing to Ezekiel's frailty as a human before the mighty God revealed in the vision. But "Son of Man" is also used in Daniel's prophecy to refer to a glorified Sovereign, the apocalyptic messianic figure who rules forever with the Ancient of Days (Dan. 7:13–14). This latter sense of the expression found its way into use in Judaism, in the pseudepigraphal writings *1 Enoch* and 2 Esdras 13 (or *4 Ezra* 13). The reference in *1 Enoch* is particularly interesting because it precedes the time of Jesus: "...pain shall seize them when they see that Son of Man sitting on the throne of his glory. [These] kings, governors, and all the landlords shall [try to] bless, glorify, extol him who rules over everything, him who has been concealed. For the Son of Man was concealed from the beginning, and the Most High One preserved him in the presence of his power; then he revealed him to the holy and the elect ones" (*1 En.* 62:5–7).[A-55]

With such a general ambiguity, "Son of Man" is convenient for Jesus to use to give instruction about his true identity. It does not have popular associations attached to it, such as were attached to titles like "Messiah," "Son of David," or even "Son of God." Instead, he can teach the meaning of his true identity by referring to himself with the expression, which indeed is his favorite self-designation. With a general threefold progression, Jesus uses the expression to clarify exactly who he is and what is his ministry.

- The Son of Man is the humble Servant, who has come to forgive sins of common sinners in his earthly ministry.[A-56]
- The Son of Man is the suffering Servant, whose atoning death and resurrection will redeem his people.[A-57]
- The Son of Man is the glorious King and Judge, who will return to bring the kingdom of heaven to earth.[A-58]

Jesus' mission is not always understood because of the misperceptions and faulty expectations of the people, the religious leaders, and even his own disciples. But at the end, it is perfectly clear that he is claiming to be the divine Messiah of Israel (cf. 26:63–68).

Another disciple said to him (8:21). This is not one of the Twelve, but one of the broader circle of followers who gather around Jesus, not yet fully understanding what his form of discipleship will entail. Like the teacher of the law, this person desires to be a disciple of Jesus and is even perceived to be one in the loose sense of the term.[150]

Lord, first let me go and bury my father (8:21). Burial of the dead supersedes other religious obligations in Israel, even for the priests, who were allowed to be defiled by touching the dead if it was for a family member (Lev. 21:2). The obligation to care for the dead comes implicitly from the command to "honor your father and mother," which is among the greatest commandments[151]; this was made explicit in later Jewish practice.[152] Surprisingly, the practice began to supersede other religious obligations: "He whose dead lies unburied before him is exempt from reciting the *Shema*, from saying the *Tefillah* and from wearing phy-

▶

BURIAL TOMBS

These date from the Maccabean era.

lacteries" (*m. Ber.* 3:1). The Talmudic interpretation carries it even one step further: "He who is confronted by a dead relative is freed from reciting the *Shema*, from the Eighteen Benedictions, and from all the commandments stated in the Torah" (*b. Ber.* 31a).

Follow me, and let the dead bury their own dead (8:22). Jesus will later rebuke the Pharisees and teachers of the law for not rightly honoring father and mother (15:1–9), so he is not advocating the contravening of the Old Testament prescription. Trying to understand Jesus' response has led to a number of explanations. Some think that the person's father has not yet died and that he wants to stay with him until then. Or perhaps he is returning to fulfill the second stage of burial by the transfer of the bones of his father a year after death to an ossuary. Others look for explanation in a metaphorical allusion in Jesus' language, so that he intends to mean something like "let those who are *spiritually* dead bury the *physically* dead." In any case, Jesus perceives the real problem with this disciple: He had not yet understood clearly the place that Jesus must have as the primary allegiance of his life.

Calming a Storm (8:23–27)

Without warning, a furious storm came up on the lake (8:24). The lake's low elevation (at least 636 feet [212 meters] below sea level) provides it with relatively mild year-round temperatures. However, encompassed with mountain ranges to the east and west that rise over 2,650 feet from the level of the lake, especially infamous is an east wind that blows in over the mountains, particularly during the spring and fall (cf. 14:19, 24; John 6:1–4). The lake's low-lying setting results in sudden violent downdrafts and storms (cf. Mark 4:37; Luke 8:23; John 6:18) that can produce waves seven feet and more, easily able to swamp a boat.[153]

But Jesus was sleeping (8:24). Traversing the Sea of Galilee by night was a common experience for fishermen, where trammel nets were used throughout the night (cf. 4:16–20; on the type of boat used, see comments on 4:21).[154] The boat was equipped for cooking during nightlong commercial fishing expeditions on the lake, with enough room for a person to lie down in the stern and sleep when not on duty, with perhaps a ballast sandbag for a pillow (cf. Mark 4:38).[155]

Then he got up and rebuked the winds and the waves, and it was completely calm (8:26). To "rebuke" indicates that Jesus is able to command even the forces of nature, in the same way that in the Old

◀

A GALILEAN FISHING BOAT

This mosaic depiction was found at Bethsaida and dates to the late Roman period.

Testament God "rebukes" the sea, a demonstration of his sovereign control over all of nature.[156]

Exorcising the Demoniacs (8:28–34)

When he arrived at the other side in the region of the Gadarenes (8:28). The "other side" is often a reference to the movement from a Jewish to a Gentile region. "Gadarenes" refers to both the village of Gadara, located about five miles southeast of the Sea of Galilee, and to the surrounding region,[157] which probably included a little village that lay on the eastern shore of the Sea of Galilee called Gerasa (modern Khersa or Kursi), the traditional site of the exorcism.[158]

Two demon-possessed men coming from the tombs (8:28). Contact with the dead rendered a Jew ceremonially unclean,[159] which may have been the reason for the demon-possessed men to accost this Jewish contingent. The book of *Jubilees* views Gentiles as unclean because they "slaughter their sacrifices to the dead, and to demons they bow down. And they eat in tombs" (*Jub.* 22:16–17).

Matthew apparently has independent knowledge of a second demonized man, because Mark (5:1–20) and Luke

REFLECTIONS

"WHO REALLY IS THIS JESUS?" the disciples are wondering. As a man Jesus was extremely tired after the exhausting day, but with divine power he quieted the storm by a mere word of command. He is far more than they ever could have understood. And Jesus is far more than what we have often understood. It is a challenge for all of us to look clearly at Jesus as the divine-human Messiah and allow him to amaze us and move us to follow him as his true disciples. And it won't hurt to humble ourselves to call on him at our time of need, as self-sufficient as we might think that we are!

(8:26–39) specify only one such person. Matthew is often concerned only with giving general details of the narrative, so he merely mentions that there are two demoniacs; Mark and Luke, giving a more detailed account, single out the spokesman of the two and describe him in more detail. This is similar to the incident where Matthew describes the healing of two blind men (20:29–34), but Mark (10:46–52) and Luke (18:35–43) mention only one. Again, they go into more detail in the incident, with Mark even explicitly identifying the blind man as Bartimaeus, the son of Timaeus (Mark 10:46).

Have you come here to torture us before the appointed time? (8:29). The author of *1 Enoch* 16:1 says graphically that evil spirits "will corrupt until the day of the great conclusion, until the great age is consummated, until everything is concluded (upon) the Watchers[160] and the wicked ones."[161] The demons question whether Jesus has come to torment them before that appointed time arrives.

Some distance from them a large herd of pigs was feeding (8:30). The east shore of the Sea of Galilee is a Gentile region.

Jews would not be raising pigs, since they were unclean (Lev. 11:7; Deut. 14:8).

The whole town . . . pleaded with him to leave their region (8:34). Jesus has given a special witness to the Gentiles of this region, but there is a terrible perversion of values. Instead of rejoicing at the release and restoration of two human beings, the townspeople weep over the loss of pigs.

Healing the Paralytic (9:1–8)

Jesus stepped into a boat, crossed over and came to his own town (9:1). Jesus "crosses over," which marks the transition from the Gentile to the Jewish regions surrounding the Sea of Galilee. He comes back to the town explicitly named Capernaum in Mark's narrative (cf. Mark 2:1; 5:18), which is now "his own town," the home base of Jesus' ministry in the Galilee region (cf. 4:17; 8:5; 11:23).

Take heart, son; your sins are forgiven (9:2). Individual sin is not always the direct cause of a person's disease or illness (John 9:2–3), but at the heart of humanity's problem is sin. Healing has confirmed Jesus' authority to announce the arrival of the kingdom of heaven (4:23–25), and healing now confirms that forgiveness of sin accompanies the arrival of the kingdom. Once sin is forgiven and redemption has occurred, all sickness and death will ultimately be abolished (cf. Isa. 25:8–9).

This fellow is blaspheming! (9:3). Blasphemy is an act in which a human insults the honor of God. This extends to misusing the name of God, which is cursed or reviled instead of being honored, the penalty for which is death by stoning (Lev. 24:10–23; 1 Kings 21:9ff.). The

SEA OF GALILEE REGION

▼

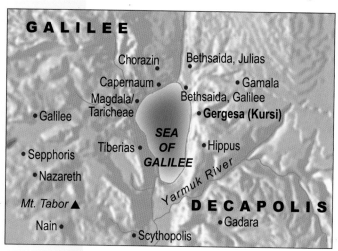

teachers of the law charge Jesus with blasphemy because they believe that he is dishonoring God by taking to himself the prerogative to forgive sins, something that only God can do (cf. Mark 2:7; Luke 5:21).

Matthew Called (9:9–13)

A man named Matthew sitting at the tax collector's booth (9:9). Taxes in ancient Rome were collected by persons who were the highest bidders for a collection contract (*ordo publicanorum*, Livy, *History* 25.3.8–19). But in Palestine, tax collectors were employed as representatives of the Roman governing authorities, collecting the prescribed duties and generally seeing to public order. They usually were enlisted from the native population, because they needed to know local people and local customs to avoid being deceived. They were expected to collect a certain amount of tax money for the Roman authorities, and whatever extra they collected constituted their own commission. A tendency to resort to excessive extortion made them despised and hated by their own people (cf. Luke 19:8), and they became proverbial of a person with a self-seeking outlook (Matt. 5:46).

Matthew's tax collection booth must have stood at some place where the Via Maris passed close by the lakeshore on the outskirts of Capernaum (cf. 4:13).[162] He may have been collecting tolls from the commercial traffic traveling through the area or collecting taxes for the fish caught on the Sea of Galilee, for both of which Herod Antipas was responsible. Josephus says that Herod Antipas received annual revenue of two hundred talents from Galilee and Perea, his taxation region[163]—approximately five million dollars a year.

"Follow me," he told him, and Matthew got up and followed him (9:9). The wording implies following Jesus as his disciple. Like the two sets of brothers called earlier (cf. comments on 4:18–22; see also John 1:35–51), Matthew had been under the influence of Jesus' preaching for some time prior to this and is now ready to join him as one of his disciples. Little is known of Matthew Levi, except for the widely attested tradition from the second century on that he is the author of the Gospel that now bears his name. As a tax collector he has been trained in secular scribal techniques, and as a Galilean Jewish Christian he would have been able to interpret the life of Jesus from the perspective of the Old Testament expectations.[164]

Why does your teacher eat with tax collectors and "sinners"? (9:11). Table fellowship was an important social and religious convention among many groups in the ancient world. Boundaries were established that designated who was included and excluded from the meal, and also served to delineate religious and ethical obligations toward the participants. Within Judaism, the Therapeutae, Essenes, and Pharisees were especially known for the role that table fellowship played in defining their group identities.[165] The shared meal was a formal occasion when group members consumed food made sacred through various ritual practices such as ceremonial washings or tithing. Participants were often marked out by a prior required initiation.[166]

The derision that many felt generally for tax collectors was aggravated because they were regarded as ceremonially unclean because of their continual contact with Gentiles and because of their compromise of the Sabbath by working on it.[167] The term "sinner" (*hamartōlos*) was often used by the Pharisees to point to an identifiable segment of the people who were opposed to God's will as reflected in their understanding of proper obedience to the law and their *halakah*. But "sinner" is normally used more generally to designate the person who commits acts of sin defined by the law (e.g., Luke 7:36–50; cf. Matt. 26:45).[168] In the minds of the Pharisees, for Jesus to share a meal with these types of persons indicates that he includes them within his own fellowship; it also suggests that he condones their behavior. Jesus must now clarify who he is and what his mission entails.

It is not the healthy who need a doctor, but the sick (9:12). The Pharisees considered themselves to be righteously healthy before God, because they defined righteousness by their observance of the law—their "sacrifice." But they are blind to their real sinfulness before God. Jesus' offer of salvation to sinners apart from sectarian observances threatens the foundation and way of life of the Pharisees, yet is at the heart of the gospel he has come announcing.[169]

Discipleship and Religious Traditions (9:14–17)

Then John's disciples came (9:14). The "disciples of John" are committed followers of the prophet John the Baptist. They gathered around him as the prophet who would usher in the messianic age. They have assisted John in baptizing those who came to him and engaged in strict religious practices John taught, such as fasting and prayer (Luke 5:33; 11:1). The "disciples of the Pharisees" (see Mark 2:18; cf. Matt. 22:16) are most likely those in training to become

full initiates to their brotherhood. They have been immersed in the Pharisaic commitment of the oral law and rigorous practice of their traditions.

How is it that we and the Pharisees fast, but your disciples do not fast? (9:14). For fasting in the Old Testament and in Jewish tradition, see comments on 6:16–18. John's disciples do not understand why Jesus' disciples do not regularly fast as a sign of repentance.

How can the guests of the bridegroom mourn while he is with them? (9:15). Jesus now alludes to himself as the "bridegroom," who in the Old Testament is Yahweh (cf. Isa. 62:5; Hos. 2:19–20). The arrival of the kingdom of heaven has brought to fulfillment the promises of Israel, which should cause a time of rejoicing, like what would be experienced during marriage ceremonies (cf. Matt. 25:12–13).

No one sews a patch of unshrunk cloth on an old garment (9:16). Using two examples from everyday life, Jesus emphasizes that he has not come simply to provide a corrective to the traditional practices of the Jews. Rather, he has come to offer an entirely new approach to God, which will be incompatible with rigid traditionalism. Jesus' kingdom life is an entirely new garment and entirely new wine, which must have appropriate traditional practices.

Healing the Ruler's Daughter and the Hemorrhaging Woman (9:18–26)

A ruler came and knelt before him (9:18). Mark 5:22 and Luke 8:41 give the man's name as Jairus; Matthew simply calls him a "ruler" (*archōn*), which can

be used of either a community leader or a head of a synagogue board. Mark and Luke specify him as the latter, though Jairus may in fact function as both a community and a synagogue leader.[170] By kneeling before Jesus he indicates the extreme honor he gives to him, for kneeling is the appropriate position one takes before God[171] or a king or superior.[172]

Just then a woman who had been subject to bleeding for twelve years (9:20). The woman's bleeding could have been from some sort of internal disease or hemophilia, although the latter is mostly a male disorder. The term *haimorroeō*, "subject to bleeding," was used in Greek medical writings and in Leviticus 15:33 (LXX) to mean "menstruous." This most likely indicates that the woman had menorrhagia, a disease in which the menstrual flow is abnormally prolonged, usually producing anemia as well.[173] The

condition was all the more difficult because she would have been considered ritually unclean and excluded from normal social and religious relations, since others making contact with her would become unclean as well (Lev. 15:25–30).

Came up behind him and touched the edge of his cloak (9:20). The expression "edge of his cloak" is *kraspeda*, which in some contexts can refer to the outer fringe (decorated or plain) of a garment (cf. 14:26). However, the term is rendered "tassel" in 23:5, which may be the meaning here as well. Attached to the four corners of a garment worn by men were "tassels" (Heb. *ṣîṣît*) that had a blue cord. The tassels reminded an individual to obey God's commands and to be holy to God (Num. 15:40).

When Jesus entered the ruler's house and saw the flute players and the noisy crowd (9:23). Music was long considered an important element at both times of mourning and at times of gladness. The music of the dirge (*qînâ*); David's lament over Saul and Jonathan (2 Sam. 1:18–27) is an example of the music that accompanied a time of mourning. Professional mourners were customarily hired to assist at funerals, usually including flautists and wailing women. Rabbi Judah later said, "Even the poorest in Israel should hire not less than two flutes and one wailing woman."[174] In the family of a prominent person like the ruler, many professional mourners would have joined the family and friends in expressing their grief. Mourning was considered an important way of dealing with the reality of death, and various rites encompassed the mourner's clothing, diet, relationships, and religious activities, usually for a period of seven days.[175]

◀ *left*

GOATSKINS

Skins such as these were used as wine containers in the first century.

After the crowd had been put outside, he went in and took the girl by the hand, and she got up (9:25). Touching a corpse renders a person unclean for a period of seven days (Num. 19:11–21), but Jesus brings the girl to life, which transforms uncleanness to purity.

The Messiah at Work (9:27–38)

Two blind men followed him, calling out, "Have mercy on us, Son of David!" (9:27). The blind men understand Jesus to be the "Son of David," a reference to the promise of the messianic deliverer from the line of David whose kingdom would have no end (2 Sam. 7:12–16; cf. *Pss. Sol.* 17:23). The messianic age promised to bring healing to the blind (Isa. 29:18; 35:5; 42:7), which Jesus told John the Baptist was one of the signs that he indeed was the Expected One (11:2–6).

A man who was demon-possessed and could not talk was brought to Jesus (9:32). Demon-possession took a variety of external forms. In the case of those in 8:28, it produced violent behavior that threatened people. Here the phenomenon prohibits a man from speaking (see also 12:22). The term for "could not talk" is *kōphos*, "dull," which can be used of dull of hearing (i.e., deaf, 11:1) or dull of speech (i.e., mute, as here).

He had compassion on them, because they were harassed and helpless, like sheep without a shepherd (9:36). The leaders in Israel's history had been likened to shepherds. Joshua was appointed as leader after Moses, so that "the LORD's people will not be like sheep without a shepherd" (Num. 27:17).[176] That is what Israel is like in Jesus' day. The leaders have not fulfilled their responsibility to guide and protect the people, so the crowds are harassed (*skyllō*) and helpless (*rhiptō*), descriptions that indicate that they are experiencing distressing difficulties and are unable to care for themselves.

The harvest is plentiful but the workers are few (9:37). The theme of harvest was

right ▶

WHEAT HARVEST

Women gathering wheat in the hills of Judea.

common in Judaism. A rabbinic saying from around A.D. 130 gives a similar emphasis: "R. Tarfon said: The day is short and the task is great and the labourers are idle and the wage is abundant and the master of the house is urgent" (*m. ʾAbot* 2.15). Jesus will draw on the harvest metaphor elsewhere in an eschatological context, but there it is harvest time of judgment (13:30, 39; cf. Isa. 17:11; Joel 3:13; Rev. 14:14–20).

Instructions for the Short Term Mission to Israel (10:1–15)

He called his twelve disciples to him (10:1). The number "twelve" has obvious salvation-historical significance, corresponding with the twelve patriarchs of Israel, the sons of Jacob, from whom the tribes of Israel descended. The twelve disciples symbolize the continuity of salvation-history in God's program, as Jesus now sends out the Twelve to proclaim to the lost sheep of the house of Israel that the kingdom of heaven has arrived (cf. 10:5–6).[177] In the future age, the twelve apostles will sit on twelve thrones judging the house of Israel (cf. 19:28).

These are the names of the twelve apostles (10:2). "Apostle" has narrow and wide meanings in the New Testament. The narrow sense, as here, is the usual meaning, signifying the special authoritative representatives chosen by Jesus to play a foundational role in the establishment of the church.[178] Paul normally used the term to refer to the Twelve, but includes himself among them as a special apostle to the Gentiles (1 Cor. 15:8–10). The wide sense of apostle derives from the common verb *apostellō*, "I send" (e.g., 10:5), and therefore can mean merely "messenger" (John 13:16), refer to Jesus as "the apostle and high priest whom we confess"

(Heb. 3:1), or designate an individual such as Barnabas, Titus, or Epaphroditus within the group of missionaries that is larger than the Twelve and Paul.[179]

Do not go among the Gentiles or enter any town of the Samaritans. Go rather to the lost sheep of Israel (10:5–6). Jesus goes first to Israel (cf. 15:21–28) to fulfill the salvation-historical order that God established with Israel, who was the tool that God intended to use to bring blessing to the world.[180] The Twelve symbolize the continuity of salvation-history in God's program. According to Paul, God's offer of salvation to the world was "first for the Jew, then for the Gentile" (Rom. 1:16). Once Israel has had her chance to receive the offer of the kingdom, the offer is proclaimed equally to all the nations, including both Jew and Gentile (see 28:19–20).

ISRAEL

Samaria was excluded from this mission. ▼

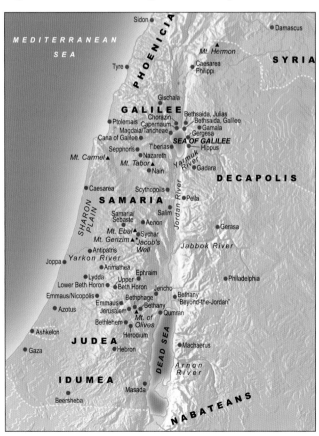

REFLECTIONS

THE TWELVE DISCIPLES/APOSTLES ARE NOT TO BE idealized. When we look at these men, and the many other men and women who were Jesus' followers, we find that they are not much different from you or me. Look at the brief description of each and see if you can identify with one or more. If Jesus could transform their lives, he can transform ours as well. That is the overwhelming story of Jesus' ministry. He came to change lives.

Simon (who is called Peter)—a successful businessman in the fishing industry, who was regularly in a leadership position.

His brother Andrew—a person highly sensitive to God's leading, but overshadowed by his brother Peter.

James son of Zebedee—left a successful family business to follow Jesus, but was the first apostle martyred.

His brother John—had a fiery temper but also a profound love for God.

Philip—never quite one of the inner circle, yet took a leadership role among the lesser-known apostles.

Bartholomew—known for his outspoken honesty (he is probably the one called Nathaniel in John 1:43–51).

Thomas—a skeptical rationalist, but eventually had one of the most profound theological understandings of Jesus' identity as the God-man.

Matthew the tax collector—formerly a traitor to his own people to save his neck and make money; became a missionary to them by writing his Gospel.

James son of Alphaeus—either younger, shorter, or less well-known than the other James; was faithful throughout his life, but never given much recognition for it.

Thaddaeus (or, Lebbaeus)—also called Judas son of James, often confused with Judas Iscariot and didn't develop much of his own reputation.

Simon the Zealot—before accepting Jesus as Messiah, a guerrilla warfare fighter who wanted to bring in God's kingdom by force.

Judas Iscariot, who betrayed him—his love of money and power may have drawn him to abandon and betray even his closest friends.

As you go, preach this message: "The kingdom of heaven is near" (10:7). The disciples are to go with the same message that both John the Baptist and Jesus preached (see comments on 3:2; 4:17).

Heal the sick, raise the dead, cleanse those who have leprosy, drive out demons (10:8). Not only do they go with the same message, but they also go with the same authority as Jesus (10:1), who performed each of these miracles (cf. chs. 8–9).

For the worker is worth his keep (10:10). The apostle Paul will call on this principle as a rationale for the support of full-time Christian workers (1 Cor. 9:14; cf. *Did.* 13:1–2). In 1 Timothy 5:18 he quotes the parallel passage in Luke 10:7, giving it the stature of "Scripture." Although the disciples are not to charge for their ministry, they are to accept the hospitality extended to them as traveling missionaries (10:11), so they will have no need to take along money ("gold or silver or copper") or extra clothing or typical traveling equipment (10:9–10). It is the responsibility of those to whom they minister to support their mission (10:10).

Search for some worthy person there and stay at his house until you leave (10:11). If a household does not receive God's messenger, then they are to shake the dust off of their feet when they leave, a sign used by Jews when leaving Gentile regions that they have removed completely unclean elements (*b. Sanh.* 12a). Paul practiced this symbol when leaving regions where his message was rejected (Acts 13:51).

Instructions for the Long-Term Mission to the World (10:16–23)

I am sending you out like sheep among wolves (10:16). Jesus reverses the metaphor. Before this the disciples were to go to the sheep (9:36; 10:6), but now they themselves are the sheep going out among wolves. In 10:5–15, Jesus gave instructions to the disciples about their short-term mission to Israel during Jesus' earthly ministry. In 10:16–23, Jesus gives instructions to the disciple/apostles about their long-term mission throughout the world until his return.

They will hand you over to the local councils and flog you in their synagogues (10:17). The synagogue was not only the place of assembly for worship, but was also an assembly of justice where discipline was exercised (cf. John 9:35).

All men will hate you because of me (10:22). The phrase "because of me" is literally "because of my name" and is an important Christological expression (cf. 5:11; 24:9) that harks back to the Old Testament significance of God's name as the representation of his person as the sole focus of Israel's worship and allegiance (e.g., Ex. 3:15; 6:3; 9:16; 20:7). Jesus' disciples will have the privilege of carrying his name, but that also brings with it suffering insofar as the antagonism and hatred directed to him will naturally fall on his followers.[181]

▶ Flogging in the Synagogue

The Old Testament gave prescriptions for exercising discipline and punishment (Deut. 25:1–3), which later Judaism applied to the responsibility of the synagogue. Flogging (*mastigoō*) was prescribed as a punishment for various sins, such as slandering a woman, incest, or entering the temple while unclean.[A-59] The lifting of the ban upon eating certain meats (e.g., Acts 10:9–16) would make a Jewish convert to Christ unclean in the eyes of the synagogue officials and subject to flogging (*m. Mak.* 3:2). After a decision by the court of judges the person was made to lie down in front of the judge and be whipped. The standard number of lashes was forty, although the number could be adjusted to make it appropriate for the crime. But no more than forty lashes could be given, because more than forty would be inhumane (Deut. 25:1–3). The number normally applied was forty less one, in case they miscounted (*m. Mak.* 3:2, 10; cf. 2 Cor. 11:24).

The Mishnah tractates *Sanhedrin* and *Makkot* ("stripes"), originally one book, give later rabbinic prescriptions for flogging. Three judges rendered the decision, although as many as twenty-three may be needed (*m. Sanh.* 1:2). The person's hands were tied to a pillar and the *ḥazzan* (administrator) of the synagogue removed the garments of the accused to bare his chest and back. The *ḥazzan* stood on a stone and gave him one-third of the prescribed stripes on the chest, and two-thirds on the back, while the person neither stood nor sat, but bent low to the ground. During the flogging the reader read Deuteronomy 28:58–9, a second person counted the blows, and a third gave the commands. The instrument of flogging was a whip (*mastix*), a strap of calf leather divided into four thongs through which smaller thongs were plaited to make it stronger, and the handle contained a device to make the strap longer or shorter. Flogging could be administered to either a man or a woman. If the accused appeared to be near death, the flogging was stopped, although there are records of people dying (*m. Mak.* 3:14).[A-60]

You will not finish going through the cities of Israel before the Son of Man comes (10:23). This is a reference, similar to the admonitions of the Olivet Discourse, that the mission to Israel will not be completed until Jesus returns to establish his kingdom on the earth (see comments on 24:1–31).

Characteristics of Missionary Disciples (10:24–42)

It is enough for the student to be like his teacher, and the servant like his master (10:25). The word "student" (*mathētēs*) is the common word for "disciple." The ultimate goal of a disciple is to be like the master—a general principle of master-disciple relations in Judaism and the Greco-Roman world. The harsh treatment that Jesus is now beginning to receive from the religious leaders will be the lot of his disciples as well.

If the head of the house has been called Beelzebub, how much more the members of his household! (10:25). The Pharisees have accused Jesus of casting out demons by the "prince of demons" (9:34), another name for Satan. That identity is further revealed to be "Beelzebub"[182] or better, "*Beelzeboul*"[183] (see comments on 12:24, 27), meaning "master of the house," as Jesus' translation and play on words with "head of the house" (*oikodespotēs*) indicates.[184] The term most likely comes from an identification of the chief of the evil spirits with Baal Shamayim, whose worship was installed in the temple by Antiochus IV Epiphanes.[185]

Do not be afraid of those who kill the body but cannot kill the soul (10:28). A Jewish parallel may be found in the saying, "With all our hearts let us consecrate ourselves unto God, who gave us our souls. . . . Let us have no fear of him who thinks he kills" (*4 Macc.* 13:13–14). This was a call to courage in the face of persecution from humans.

I did not come to bring peace, but a sword (10:34). This is a metaphorical sword, as is indicated by Jesus' rebuke of those who take up a sword to defend him in the Garden of Gethsemane (26:52). The sword can be a metaphor of God's divine judgment (Ps. 7:12) and, as here, a metaphor of separation between those who believe and those who do not, even if it is in one's family.

Anyone who loves his father or mother . . . his son or daughter . . . more than me is not worthy of me (10:37). This saying reminds one of Jesus' statement to the disciple who wanted to return to bury his father (see comments on 8:21–22). Jesus' form of discipleship calls for giving him ultimate supremacy beyond parents or children, something that not even the most esteemed rabbi would demand. Therefore, this is an implicit declaration of his deity, because only God deserves a higher place of honor than one's father and mother. A precedent for giving supremacy to God, even over parents, is found in the commendation to the tribe of Levi: "He said of his father and mother, 'I have no regard for them.' He did not recognize his brothers or acknowledge his own children, but he watched over your word and guarded your covenant" (Deut. 33:9–10).

Anyone who does not take his cross and follow me is not worthy of me (10:38). See comments on 16:24–26.

Anyone who receives a prophet . . . and anyone who receives a righteous man (10:41). The "prophets" and the "righteous" are linked elsewhere, indicating Old Testament luminaries (13:17; 23:29), but here they refer to Christian prophets (cf. 23:34) and righteous persons (cf. 13:43, 49; 25:37, 46). These distinctions are not mutually exclusive. "Prophet" refers to those who speak for God and for those with whom Jesus' followers are aligned (cf. 5:10–12; 7:15–23), and "righteous man" is a generic category that refers to all who are righteous in Christ Jesus (cf. 5:20), including the righteous people of earlier generations.

If anyone gives even a cup of cold water to one of these little ones because he is my disciple (10:42). "Little ones" points explicitly to needy disciples, which may include prophets and the righteous who are in need. As in 25:40, 45, the expression helps to emphasize that needy disciples are often the ones who are excluded from

care, while attention is given to the prominent members of the discipleship community (see 18:1–5).

John the Baptist Questions Jesus (11:1–6)

After Jesus had finished instructing his twelve disciples (11:1). Matthew uses the familiar stylized conclusion to the missionary discourse (cf. 7:28; 13:53; 19:1; 26:1) as he transitions to the next section of narrative (chs. 11–12). The narrative draws attention to the gathering opposition to Jesus, which comes innocently enough from John the Baptist (11:2–19) but with outright hostility from the Jewish religious leaders (12:1–45).

When John heard in prison what Christ was doing (11:2). John has been imprisoned by Herod Antipas at the fortress Machaerus, where ultimately he was put to death (see 14:1–14). Imprisoned for upwards of a year or more, John sends his disciples to query Jesus about the messianic program.

He sent his disciples (11:2). John's disciples (see comments on 9:14) apparently stay as close to John as they can while he

ISRAEL

Machaerus is located near the east shore of the Dead Sea.

is in prison. They probably travel from the fortress Machaerus north through Perea along the Jordan River, crossing into Galilee where Jesus is ministering.

Are you the one who was to come, or should we expect someone else? (11:3). The expression "the one who was to come" is an allusion to the Messiah, the Coming One, the expression John used to refer to Jesus at the beginning of his public ministry (3:11). The expression recalls Zechariah's prophecy, which is the prophecy fulfilled at Jesus' entry to Jerusalem (cf. Zech. 9:9; Matt. 21:4). It would be natural for John to experience some perplexity as he languishes in prison, much as had earlier prophets such as Elijah (e.g., 1 Kings 19:1–18).

Go back and report to John what you hear and see (11:4). The way that Jesus' ministry has unfolded (chs. 8–9) is in line with the prophetic promises. Isaiah's Coming One was described in these very terms: "The blind receive sight (Isa. 29:18; 35:5), the lame walk (35:6), those who have leprosy are cured (cf. 53:4; Matt. 8:1–4), the deaf hear (Isa. 29:18–19; 35:5), the dead are raised (26:18–19), and the good news is preached to the poor" (61:1).

Jesus' Tribute to John (11:7–19)

What did you go out into the desert to see? A reed swayed by the wind? (11:7). The metaphor of tall reed grasses growing along the shores of the Jordan suggests weakness and vacillation with every changing wind of opportunity or challenge.

▶ The Fortress Machaerus

Machaerus[A-61] was an important fortress east of the Dead Sea, near the southern frontier of the region of Perea. It was originally built by the Hasmonean ruler Alexander Jannaeus[A-62] around 90 B.C., destroyed by the Roman commander Gabinius in 57 B.C., and then rebuilt by Herod the Great[A-63] around 30 B.C. as one of the series of fortresses guarding the eastern frontier of Palestine (Masada, the Herodium, etc.). Pliny the Elder called Machaerus "the most important Jewish stone fortress immediately after Jerusalem."[A-64] The name of the fortress probably derives from *machaira*, "dagger," and it sits perched atop a rocky mountain with steep sides rising to an elevation seven hundred meters (1,600 feet) above sea level, protected by deep ravines on three sides.[A-65]

After the death of Herod the Great the fortress was assigned to the tetrarch of his son Herod Antipas. Here, according to Josephus,[A-66] Herod Antipas imprisoned John the Baptist and later had him put to death (see comments on 14:1–12). When Perea was added to the province of Judea (A.D. 44), Machaerus was occupied by a Roman garrison and remained in Roman control until the Jewish revolt in A.D. 66. The Jewish insurgents occupied Machaerus until A.D. 71–72, when they were besieged and finally surrendered to the Roman forces under governor Lucilius Bassus.[A-67]

Among those born of women there has not risen anyone greater than John the Baptist (11:11). "Among those born of women" is a Jewish idiom that contrasts ordinary human birth (Job 14:1; 15:14; 25:4) with the birth of those into the kingdom of heaven. The contrast is not between human accomplishments but between eras. The arrival of the kingdom of heaven ushers in an incomparably greater era than any preceding it.

The kingdom of heaven has been forcefully advancing, and forceful men lay hold of it (11:12). Since the announcement of the kingdom of heaven in John's ministry, it has received opposition from the religious establishment of Israel. Now John has received opposition from Herod Antipas, a violent man who will put John to death violently.

If you are willing to accept it, he is the Elijah who was to come (11:14). Malachi prophesied that Elijah would prepare the way for the Messiah (Mal. 3:1; 4:5). Malachi did not imply a reincarnation of Elijah or a return to life in a whirlwind (in the way he left). Rather, at John the Baptist's conception he was designated as the one who ministers in the "spirit and power of Elijah" (Luke 1:17). For those who receive John's ministry, he is the fulfillment of Malachi's prophecy (see Matt. 17:10–13).

But wisdom is proved right by her actions (11:19). Wisdom was often personified in Judaism (Prov. 8; Wisd. Sol. 7–8) to exemplify the way in which those who are guided by God's practical approach to life will make right decisions. This saying appears to be proverbial.

The Privileged Unrepentant Cities (11:20–24)

Woe to you, Korazin! Woe to you, Bethsaida! (11:21). Capernaum, Korazin (or Chorazin), and Bethsaida were the cities in which most of Jesus' miracles had been performed (11:20). The people there have had the greatest privilege and opportunity to meet Jesus, but with that comes greater accountability and responsibility.

If the miracles that were performed in you had been performed in Tyre and Sidon (11:21). Tyre and Sidon were Gentile cities in northwest Philistia/Phoenicia, an ancient region that bordered Galilee to the west along the coast of the Mediterranean Sea. These two cities were known throughout the ancient world as powerful maritime commercial centers. In Israel they became proverbial for pagan peoples, often linked as the

NORTHERN PALESTINE
▼

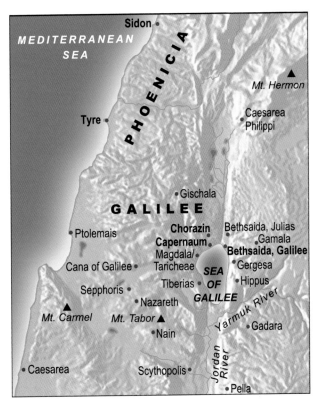

▶Korazin and Bethsaida

Jesus' public ministry has centered in the region surrounding the towns of Capernaum, Korazin, and Bethsaida, what some call the "Evangelical Triangle" (for Capernaum see comments on 4:17; 8:5; 9:1).

Korazin (Khirbet Kerazeh) is only 2-1/2 miles (4 kilometers) north of Capernaum. Little evidence from the time of Jesus remains, but by the third to fourth centuries it was described in rabbinic literature as a "medium-size town."[A-68] The black basalt ruins of a large synagogue from that later era have been excavated, with the famous "seat of Moses" (cf. 23:2) discovered in the ruins. The city was destroyed by an earthquake and rebuilt in the fifth century, only to be destroyed again in the seventh or eighth century.[A-69]

Bethsaida (Aram. "house of fishermen") was the birthplace of Peter, Andrew, and Philip (John 1:44; 12:21), and possibly others of the disciples including James and John, the sons of Zebedee. It is mentioned more often in the New Testament than any city except Jerusalem and Capernaum. It is located four miles northeast of Capernaum at the northernmost tip of the Sea of Galilee at the place where the Jordan River enters the sea. The city was built by Herod Philip (cf. 16:13), son of Herod the Great and half-brother of Herod Antipas, and lay in the region under Philip's governance. During Jesus' time the Jordan delta extended further inland at that point (perhaps as much as 1-1/2 miles further than presently[A-70]), giving it one of the largest harbors on the Sea of Galilee and making it an important fishing center.[A-71]

object of condemnation from Old Testament prophets for their Baal worship and arrogant pride in their power and wealth, and therefore deserving of judgment.[186]

They would have repented long ago in sackcloth and ashes (11:21). "Sackcloth and ashes" were familiar symbols of repentance. The rough cloth woven from camel or goat's hair was worn close to the skin as a symbolic rejection of comfort and ease in cases of mourning, national disaster, or repentance (e.g., Jonah 3:5–8). Ashes symbolized loss, whether sprinkled over one's head or lying in them (Est. 4:1–3; *Jos. Asen.* 10:8–15).

You, Capernaum, will you be lifted up to the skies? No, you will go down to the depths (11:23). Jesus uses a strikingly

familiar reference to prideful ancient Babylon (Isa. 14:12–15) to emphasize the consequence of Capernaum's satanically stimulated refusal to repent.

If the miracles that were performed in you had been performed in Sodom, it would have remained to this day (11:23). If Tyre and Sidon are stereotypes of pagan worship and prideful arrogance, Sodom is the consummately proverbial city of sin.[187]

The Invitation to an Easy Yoke (11:25–30)

I praise you, Father, Lord of heaven and earth (11:25). The intimacy of Jesus' relationship with God is again revealed as he addresses him as "Father" (6:9; cf.

◀ *top left*

BETHSAIDA

The site of
Bethsaida.

◀ *top right*

SODOM

The salt pans south
of the Dead Sea.

◀ *middle*

CHORAZIN

Ruins of the
synagogue.

▼ *bottom*

TYRE AND SIDON

(*left*) Remains
of the Roman
hippodrome at
Tyre.

(*right*) The shore-
line at the site of
Sidon.

Sir. 51:10). "Lord of heaven and earth" is a title of sovereignty that brings comfort and security, as is expressed in Jewish literature, "Take courage, my daughter; the Lord of heaven grant you joy in place of your sorrow" (Tobit 7:16).

You have hidden these things from the wise and learned, and revealed them to little children (11:25). "The wise and learned" are not just academic specialists, but those who stubbornly and arrogantly refuse to repent and learn from Jesus the true way to God (cf. 13:10–16). "Little children" are those who innocently (not naively) receive Jesus' revelation from the Father.

Take my yoke upon you and learn from me. . . . For my yoke is easy (11:29–30). Yoke (*zygos*) can be used literally for the wooden frame joining two animals (usually oxen), or it can be used metaphorically to describe one individual's subjection to another. In that latter sense, yoke was a common metaphor in Judaism for the law: "He that takes upon himself the yoke of the Law, from him

shall be taken away the yoke of the kingdom [troubles from those in power] and the yoke of worldly care; but he that throws off the yoke of the Law, upon him shall be laid the yoke of the kingdom and the yoke of worldly care" (*m. ʾAbot* 3:5; cf. *m. Ber.* 2:2). Sirach invited people to the yoke of studying Torah to gain wisdom: "Acquire wisdom for yourselves without money. Put your neck under her yoke, and let your souls receive instruction; it is to be found close by" (Sir. 51:25–26; cf. 6:23–31). The New Testament refers to the yoke of legalism (Acts 15:10; Gal. 5:1). But Jesus' yoke is none other than commitment to him, gaining his authoritative understanding of God's truth. To learn from Jesus is to receive his revelation of what the law truly intends (cf. Matt. 5:17–48).

Lord of the Sabbath (12:1–21)

God had given the Sabbath as a day of rest and holiness to God. The fourth commandment specified that no work be performed on the Sabbath, so that the day would be kept holy to God. Over time the Sabbath became one of the most distinctive characteristics of the Jewish people, along with circumcision and dietary laws. The legal mandate not to work had to be interpreted for the people, so the Pharisees developed an extensive set of laws to guide them so that they would not violate the Sabbath.

At that time Jesus went through the grainfields on the Sabbath (12:1). Exodus 16:29 set a standard for travel on the Sabbath, admonishing people not to go out in order to observe the Sabbath rest. The Qumran community interpreted the admonition to mean that a person could not walk more than one thousand cubits

---

R E F L E C T I O N S

JESUS' EASY YOKE IS IN STARK CONTRAST TO THE burden of Pharisaic Judaism. The Pharisees spoke of 613 commandments, and their *halakot* (binding interpretations) produced an overwhelmingly complicated approach to life. In our quest to know God's Word it is good to remember that we can turn Jesus' yoke into an equally unbearable burden unless we consciously recognize that discipleship to Jesus is not essentially a religious obligation. Rather, ours is an intimate relationship with the One who calls, "Come to me" and "learn from me." As complicated as life may become, discipleship at heart simply means walking with Jesus in the real world and having him teach us moment by moment how to live life his way.

outside the city" (CD 10:21), while the rabbis allowed a combination of a thousand cubits to travel a distance of two thousand cubits (e.g., *m. Soṭah* 5:3)—approximately three thousand feet or a little over half of a mile.[188]

His disciples were hungry and began to pick some heads of grain and eat them (12:1). The law made provision for people who were hungry to eat from a neighbor's field: "If you enter your neighbor's vineyard, you may eat all the grapes you want, but do not put any in your basket. If you enter your neighbor's grainfield, you may pick kernels with your hands, but you must not put a sickle to his standing grain" (Deut. 23:24–25). Similarly, the edges of a field were not normally harvested, so that the poor and hungry, the foreign travelers, the orphans, and the widows would have grain available to them. This also included olives and grapes left after the first harvest (24:19–22; cf. Ruth 2:2–3).

Look! Your disciples are doing what is unlawful on the Sabbath (12:2). A later ruling stated that there were thirty-nine ("forty less one") main classes of work prohibited on the Sabbath, among them "sowing, ploughing, reaping, binding sheaves, threshing, winnowing, cleansing crops, grinding, sifting" (*m. Šabb.* 7:2). The disciples could have been guilty of several of these in the eyes of the Pharisees as they plucked the grain heads, separated the chaff from the grain, and ground the grain in their hands to prepare it to eat.

I tell you that one greater than the temple is here (12:6). The Old Testament priests regularly violated the Sabbath when they performed their duties on the Sabbath, yet they were considered guilt-less. Using typical rabbinic logic, *qal wāḥômer* (lit., "light and weighty," usually trans. "how much more"), Jesus emphasizes that if the guardians of the temple are allowed to violate the Sabbath for the greater good of conducting priestly rituals, how much more should Jesus and his disciples be considered guiltless when doing God's work. After all, someone greater than the temple is here. The "greater" points either to the ministry of Jesus and his disciples in proclaiming the arrival of the kingdom of heaven or to Jesus himself.

For the Son of Man is Lord of the Sabbath (12:8). As Messiah, Jesus has supremacy over the temple, and he has the authority to give the true interpretation of the law (5:17–48), including the role of the Sabbath. Jesus does not challenge the Sabbath law itself, but the prevailing Pharisaic interpretation of it.

Is it lawful to heal on the Sabbath? (12:10). Rabbinic teaching allowed that only in extreme cases of life and death could the Sabbath be violated: "If a man has a pain in his throat they may drop medicine into his mouth on the Sabbath, since there is doubt whether life is in danger, and whenever there is doubt whether life is in danger this overrides the Sabbath" (*m. Yoma* 8:6). The person with a withered hand has quite likely had the condition for some time; thus, his life certainly is not in danger, so he can wait until the next day.

If any of you has a sheep and it falls into a pit on the Sabbath, will you not take hold of it and lift it out? (12:11). There was active debate in Judaism at the time on just such a point. In many ways the debate centered on how much a person was willing to sacrifice to give honor to

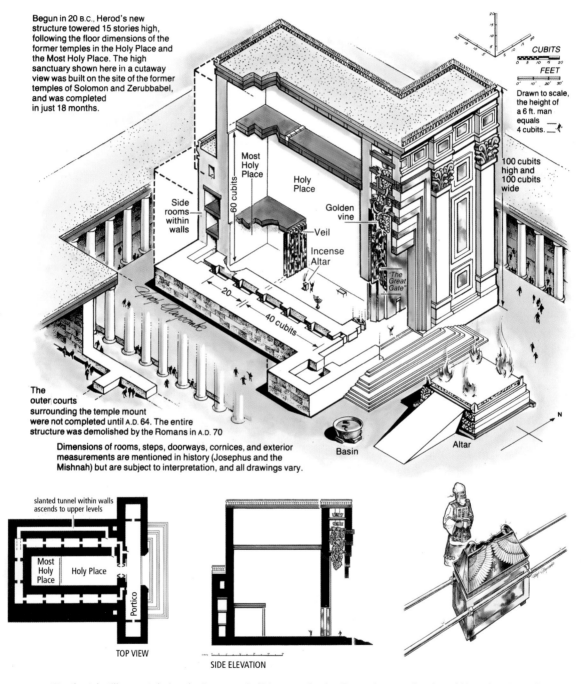

Begun in 20 B.C., Herod's new structure towered 15 stories high, following the floor dimensions of the former temples in the Holy Place and the Most Holy Place. The high sanctuary shown here in a cutaway view was built on the site of the former temples of Solomon and Zerubbabel, and was completed in just 18 months.

CUBITS

FEET

Drawn to scale, the height of a 6 ft. man equals 4 cubits.

Most Holy Place

60 cubits

Side rooms within walls

Holy Place

Golden vine

Veil

Incense Altar

100 cubits high and 100 cubits wide

"The Great Gate"

20

40 cubits

The outer courts surrounding the temple mount were not completed until A.D. 64. The entire structure was demolished by the Romans in A.D. 70.

Basin

Altar

N

Dimensions of rooms, steps, doorways, cornices, and exterior measurements are mentioned in history (Josephus and the Mishnah) but are subject to interpretation, and all drawings vary.

slanted tunnel within walls ascends to upper levels

Most Holy Place | Holy Place

Portico

TOP VIEW

SIDE ELEVATION

Was the Ark still present during the Roman period? Josephus describes the Most Holy Place as having "nothing at all" which was accurate on the day he wrote it. Yet the Mishnah hints that the Ark was hidden (Shekalim 6:12).

Fearing Roman intervention, it could have been secretly moved into the Temple interior for use only on the Day of Atonement. It may be hidden underground to this day.

God and his holy day. The Qumran community was more rigorous on this matter than most others: "No one should help an animal give birth on the Sabbath day. And if he makes it fall into a well or a pit, he should not take it out on the Sabbath" (CD 11:13–14). In the same document the community contends that even if a living man fell into water, they were not to take him out by using a ladder or a rope or a utensil (CD 11:16–17).

The Pharisees went out and plotted how they might kill Jesus (12:14). The law prescribed the death penalty to be carried out in cases of extreme Sabbath desecration (Ex. 31:14; 35:2), but under the Roman occupation the Jews did not have arbitrary power to impose or to carry out a death penalty (cf. John 18:31). The collaboration and plotting of the Pharisees with Caiaphas, the chief priests, and the rest of the Sanhedrin was sufficient to persuade the Romans to put Jesus to death for them.

Here is my servant whom I have chosen, the one I love, in whom I delight (12:18). Matthew identifies Jesus with the messianic Servant of Isaiah 42:1–4. The identity of the Servant in Isaiah is perplexing, because it vacillates between the nation Israel as the Servant[189] and an individual who leads the nation.[190] Jesus emerges as the Servant Messiah who has a ministry and mission both to Israel and the nations and who is the gentle Spirit-endowed Servant with a mission of justice to the nations.

Beelzebul and the Blasphemy Against the Spirit (12:22–37)

All the people were astonished and said, "Could this be the Son of David?" (12:23). The different sectarian groups had difficulty putting together all of the varied messianic promises of the Old Testament, so the common people especially seemed to focus on one strand of the prophecies. In their mind, because King David was a warrior, the messianic son of David would be a liberator. Although David is the only person recorded to have exorcised a demon in the Old Testament, he was not considered a miracle worker. Yet the Son of David would bring a time of eschatological fulfillment, including the healing of all illnesses. It is astonishing to recognize that the gentle healing Servant Messiah (8:17; 12:18–21) is indeed the Son of David who will shepherd his people and bring the time of covenantal peace (Ezek. 34:23–31; 37:24–28).

It is only by Beelzebub, the prince of demons, that this fellow drives out demons (12:24). The ancient world regularly drew on magical incantations to manipulate the spirit world. The Pharisees accuse Jesus of drawing on the power of "the prince of demons," *Beelzebub*, or better, *Beelzeboul*, "master of the house," to cast out the demon from the blind and mute man (12:22). *Beelzeboul* most likely comes from an identification of the chief of the evil spirits with Baal Shamayim, whose worship was installed in the temple by Antiochus IV Epiphanes[191] and came to be another title for Satan in Judaism: "I am Beelzeboul, the ruler of the demons" (*T. Sol.* 3:6). The Pharisees do not deny the miracle but instead attribute Jesus' power to Satan. Judaism continued this charge into the early centuries of the church era, branding him a sorcerer (e.g., *b. Sanh.* 107b; *b. Šabb.* 104b).

If I drive out demons by Beelzebub, by whom do your people drive them out? So then, they will be your judges (12:27).

Some of those exorcisms were well known among the Jews. Josephus gives a peculiar perspective of Solomon developing the art of incantations for healing and exorcism. That art was passed down to Eleazar, a Jewish exorcist of Josephus's day. Eleazar used a signet ring with part of a root to draw out a demon through the nostrils of a possessed man and then commanded the demon to overturn a cup of water to demonstrate the reality of the exorcism.[192] The legendary Tobias exorcised the demon Asmodeus from his wife, Sarah, on their wedding night by forcing the demon to smell a fish's liver and heart (Tobit 8:1–3). These accounts are obvious clashes of God's power against Satan's.

How can anyone enter a strong man's house and carry off his possessions unless he first ties up the strong man? (12:29). *Testament of Levi* 18:12 refers to the eschatological priest-king who inaugurates the age of blessing as he binds Satan, "And Beliar [Satan; cf. 2 Cor. 6:15] shall be bound by him. And he shall grant to his children the authority to trample on wicked spirits."[193] The analogy refers to Jesus' "binding" Satan and then releasing those held captive by demons through his exorcisms.

Anyone who speaks against the Holy Spirit will not be forgiven (12:32). The Old Testament regarded deliberate, defiant sin against God and his ordinances to be blasphemy, the guilt of which remained (Num. 15:30–31). Such defiant sin was considered within Judaism to be unforgivable: "And there is therefore for them no forgiveness or pardon so that they might be pardoned and forgiven from all of the sins of this eternal error" (*Jub.* 15:34). Rejection of Jesus' ministry as validated by the Spirit is the same sort of defiant, deliberate sin. Thus the only

"unpardonable sin" occurs when a person consciously and willfully rejects the operation of the Spirit bearing witness to the reality of Jesus as the Savior and rejects the convicting power of the Spirit in his or her life. The person who does not receive this work of the Spirit cannot come to Jesus and therefore cannot receive forgiveness.

You brood of vipers, how can you who are evil say anything good? (12:34). Jesus uses the same harsh title that John used for the Pharisees and Sadducees, "brood of vipers" (cf. 3:7; 23:33). Vipers are proverbial for their subtle approach and attack, as was the original serpent (Gen. 3).

The Sign of Jonah (12:38–42)

Teacher, we want to see a miraculous sign from you (12:38). A "sign" (*sēmeion*) is some kind of visible mark or action that conveys an unmistakable message, such as the mark of Cain that warned people not to kill him (Gen. 4:15) or that act of speaking in tongues that is a sign to unbelievers of the reality of the gospel message (1 Cor. 14:22). Jesus' return as the glorious Son of Man is the sign that announces the eschatological consummation of the age (see Matt. 24:29; cf. 16:27; 26:64), but Judas's kiss of death is the sign that marks out Jesus' identity to the arresting forces (26:48). "Signs and wonders" will be the proof of God's activity in the proclamation of the gospel in the early church (Acts 2:22, 43; 4:30; Rom. 15:19).

The problem with a sign is that it can be interpreted different ways.[194] The Pharisees are asking Jesus to perform some kind of on-demand spectacular display of power that will irrefutably convince them that his power is from God, not from Satan. Although their request appears innocent enough, they are not asking in good faith. They are asking for a sign they can use against him.

None will be given it except the sign of the prophet Jonah (12:39). The sign of Jonah is not some kind of sign that Jonah brings. Rather, Jonah *is* the sign.[195] When Jonah himself appeared among the people of Nineveh, he was the sign to the people of Nineveh that his message was from the God who had rescued him from death (Jonah 3:1–5). The generation that has heard Jesus' message and seen his ministry has enough validating proof in his miracles that he is the Messiah. Instead of repenting when they see his miracles (cf. Matt. 12:9–14, 22), however, they attempt to use them as the basis of the charge that he is in league with Satan (12:24). Because of their evil intention, the only other sign Jesus will give to them will be a sign of God's coming judgment on them, as Jonah was to the people of Nineveh.

As Jonah … so the Son of Man will be three days and three nights in the heart of the earth (12:40). The Old Testament regularly reckoned a part of a day as a whole day[196]; in rabbinic thought, a part of a day was considered to be a whole day: "A day and a night constitute an *ōnâh* (a full day), and part of an *ōnâh* counts as a whole."[197] Three days and three nights is a proverbial expression and means no more than three days or the combination of any part of three separate days. See "The Days of the Lord's Supper and Crucifixion During the Passion Week" at 26:16.

The Queen of the South will rise at the judgment with this generation and condemn it (12:42). The Queen of the South is the queen of Sheba (1 Kings 10:1–29). Sheba is most likely the home of the Sabaeans in southwestern Arabia in present-day Yemen. It was known for its strong agricultural base, but even more for being one of the most important trade centers involving Africa, India, and the Mediterranean countries. Solomon's wisdom was so widely renowned that the queen went to question him and found his wisdom to be more than she had anticipated. She and the people of Nineveh had allowed the revelation of God to penetrate to their pagan hearts and so will be God's eternal witnesses against the Jewish religious leaders that they have not opened their heart to Jesus, the preeminent revelation of God.

The Return of the Unclean Spirit (12:43–45)

An evil spirit … goes through arid places seeking rest and does not find it (12:43). Demons are often associated with desert (waterless) places as their home.[198] These spirits are evil, and their intent is to find a suitable place to work even greater evil. The demon seeks ownership of the person, which he calls, literally, "*my house.*" That is why it is called demon *possession.*

Takes with it seven other spirits more wicked than itself, and they go in and live there (12:45). The number seven is linked in Scripture with completion, fulfillment, and perfection.[199] Here it may point to the completeness of demon-possession once the demon returns.

Jesus' Disciples Are His True Family (12:46–50)

His mother and brothers stood outside, wanting to speak to him (12:46). The omission of "father" may indicate that

Joseph has died by this time. No reason is given for why his family wishes to speak to him. Mark indicates that his family wants to take control of Jesus and alter his ministry, because people think he is crazy (Mark 3:21; cf. John 7:5).

Pointing to his disciples, he said, "Here are my mother and my brothers" (12:49). Jesus has already accentuated to his disciples the inevitable separation that will occur between family members because of the decision to make a commitment to him (10:34–39; cf. 8:21–22). Jesus did not come to abolish the family, because he will continue to uphold the law that demands children to honor their father and mother (15:4). Instead, he stresses preeminence of a person's commitment to Jesus and the kingdom of heaven above all other commitments. This will form a new spiritual family of disciples of Jesus.

Whoever does the will of my Father in heaven is my brother and sister and mother (12:50). Jesus intentionally broadens the gender reference to include women as disciples by stating "sister." This was a unique form of discipleship in Judaism at that time, especially among the rabbis, because only men could become a disciple of a rabbi and study Torah. A later passage in the Mishnah gives what probably was a general feature during Jesus' time. It discourages too much conversation between men and women, even one's own wife, because it distracts the rabbinic disciple from studying Torah: "He that talks much with womankind brings evil upon himself and neglects the study of the Law and at the last will inherit Gehenna" (*m. ʾAbot* 1:5). But with Jesus, any person—woman or man, young or old, Gentile or Jew—who responds to the gospel of the kingdom and believes on him for eternal life is his disciple and will be taught to obey all that Jesus commands (cf. 28:19–20).

The Parable of the Soils (13:1–23)

He got into a boat and sat in it, while all the people stood on the shore (13:2). Local tradition locates the place of this discourse at a distinctive inlet called the "Cove of the Parables." It lies approximately a mile (1.5 km) southwest of Capernaum, halfway to the traditional site of the Sermon on the Mount near Tabgha. The land slopes down like a natural, horseshoe-shaped amphitheater around the cove, providing environmental acoustics for Jesus' voice to have carried over one hundred meters from the boat to a crowd of perhaps hundreds gathered on the shore. Israeli scientists have tested the acoustics in modern

R E F L E C T I O N S

EXORCISM WAS CONVINCING EVIDENCE THAT JESUS had brought the kingdom of heaven to Israel (12:28). Experiencing an exorcism was important enough, but the exorcised person must then respond to Jesus' invitation to believe and enter the kingdom of God and experience its new life in Christ through his Spirit. If not, the exorcised person is more vulnerable to the renewed and persistent attack of the demon world to take back ownership of him or her. No fundamental change has taken place in the person that prevents the return of the demon. This is truly spiritual warfare, and the battle is over the lives of people. An exorcised person when repossessed will be worse off because of the persistent battle to take full control of him or her. Exorcism is the first step, but the most important step is to enter the kingdom of heaven and receive the resources necessary to resist the devil, including a regenerated heart, the presence of Jesus, and the power of the Spirit.

times and found them to be realistic for Jesus' parables to have been heard.[200]

Then he told them many things in parables (13:3). Jesus speaks (*laleō*, not "teaches") to the crowd (*ochlos*, not "people" as NIV) many things in parables. Later, Jesus will explain the parables to his disciples (13:10–23, 36–43). Parables have distinctively different purposes for the crowd and for the disciples. Jesus has already given several parables,[201] but this is the first time that Matthew uses the term "parable" (*parabolē*). Underlying the term *parable* is the Hebrew *māšāl*, which refers to a wide spectrum of ideas based on comparison or analogy, including byword, proverb, wisdom sayings, and story.[202] As used by Jesus, the parable is a way of communicating truth through a narrative analogy in the service of moral or spiritual argument. They are often deeply, even frustratingly, perplexing.[203] The analogies or comparisons Jesus uses to make his point come from everyday experiences, but they press the listener to search for the intended meaning. That is why in popular preaching Jesus' parables are often referred to as "an earthly story with a heavenly meaning."

A farmer went out to sow his seed (13:3). Jesus' listeners are well aware of farming techniques, because most everyone took care of his own fields and gardens or worked the fields of his landlord. We are not certain of the type of seed that the sower (NIV "farmer") was sowing, but we may think of wheat to help illustrate the scene, since wheat was one of the most important crops in Israel,[204] and it appears as the subject of a later parable (13:24–30).

Some fell along the path, and the birds came and ate it up (13:4). Seed was sown "broadcast" style by scattering it in all directions by hand while walking up and down the field. The average rate of sowing wheat varies from twenty pounds

per acre (22.5 kilograms per hectare) upward, which allowed for wasted seed. Fields were apparently plowed both before the seed was sown and after, plowing across the original furrows to cover the seeds with soil. The desired depth of plowing under wheat seed was usually one to three inches (2.5 to 7.5 centimetres), but it could be less in certain areas where the topsoil was shallow. In the rabbinic listing of the thirty-nine main classes of work, plowing follows sowing (*m. Šabb.* 7:2). It was common for seed to be scattered on the hard paths that surrounded the fields. Birds would swoop down as the farmer walked on and eat the seed.

Some fell on rocky places, where it did not have much soil (13:5). Conditions for farming in many areas of Israel were not favorable. The hardships that many people experienced included insufficient amounts of water and soil. The terrain in most cases was uneven and rocky, with only thin layers of soil covering the rock. Seed that landed on this shallow soil could begin to germinate, but it couldn't put down deep roots to collect what little moisture was in that parched thin layer of earth.[205] Sprouting seed would soon wither and die in the hot sun (13:6). James gives a fitting commentary: "For the sun rises with scorching heat and withers the plant; its blossom falls and its beauty is destroyed" (James 1:11).

Still other seed fell on good soil, where it produced a crop—a hundred, sixty or thirty times what was sown (13:8). In the fourth example, seed falls on what is described as "good soil." As the seeds germinate and mature, they keep on yielding a range of a hundred, sixty, or thirty times what is sown, signifying a good harvest, typical of what a harvest blessed by God would yield,[206] such as Isaac's harvest: "Isaac planted crops in that land and the same year reaped a hundredfold, because the LORD blessed him" (Gen. 26:12).

The knowledge of the secrets of the kingdom of heaven has been given to you, but not to them (13:11). Jesus speaks to the crowd in parables because God has given (cf. the divine passive "has been given") the secrets of the kingdom of heaven to the disciples, not to the crowd, to know. "Secrets" (NIV) is the Greek *mystēria* (lit., "mysteries"), which draws on a Semitic background of an eschatological secret passed on in veiled speech

to God's chosen. The term is found explicitly in Daniel: "During the night the mystery was revealed to Daniel in a vision" (Dan. 2:18–19; cf. 2:27–30, 47; 4:9). The idea of God revealing his secrets is also found as a powerful theme elsewhere in the Old Testament.[207]

Though seeing, they do not see; though hearing, they do not hear or understand (13:13). The crowd in Jesus' ministry mirrors the people of Israel to whom the prophet Isaiah ministered (Isa. 6:9–10). They reject the message because they are spiritually deadened.

Listen then to what the parable of the sower means (13:18). To his disciples, not to the crowd, Jesus gives the intended meaning behind the parable of the soils and sower. A similar parable, but with a different emphasis, is found in Jewish literature: "For just as the farmer sows many seeds upon the ground and plants a multitude of seedlings, and yet not all that have been sown will come up in due season, and not all that were planted will take root; so all those who have been sown in the world will not be saved" (4 Ezra 8:41). In this parable the chief character is the farmer; that is, God. The fate of the seed depends on his action, especially his distributing the right amount of water at the correct time (4 Ezra 8:42–45). Jesus' emphasis is on the spiritual responsiveness and responsibility of the types of soil that represent the lives of those who hear the message of the kingdom.

The evil one comes and snatches away what was sown in his heart (13:19). Satan is the prince of demons (12:24–27), the prince of the power of the air (Eph. 2:2). *Jubilees* refers to him as "Prince Mastema," likening him to a swooping bird leading a pack of other birds: "Prince Mastema sent crows and birds so that they might eat the seed which was being sown in the earth in order to spoil the earth so that they might rob mankind of their labors. Before they plowed in the seed, the crows picked it off the surface of the earth" (*Jub.* 11:10–11; cf. *b. Sanh.* 107a).

Further Parables (13:24–58)

The kingdom of heaven is like a man who sowed good seed in his field (13:24). Satan operates in this world both as a swooping bird (13:19) and as the enemy farmer attempting to disrupt the growth of good wheat (disciples) by sowing among it *zizanion* (*Lolium temulentum*), a kind of weed referred to also as "darnel" or "tares." It is a weedy rye grass with poisonous seeds, which in early stages of growth looks like wheat, but can

R E F L E C T I O N S

A "CROP" WILL BE PRODUCED IN THE LIFE OF THE person who is "good soil" for the kingdom of heaven to operate. Many think that this "crop" refers to converts won to Christ through the believer. This no doubt is partially correct, but in this context it refers to something more fundamental—the transformation of a person who has encountered the kingdom of heaven. In the fourth soil the crop represents the outworking of the life of the divine seed (cf. 1 John 3:9), with special reference to the production of the fruit of the Spirit (cf. Gal. 5:22–23), and the outworking of the Spirit in the gifts of the Spirit in the believer's life (1 Cor. 12). This results in personal characteristics produced by the Spirit (Gal. 5:22–23), the external creation of Spirit-produced righteousness and good works (e.g., Col. 1:10), and indeed, new converts won through the believer's testimony (e.g., Rom. 1:13). The "crop" produced is the outward evidence of the reality of inward life of the kingdom of heaven.

be distinguished easily in its mature state at the time of harvesting.

The kingdom of heaven is like a mustard seed (13:31). The seed of the mustard plant was proverbially small (cf. 17:20). Rabbinic literature gives similar contrasting metaphors using the mustard seed. The mustard seed exemplifies the smallest quantity of blood (y. Ber. 5:8d; b. Ber. 31a), while the Galilean Rabbi Simeon ben Halafta (2d cent. A.D.) asserts that he climbed a mustard bush that was as tall as a fig tree (y. Pe'ah 7:20b).[208] The metaphor contrasts the small beginnings of the kingdom of heaven with its growth.

So that the birds of the air come and perch in its branches (13:32). The image of a large tree with birds alighting on its branches recalls several Old Testament references to a great kingdom (cf. Ezek. 17:22–24; 31:2–18; Dan. 4:9–27).

The kingdom of heaven is like yeast (13:33). Yeast is any number of different forms of fungi that multiply rapidly. Homemade bread required a bakers' yeast (*saccharomyces cerevisiae*) to cause it to rise, also called "leaven." Therefore, a small piece of fermenting, acidic dough, set aside from a former baking, was called a "leaven." It was "mixed" (lit., "hidden") in the flour and kneaded. A typical lump of leaven might have been no more than 2 percent of the dough weight.[209] Bread made with yeast was known as "leavened," as distinct from "unleavened" bread (Ex. 12:15).

Scripture uses leaven almost exclusively as a negative metaphor, probably because fermentation implied disintegration and corruption (Ex. 12:8, 15–20), as in the Feast of Unleavened Bread, which reminded the Israelites of their hurried departure from Egypt (Ex. 12:31–39; Deut. 16:3). But Jesus seems to reverse the connotation here to symbolize the hidden permeation of the kingdom of heaven in this world. The mustard seed emphasizes growth, while the yeast suggests permeation and transformation. In spite of its small, inauspicious beginnings, the kingdom of heaven will permeate the world.

"I will open my mouth in parables, I will utter things hidden since the creation of the world" (13:35). The psalmist Asaph reflected on Israel's history and clarified through parables the meaning of past events so that the people would learn from their history and would not be a stubborn and rebellious people with hearts hard to God (Ps. 78:2, 8). Matthew's standard fulfillment formula says that Jesus has done a similar service to Israel in his day, revealing in his parables the mysteries of the kingdom of heaven that have been hidden since the beginning. Once again, the difference is in the response of the audience. Those spiritually alive will come to Jesus for further clarification and understanding, while those spiritually deadened will turn away.

LEAVENED AND UNLEAVENED BREAD

Also depicting a container of yeast.

▼

The kingdom of heaven is like treasure hidden in a field (13:44). Treasures were often hidden in fields, because there were no formal banks as we know them today. The intriguing Copper Scroll found at Qumran lists sixty-four places in Palestine where treasures were supposed to be hidden: e.g., "In the ruin which is in the valley, pass under the steps leading to the East forty cubits . . . [there is] a chest of money and its total: the weight of seventeen talents" (3QCopper Scroll 1:1–3). Jesus speaks of a treasure hidden in a field. If the field is the world (cf. 13:38), then the treasure is the kingdom of heaven that lies unnoticed because of its small, inconsequential nature. The emphasis is on the supreme worth of that treasure unseen by others; it is worth far more than any sacrifice one might make to acquire it.

Once again, the kingdom of heaven is like a net (13:47). The net (*sagēnē*) is the large *seine* or "dragnet," the oldest type of net used and until recently the most important fishing method on the Sea of Galilee. It was shaped like a long 750 to 1,000 foot wall, upwards of twenty-five feet high at the center and five feet high at the ends. The foot-rope was weighted with sinkers, while the head-rope floated with attached corks, enabling the net wall to be dragged toward shore by both ends, trapping fish inside.[210] Bad fish would have included those without fins and scales, which were unclean (Lev. 11:9–12).

Like a large dragnet, the kingdom of heaven has all sorts respond to it in the preaching of "fishers of men" (4:19). The true nature of those who are gathered in will not always be readily apparent, as Judas Iscariot will so sadly exemplify. Only at the judgment will the full implication be known.

Brings out of his storeroom new treasures as well as old (13:52). The Torah-trained teacher of law has studied under a great rabbi, but for the one who has been made a disciple[211] of the kingdom of heaven, Jesus is the great Teacher (cf. 28:20). The true disciple knows how to draw spiritual truths from the parables properly, to balance the new teachings of Christ with the fulfilled promises of the messianic kingdom, and to understand how Jesus truly fulfills the Law and the Prophets (5:17).

He began teaching the people in their synagogue, and they were amazed (13:54). Although Capernaum had become Jesus' "own city" during his

◀ *left*

A PEARL OF GREAT PRICE

Pearls of various size.

FISHING WITH A NET

The man is fishing in the Sea of Galilee.

▼

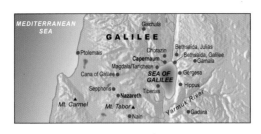

Galilean ministry (9:1), Nazareth was his "hometown" (*patris*), the land of his father and family (13:54; cf. 2:23). Most scholars see this as a thematic abridgment of the same incident recorded much more fully in Luke 4:14–30, although it is possible that this is a later return to Galilee for a second visit (cf. Mark 6:1–6). The later may be implied by the reference to wisdom and miracles, which are not a significant part of Jesus' ministry until after the visit to Nazareth as recorded in Luke.

John the Baptist Beheaded by Herod (14:1–12)

At that time Herod the tetrarch heard the reports about Jesus (14:1). Herod Antipas was the Roman client-ruler over the region where Jesus ministered. He was only seventeen years old when his father, Herod the Great, died. Herod's

kingdom was divided among three of his sons, Archelaus, Philip, and Antipas (see comments on 2:19ff.; 16:13). Herod Antipas had a long rule (4 B.C.-A.D. 39) and was the most prominent of Herod's sons in the four Gospels because he ruled the area of Galilee, the region of Jesus' primary ministry. His chief infamy comes from his execution of John the Baptist and his interview of Jesus prior to his crucifixion (cf. Luke 23:6–12).

Herod Antipas's capital city, Tiberias, was only eight miles down the coast of the Sea of Galilee from Capernaum. The news of Jesus' ministry has reached him possibly through Cuza, his steward, whose wife is part of the group of women who on occasion support and travel with the apostolic band (cf. Luke 8:1–3).

right ▶

EXCAVATIONS AT SEPPHORIS

MODERN NAZARETH
▼

This is John the Baptist; he has risen from the dead! (14:2). Herod Antipas was a Jew by religion, although he had an Idumean background. His reaction reveals a curious blend of emotion, theology, and superstition. His guilty fear for having executed John combines with a confused notion of resurrection, probably based in part on Pharisaic beliefs along with semi-pagan superstitious ideas of returning spirits. As a Roman client-ruler, he has been well versed in Roman mythology. The Herodian family had long been notorious for this syncretistic mixture of beliefs.

Now Herod had arrested John and . . . put him in prison because of Herodias, his brother Philip's wife (14:3). Herod Antipas had married the daughter of King Aretas IV of Nabataea, probably a political marriage arranged by Emperor Augustus to keep peace in the region. The marriage lasted for several years, until Antipas fell in love with Herodias, the wife of his brother Herod Philip I (not the better known half-brother, Herod Philip the tetrarch), another of Antipas's half-brothers (by Mariamne II; Mark 6:17). Herod Philip was a private citizen who lived in Rome. On a trip to Rome, Antipas stayed at the home of his half-brother and fell in love with Herodias. They determined to marry, but Herodias demanded that Antipas divorce his wife of over fifteen years.[212] Some years later (A.D. 36), King Aretas IV attacked and conquered Antipas's military forces, at least in part to seek revenge for repudiating his daughter.[213]

John had been saying to him: "It is not lawful for you to have her" (14:4). When Antipas married Herodias, the highly popular John the Baptist publicly con-

demned him for marrying his half-brother's wife, who was also his half-niece (14:3–4; Mark 6:18; Luke 3:19). This would have been considered an incestuous affront to God's law (Lev. 18:16; 20:21).

On Herod's birthday the daughter of Herodias danced for them (14:6). Herod the Great built a royal palace at the fortress Machaerus, in part because he prized the hot springs at Calirrhoe not far away. The remains of a majestic peristyle court that rose to an ornate triclinium (banquet room) have been excavated, an indication of the lavish entertaining that

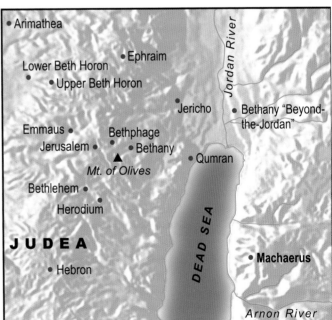

Arimathea

Ephraim

Lower Beth Horon

Upper Beth Horon

Jericho

Jordan River

Bethany "Beyond-the-Jordan"

Emmaus

Bethphage

Jerusalem

Bethany

Qumran

Mt. of Olives

Bethlehem

Herodium

JUDEA

DEAD SEA

Hebron

Machaerus

Arnon River

was held at the palatial fortress.[214] After the death of Herod the Great the fortress was assigned to the tetrarch of his son Herod Antipas. Here, according to Josephus,[215] Herod Antipas imprisoned John the Baptist and later had him put to death[216] (see "Machaerus" at 11:1–6).

Herodias had her daughter (named Salome in Josephus, *Ant.* 18.5.4 §136) perform a dance for Antipas. She was probably only twelve to fourteen years old,[217] but in that kind of degraded, deceptive setting it likely was a sensual dance.

Give me here on a platter the head of John the Baptist (14:8). Behind the scenes of the majority of the intrigues in Antipas's life was his second wife, Hero-

dias. She had demanded that Antipas divorce his first wife, the daughter of Aretas IV. Here she manipulates Antipas to execute John the Baptist. Later she will persuade Antipas to go to Emperor Gaius Caligula to denounce her brother Agrippa I, because she is envious of his success at being named "king" over Herod Philip's former region northeast of Antipas.[218] She finally got her own due on that incident, however, because the emperor was a close friend of her brother. Gaius turned the tables and banished Antipas to Gaul, where Herodius accompanied him.

During the Hasmonean reign more than a century earlier, Alexander Jannaeus performed an even more heinous

---

▶ **John the Baptist's Execution by Herod Antipas as Recorded by Josephus**

Josephus took a soldier's and politician's perspective on the arrest and execution of John the Baptist, while the evangelists tended to take more of a moral and spiritual perspective. Both accounts are necessary in order to get the full impact that John the Baptist had on Israel as he prepared the way for Jesus Messiah. Josephus's perspective follows his description of Herod Antipas's defeat at the hands of Aretas IV, his former father-in-law, who had waged war in part to seek revenge for the repudiation of his daughter by Antipas.

> To some of the Jews the destruction of Herod's army seemed to be divine vengeance, and certainly a just vengeance, for his treatment of John, surnamed the Baptist. For Herod had put him to death, though he was a good man and had exhorted the Jews to lead righteous lives, to practice justice towards their fellows and piety toward God, and so doing to join in baptism. In his view this was a necessary preliminary if baptism was to be acceptable to God. They must not employ it to gain pardon for whatever

sins they committed, but as a consecration of the body implying that the soul was already thoroughly cleansed by right behaviour. When others too joined the crowds about him, because they were aroused to the highest degree by his sermons, Herod became alarmed. Eloquence that had so great an effect on mankind might lead to some form of sedition, for it looked as if they would be guided by John in everything that they did. Herod decided therefore that it would be much better to strike first and be rid of him before his work led to an uprising, than to wait for an upheaval, get involved in a difficult situation and see his mistake. Though John, because of Herod's suspicions, was brought in chains to Machaerus, the stronghold that we have previously mentioned, and there put to death, yet the verdict of the Jews was that the destruction visited upon Herod's army was a vindication of John, since God saw fit to inflict such a blow on Herod. (Josephus, *Ant.* 18.5.2 §116–119)

act of cruelty while engaged in a riotous party: "While he feasted with his concubines in a conspicuous place, he ordered some eight hundred of the Jews to be crucified, and slaughtered their children and wives before the eyes of the still living wretches."[219]

John's disciples came and took his body and buried it. Then they went and told Jesus (14:12). John's disciples had remained loyal to the prophet throughout his imprisonment; now they perform the duties of loyal followers, since John's family are likely all deceased by this time. We hear of other disciples of John throughout the next few decades, although they are increasingly separated from his true message (Acts 19:1–7). The natural transition should have been to follow Jesus.[220]

Feeding the Five Thousand (14:13–21)

The crowds followed him on foot from the towns (14:13). The traditional site of the feeding of the five thousand is west of Capernaum, past the traditional site of the Sermon on the Mount, above the Heptapegon ("Seven Springs"), at present-day Tabgha,[221] just a mile or so beyond the "Cove of Parables" (cf. 13:1–3). This area was a favorite hideaway for Jesus. The site is supported by an ancient report from the pilgrim Egeria (c. A.D. 383–395):

Above the Lake there is also a field of grass with much hay and several palms. By it are the Seven Springs, each of which supplies a huge quantity of water. In the field the Lord fed the people with the seven loaves of bread. . . . The Stone on which the Lord placed the bread has been made into an altar. Visitors take small pieces of rock from this stone for their welfare and it brings benefit to everyone.[222]

Crowds could easily have followed Jesus from the Capernaum region to Tabgha (about two miles) or to Bethsaida (about four miles).

We have here only five loaves of bread and two fish (14:17). Bread and dried or pickled fish were food suitable for taking on a short journey into the hills. John tells us that a young boy had supplied them, indicating that they were small cakes sufficient for one person's afternoon meal, not full "loaves" found on modern grocery store shelves (John 6:9). John further reports that the bread cakes were made of barley, the chief component of the staple food in Israel, especially of the poorer people.[223]

Taking the five loaves and the two fish and looking up to heaven, he gave thanks and broke the loaves (14:19). An old tradition recounts that Jesus placed the five loaves and two fish on a large piece of rock and then gave the common Jewish *Berakah*: "Blessed art thou, O Lord our God, King of the universe, who bringest forth bread from the earth" (*m. Ber.* 6:1). The rock is visible today beneath the altar of the Church of the Multiplication

FIVE LOAVES AND TWO FISH

A mosaic in the church at Tabgha (Heptapegon)

▼

right ▶

**A GALILEAN
FISHING BOAT**

A mosaic in the
floor of the fifth-
century Byzantine
church at Beth Loya
in the southern
foothills of Judea.

at Tabgha. A mosaic of fishes and bread cakes covers the floor in the basilica next to the rock. If Tabgha was the location of the feeding, this area is probably close.[224]

The disciples picked up twelve basketfuls of broken pieces (14:20). The "basket" (*kophinos*) is a small woven container that occurs in Jewish contexts to denote a hamper for carrying kosher foods. In the feeding of the four thousand a different word for basket (*spyris*) occurs (see comments on 15:37).

Five thousand men, besides women and children (14:21). The total number may have stretched to 10,000 or more, far larger than the populations of most villages surrounding the Sea of Galilee.

The Son of God Walks on the Water (14:22–36)

After he had dismissed them, he went up on a mountainside by himself to pray (14:23). If the feeding was in the Tabgha area, Jesus may have stayed in a grotto below a hanging cliff, which tradition today calls the Eremos Cave, named after Jesus' lonely prayer vigil. For "mountainside," see comments on 28:16.

The boat was . . . buffeted by the waves because the wind was against it (14:24). The winds against the boat probably indicate that they are moving from west to east, because the most severe storms come down the mountains to the east. "A considerable distance" out on the lake in Greek is literally "many stadia." A *stadion* is 185 meters (approximately 600 feet), which would have put the disciples anywhere from a mile to even two or three miles out on the lake, which is seven miles at its widest point. The lake's low elevation (see comments on 8:24) leads it to be subject to a powerful east wind ("Sharkiyeh") that blows in over the mountains.

During the fourth watch of the night Jesus went out to them, walking on the lake (14:25). The Roman military divided the night into four "watches," based on the need to provide rotating guards throughout the night. At three hours each, the fourth watch was from 3:00 A.M. to 6:00 A.M.

The disciples . . . were terrified. "It's a ghost," they said, and cried out in fear (14:26). In Greek literature the term "ghost" (*phantasma*) is used for dream appearances or spirit appearances or apparitions, but in the Old Testament it means a "deception" (Job 20:8 LXX; Isa. 28:7; cf. Wisd. Sol. 17:14).[225] It only occurs in the New Testament here and in

SEA OF GALILEE

▼

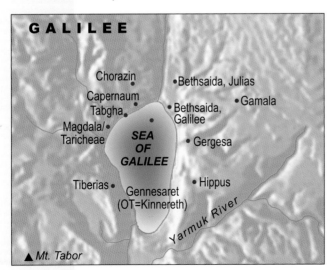

GALILEE

Chorazin
Bethsaida, Julias
Capernaum
Tabgha
Bethsaida, Galilee
Gamala
Magdala/
Taricheae
SEA OF GALILEE
Gergesa
Tiberias
Hippus
Gennesaret
(OT=Kinnereth)
Yarmuk River
▲ Mt. Tabor

REFLECTIONS

PETER'S WALKING ON THE WATER is a story that is surpassed only by the perfect walk of our Lord Jesus on the lake. Peter is often unfairly criticized by modern readers for being presumptuous to ask to go out on the lake. But Jesus does not criticize him for that request; he only mildly chides him for his ineffective faith once he gets out there. It took much courage to follow Jesus on the water, and Peter does fine until he looks at his circumstances ("seeing the wind," 14:30) and takes his eyes off of Jesus; then he finds himself afraid and in trouble. We will face many circumstances for which we are completely unprepared, and the circumstances we face from day to day will change. But the one constancy we have in this life is Jesus. As we go through life focused on an intimate walk with Jesus through each and every circumstance, we learn how to apply his consistency to our circumstances.

the parallel in Mark 6:49. The disciples may be thinking that some evil spirit is attempting to deceive them.

Take courage! It is I. Don't be afraid (14:27). The meaning behind the expression "It is I" (lit., "I am") may allude to the voice of Yahweh from the bush (Ex. 3:14) and the voice of assurance to Israel of the Lord's identity and presence as their Savior (Isa. 43:10–13).

"Lord, if it's you," Peter replied, "tell me to come to you on the water" (14:28). Peter will play an increasingly important role as a leader and spokesman for the disciples in the next several incidents

(14:28–31; 15:15; 16:17–19; 17:24–27; 18:21). Matthew emphasizes Peter's leadership role, but also shows how Peter is an imperfect leader who is in process of development, as Jesus prepares him for the early days of the church ahead.[226]

Then those who were in the boat worshiped him, saying, "Truly you are the Son of God" (14:33). All of the events evoked from the disciples an act of worship (*proskyneō*), which in Scripture is nearly always reserved for God. One may prostrate oneself before other esteemed personages as a symbol of respect, such as David before King Saul (1 Sam. 24:8) or Abigail before David (25:23). But in this context of miracles of divine significance, the disciples are gripped with the reality that Jesus is much, much more; he is the "Son of God," and so they worship him.

When they had crossed over, they landed at Gennesaret (14:34). Either coming from Bethsaida or having been blown back to the west shore (cf. 14:13), the disciples with Jesus now land at Gennesaret. This site may refer to the Old Testament town of Kinnereth, for which the Sea was named,[227] but the more usual use of the

GENNESARET

The site of Tel Kinnereth near the Sea of Galilee.

▼

▶**Gennesaret**

The region of Gennesaret did not figure prominently in Jesus' ministry as recorded in the Gospels, but the response to Jesus on this occasion was remarkable. Josephus's description captures not only the beauty of the region, but also indicates the exquisiteness of the lands surrounding the Sea of Galilee.

Skirting the Lake of Gennesar [Galilee], and also bearing that name, lies a region whose natural properties and beauty are very remarkable. There is not a plant which its fertile soil refuses to produce, and its cultivators in fact grow every species; the air is so well-tempered that it suits the most opposite varieties. The walnut, a tree which delights in the most wintry climate, grows luxuriantly, beside palm-trees, which thrive on heat, and figs and olives, which require a milder climate. One might say that nature had taken pride in this assembling, by *tour de force*, the most discordant species in a single spot, and that, by a happy rivalry, each of the seasons wished to claim this region for her own.[A-72]

name is to refer to a plain extending about 3.5 miles (5 km.) by 1.5 miles (2.5 km.) along the northwest shore of the Sea of Galilee. The plain of Gennesaret is the only easily tillable land bordering the Sea of Galilee (for Josephus's description see "Gennesaret"). It was heavily populated during Jesus' day and included the urban centers of Tiberias, Herod Antipas' elaborate and bustling capital city, and Tarichaeae/Magdala, the hometown of Mary Magdalene.[228]

Jesus and the Tradition of the Elders (15:1–20)

Why do your disciples break the tradition of the elders? (15:2). The primary point of contention between Jesus and the Pharisees was that Jesus did not recognize the binding authority of the Pharisees' oral law, here called the "tradition of the elders."

The term "tradition" comes from a noun that refers to something that has been "handed over" or "passed on" (*paradosis*). The "tradition of the elders" (15:1)

became a technical expression among the Pharisees for the interpretation of Scripture made by past esteemed rabbis that was "passed on" to later generations. This generally was connected later with Mishnah's *halakah*, "walking," that sets forth law to guide the faithful in their walking, or living, in consistency with Scripture.[229] The traditions of the elders, therefore, came to refer to "rules of Jewish life and religion which in the course of centuries had come to possess a validity and sanctity equal to that of the Written Law and which, as the 'Oral Law,' were deemed, equally with the Written Law, to be of divine origin and therefore consonant with and, for the most part, deducible from the Written Law."[230]

The tractate ʾ*Abot*, "The Fathers," in one of the most famous of rabbinic sayings, traces the traditions of the elders back to the giving of the oral law to Moses, who in turn passed it on to succeeding generations: "Moses received the Law ["Oral Law"] from Sinai and committed it to Joshua, and Joshua to the elders, and the elders to the Prophets; and the Prophets committed it to the men of the Great Synagogue" (*m. ʾAbot* 1.1). The Great Synagogue was the body of 120 elders that came up from the Exile with Ezra and committed themselves to making Scripture practically relevant by developing new rules and restrictions for its observance.[231] The saying goes on, "They said three things: Be deliberate in judgment, raise up many disciples, and make a fence around the Law" (*m. ʾAbot* 1.1).

At the time of Jesus the "traditions of the elders" was a developing system of interpretation that was the distinctive characteristic of the Pharisees.[232] It had not yet been written and codified. That was the accomplishment of post-A.D. 70 Judaism, which finally resulted in the Mishnah, promulgated by Judah the Prince around 200.

They don't wash their hands before they eat! (15:2). Bodily cleanliness was valued highly in the ancient world. The heat and dust made frequent washing necessary for both health and refreshment. Within ancient Israel, a host provided travelers with water for their feet so that they would be refreshed and cleansed from their journey and ready for a meal.[233] The hands were a particular concern for cleanliness, as something unclean could be transmitted to oneself and others, so the priests were required to wash their hands and feet prior to offering their ritual service (Ex. 30:18–21). The Pharisees and later rabbis adapted this concern for ceremonial cleanness to common Israelites, with the purpose that they would consume everyday food as though it were a sacrifice to God at the temple altar. Mishnah *Yadayim* ("hands") describes the procedure: "[To render the hands clean] a quarter-*log* or more [of water] must be poured over the hands [to suffice] for one person or even for two."[234] A quarter-log of water is equal in bulk to an egg and a half,[235] which was poured over the hands up to the wrists prior to the consumption of food. Such a small amount of water demonstrates that the concern for washing was ceremonial, not hygenic (see "Purity" at Mark 7).[236]

And why do you break the command of God for the sake of your tradition? (15:3). The traditions of the elders were not simply preferred ways of living, but were equal in authority to the written Law. Jesus contrasts what God has given with what the elders pronounced.

Whatever help you might otherwise have received from me is a gift devoted to God (15:5). The expression "gift devoted to God" reflects the Hebrew term "Corban" (Mark 7:11), a technical term designating a formal vow made to God. Such a formal vow allowed a person to be exempt from one's other responsibilities. The Pharisees developed a complicated series of rulings regarding vows and oaths that were eventually compiled in the rabbinic Mishnaic tractates *Nedarim* ("vows") and *Šebuʿot* ("oaths"). Summarized, the difference is that "a vow forbids a certain thing to be used ('Let such-a-thing be forbidden to me, or to you!'), while an oath forbids the swearer to do a certain thing although it is not a thing forbidden itself ('I swear that I will not eat such-a-thing!')."[237] Jesus addresses oaths in 5:34–37 and 23:16–22, but addresses vows here in 15:1–9. Vows are of two kinds: vows of dedication, which render a thing to be forbidden in the future for common use (as the vow in 15:5), and vows of abstention, which render forbidden those things or acts that are ordinarily permissible (*m. Ned.* 1.1).[238] The situation Jesus raises is a gift vowed for the support of the temple, which takes precedence over the support of one's parents.

Thus you nullify the word of God for the sake of your tradition (15:6). The Pharisees would not have disagreed with Jesus' emphasis on honoring parents, but their human traditions of allowing certain vows actually supplanted Scripture. They would have considered anyone who broke a vow (human law) in order to help needy parents (God's law) to have committed a serious sin.

Do you know that the Pharisees were offended when they heard this? (15:12). The Pharisees, in contrast to the Sadducees (see "Pharisees and Sadducees" at 3:7), were increasingly influential in Israel as the authoritative interpreters of Scripture and the most righteous in their daily behavior. Jesus with one swipe undercuts both of those distinctives, and his disciples report that Jesus has "offended" or "scandalized" (*skandalizō*) the Pharisees. They rightly understand that Jesus has elevated himself as critic of their entire religious tradition, which would undercut their influence with the people.

The things that come out of the mouth come from the heart, and these make a man "unclean" (15:18). Clean or unclean is ultimately God's judgment. Jesus gives

---

R E F L E C T I O N S

TRADITIONS DEVELOPED BY HUMANS CAN BE DANgerous when they supplant God's revelation. But tradition is not wrong per se. Paul uses the same term (*paradosis*) to refer to the gospel truths and doctrines that he passed to the churches (1 Cor. 11:2; 2 Thess. 2:15; 3:6), and a related verb (*paradidōmi*) to refer to the fundamental creedal truths of the cross and resurrection that he had received and passed on to the church (1 Cor. 15:1). The essential difference between these forms of tradition and those developed within Judaism rests on the fact of Jesus' incarnation. Jesus is the revelation of God embodied, and Paul declares therefore that the traditions he received and passed on to the church have derived from God himself through the revelation of Jesus the Messiah. That is a crucial dissimilarity for us to reflect upon.

God's perspective by rendering superfluous the Pharisees' fastidious and obsessive preoccupation with dietary purity laws, especially those at the center of the controversy, the washing of hands. God's evaluative judgment concerns behavior that originates in the heart of a person. The implication is that the heart is evil (cf. 7:11), and all of the sinful activity in the world around them, and even in their own lives, cannot be cleansed through the religious traditions of the elders.

Gentiles Acknowledge Jesus as the Son of David (15:21–31)

Jesus withdrew to the region of Tyre and Sidon (15:21). Tyre and Sidon were Gentile cities in northwest Philistia/Phoenicia, an ancient region that bordered Galilee to the west along the coast of the Mediterranean Sea. They were known throughout the ancient world as powerful maritime commercial centers. In Israel they became proverbial for pagan peoples, often linked as the object of condemnation from Old Testament prophets for their Baal worship and arrogant pride in their power and wealth, and therefore deserving of judgment.[239] In his denunciation of the Jewish cities of Korazin and Bethsaida, Jesus had said that if the miracles performed in them had been performed in Tyre and Sidon, they would have repented (11:21). Now they get their chance.

A Canaanite woman from that vicinity came to him, crying out, "Lord, Son of David, have mercy on me!" (15:22). The expression "Canaanite" (*Chananaia*) indicates a woman from the region that was a virtual stereotype in the Old Testament and rabbinic literature of pagan non-Jews.[240] Mark calls her "a Greek,

◀

GALILEE, TYRE, AND SIDON

Phoenicia belonged to the Roman province of Syria.

born in Syrian Phoenicia," which may indicate she was from a higher, more affluent class (see comments on Mark 7:26). Intriguingly, she demonstrates familiarity with Jewish messianic tradition by calling Jesus "Son of David" and calling for his merciful, miraculous ministry of exorcism for her daughter. Her use of "Lord" three times in the interaction (15:22, 25, 27) is probably for her a title of great respect, but she is saying more than she realizes.

I was sent only to the lost sheep of Israel (15:24). "Lost sheep of Israel" (cf. 10:5–6) does not mean the lost sheep *among* Israel, as though some are lost and others not. The expression indicates the lost sheep *who are* the house of Israel. Jesus comes as the Suffering Servant to save all of Israel. The prophet Isaiah laments, "We all, like sheep, have gone astray, each of us has turned to his own way; and the LORD has laid on him the iniquity of us all" (Isa. 53:6). Jesus must first go to Israel with the fulfillment of the promises made to the nation (cf. 53:6–8), so that the Gentiles themselves will glorify God for his promises made to his people (cf. Rom. 15:8–9).

"Lord, help me!" she said (15:25). This recalls a prior Gentile woman from Sidon (1 Kings 17:7–24) who was persistent in her desire for the prophet Elijah to heal her son.

It is not right to take the children's bread and toss it to their dogs (15:26). The "children's bread" emphasizes the care that God promised to provide for his covenant children, Israel: "You are the children of the LORD your God . . . for you are a people holy to the LORD your God. Out of all the peoples on the face of the earth, the LORD has chosen you to be his treasured possession" (Deut. 14:1–2; Hos. 11:1). As a metaphor, "dogs" is a humiliating label for those apart from, or enemies of, Israel's covenant community (cf. 7:6).[241] Some suggest that the diminutive form for dog used here (*kynarion*) conjures up an image of a little puppy dog, so that Jesus is using the term as an endearing metaphor. More likely, the diminutive form parallels "children's bread" and suggests a dog that has been domesticated, but is nonetheless still a dog. Jesus is contrasting God's care for those of his family with those who are not. He is not condoning the use of a derogatory title, as the response of the woman indicates.

Even the dogs eat the crumbs that fall from their masters' table (15:27). The woman continues the metaphor but uses it to emphasize that dogs too have a caring relationship with "their master." Most dogs were not domesticated, living in squalor, running the streets, and scavenging for food (Ps. 59:14–15). Some dogs were trained for guarding flocks (Job 30:1) and humans (Isa. 56:10; Tobit 6:2; 11:4), but were not normally brought into the home. However, some dogs were domesticated and trained as household watchdogs; they were fed in the house (cf. *Jos. Asen.* 10:13). This perceptive woman, who had already confessed Jesus as the messianic Son of David, presses Jesus by calling on the extended blessings promised to the Gentiles. Although Israel receives the primary blessings of the covenant, Gentiles also were to be the recipient of blessing through them, a promise central to the Abrahamic covenant.[242]

Feeding the Four Thousand (15:32–39)

This is now the second time that Jesus feeds a crowd of thousands miraculously, although now he is in the primarily Gentile region of Decapolis. For comments on the feeding of the five thousand see 14:13–21.

Went up on a mountainside (15:29). See comments on 28:16 for the meaning of this phrase.

"How many loaves do you have?" Jesus asked. "Seven," they replied, "and a few small fish" (15:34). In this feeding the

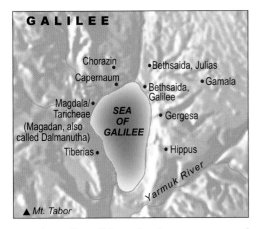

GALILEE

- Chorazin
- Capernaum
- Bethsaida, Julias
- Gamala
- Bethsaida, Galilee
- Magdala/ Taricheae (Magadan, also called Dalmanutha)
- SEA OF GALILEE
- Gergesa
- Tiberias
- Hippus
- Yarmuk River
- ▲ Mt. Tabor

Tabgah.[245] A more promising proposal is that Magadan is actually a variant spelling for Magdala, the home of Mary, called Magdalene (27:55; cf. Luke 8:2).[246]

Magdala is generally identified with Migdal Nunya ("Tower of Fish") of Talmudic times (*b. Pesah.* 46b), located about three miles north of Tiberias on the Gennesaret plain, which is usually connected with the town about which Josephus writes, the Greek name of which was Taricheae, roughly translated "the place where fish were salted."[247] During Jesus' day and up to Talmudic times, Magdala-Taricheae was the center of Galilee's fish-processing industry, making it one of the most important fishing centers on the Sea of Galilee and the administrative seat of the surrounding region.[248] Archaeologists uncovered in Magdala a decorative mosaic depicting a boat with a mast for sailing and oars for rowing in the ruins of a first century A.D. home,[249] and discovered about a mile north of the town the remains of the famous first-century A.D. "Kinneret boat" (see comments on 4:21). These discoveries have been invaluable for recreating life in first-century A.D. Galilee.

◀ *left*

GALILEE

Showing Magadan, or Dalmanutha.

number of small bread cakes is seven, and there are seven baskets left over (15:37). If the number of twelve baskets left over in the feeding of the five thousand is symbolic of Israel, as most suppose, then the number seven here—normally symbolic of perfection or completion—may symbolize the completion or fullness of God meeting the needs of all peoples, now including Gentiles. The word for basket in 15:37 is *spyris*, a large, flexible basket, often with handles, used for carrying provisions. This word contrasts with the smaller "basket" (*kophinos*) in the feeding of the five thousand (see comments on 14:20).[243]

Jesus . . . got into the boat and went to the vicinity of Magadan (15:39). The name Magadan occurs only here in the New Testament, while the parallel in Mark 8:10 has Dalmanutha. The identity of the town or region is puzzling, because there are no historical or archaeological records to confirm the identity. One suggestion is that it is an ancient Canaanite name, "ma-gadan" or "may-gad," which may have meant "the Waters of (the Canaanite god of springs) Gad,"[244] or perhaps "Waters of Good Luck." This identification links it with the place called in Greek, Heptapegon, "the Seven Springs," later shortened into the Arabic,

Another Request for a Sign Denied (16:1–4)

Tested him by asking him to show them a sign from heaven (16:1). For "sign," see comments on 12:38ff. "Heaven" is often used as a circumlocution for the name of God, as in the expression "kingdom of heaven" (cf. 3:2; 4:17). The problem with a sign is that it can be interpreted differently ways.[250] The Pharisees and Sadducees want a sign from God, but most likely want one that will be displayed in the skies.[251] They are looking to "test" or "tempt" Jesus, the same word used for

Jesus' temptations by Satan (*peirazō*; see comments on 4:1). That is, they are asking for a sign they can use against him.

When evening comes, you say, "It will be fair weather, for the sky is red," and in the morning, "Today it will be stormy, for the sky is red and overcast" (16:2–3). People who live close to nature are aware of daily patterns and irregularities in those patterns that may portend future natural phenomena. There are numerous proverbial expressions that capture signals from nature. Mariners are famous for maxims that predict the patterns of weather, which they must heed daily, if not hourly, in order to conduct safe passage on the seas, such as the well-known saying, "Red skies at night, sailor's delight; red skies in the morning, sailor's warning."

The sign of Jonah (16:4). See comments on 12:39–41.

Spiritual Leaven (16:5–12)

Be on your guard against the yeast of the Pharisees and Sadducees (16:6). Jesus earlier used yeast in a positive metaphorical sense to point to the permeating nature of the kingdom of heaven (cf. 13:33). Now he returns to the more consistent use of yeast in Scripture as a negative metaphor to indicate the evil of

disintegration and corruption that can permeate what is good (e.g., Ex. 12:8, 15–20).

Against the teaching of the Pharisees and Sadducees (16:12). Josephus testifies to the "controversies and serious differences" between the Pharisees and Sadducees.[252] Jesus does not suggest that these two religious groups share the same overall theological teaching, but emphasizes that they have a united opposition to Jesus.

The Christ, the Son of the Living God (16:13–20)

Jesus came to the region of Caesarea Philippi (16:13). Jesus continues to move away from Galilee, extending his ministry into a predominantly Gentile area to the north-northeast of the Sea of Galilee. This region was governed by Philip the Tetrarch, one of Herod the Great's three sons (see "Herod Philip the Tetrarch and Caesarea Philippi").

"Who do people say the Son of Man is?" . . . "Some say John the Baptist; others say Elijah; and still others, Jeremiah or one of the prophets" (16:13–14). Each response to Jesus' question indicates a prophet, in line with one of the popular messianic expectations held in Israel. This goes back to the strand of Old Testament predictions about a great prophet that would arise. Included in this strand are the eschatological Prophet of Moses' prophecy (Deut. 18:15–18),[253] the return of Elijah (Mal. 4:5), and the hope of the return of great Old Testament prophetic figures such as Isaiah and Jeremiah (*4 Ezra* 2:18).

You are the Christ (16:16). *Christ* as a title (cf. 1:1) draws on the promise to

MEDITERRANEAN SEA

PHOENICIA

Mt. Hermon

Tyre

Caesarea Philippi

Gischala

GALILEE

Ptolemais

Chorazin
Capernaum
Magdala/
Taricheae

Bethsaida, Julias
Gamala
Bethsaida, Galilee

Cana of Galilee

SEA OF GALILEE

Gergesa
Hippus

Sepphoris

Tiberias

Nazareth

Yarmuk River

Mt. Carmel

Mt. Tabor

Gadara

Nain

David of a perpetual heir to his throne (2 Sam. 7:14), which became a fixture of the hope of a coming age of blessing for the nation (e.g., Isa. 26–29, 40), inaugurated by a figure who would bring to reality the promise of the end-time reign of David's line (cf. Ps. 2:2; Dan. 9:25–26). By the first century, many Jews referred the term *Messiah* or *Christ*, although understood in a variety of ways,[254] to a kingly figure who, like David, would triumph in the last days over Israel's enemies.[255]

The Son of the living God (16:16). "Son of the living God" also points back to the profound prophecy of David's line, "I will be his father, and he will be my son" (2 Sam. 7:14). This spoke immediately of Solomon, but also of the future messianic line. The successor to the line was to be God's Son, as the Old Testament and later Jewish writings reveal. One of the magnificent Royal Psalms that speaks of the anointing and coronation of the Lord's Anointed, the Davidic King, declares, "I will proclaim the decree of the LORD: He said to me, 'You are my Son; today I have become your Father'" (Ps. 2:7; cf. 89:27). The first-century B.C. *Psalms of Solomon* express a combined hope of son and king, "Behold, O Lord, and raise up unto them their king, the son of David, at the time you have foreseen, O God, to rule over Israel your servant."[256] The *Florilegium* from the Qumran community, in commenting on 2 Samuel 7:12–14, says, "This refers to the 'branch of David,' who will arise with the Interpreter of the law who will rise up in Zion in the last days."[257] The expression "living God" would have special significance in the area of Caesarea Phillippi with its ancient Baal, Pan, and Caesar worship.

◀ *left*

GALILEE AND CAESAREA PHILIPPI

CAESAREA PHILIPPI

(bottom left)
Aerial view of the Jordan river near Caesarea Philippi (modern Banias).

(bottom right)
Niches in the stone for the worship of the god Pan at Caesarea Philippi.

▼

Blessed are you, Simon son of Jonah, for this was not revealed to you by man, but by my Father in heaven (16:17). "Blessed" (*makarios*) is the same word found in the Beatitudes of the Sermon on the Mount (cf. 5:3ff.); as there, this is not a *conferral* of blessing but an *acknowledgment* that Peter has been blessed personally by a revelation from God, Jesus' Father (cf. 5:3–11; 11:6; 13:16; 24:46).

You are Peter, and on this rock I will build my church (16:18). In Aramaic, almost certainly the language Jesus spoke on this occasion, the same word, *kēpha'*, would have been used for both "Peter" and "rock." Translating the wordplay into Greek, Matthew most naturally uses the feminine noun *petra*, because it is the closest equivalent to *kēpha'*, a common noun in Aramaic texts found in the Qumran caves, meaning "rock" or "crag" or "a part of a mountainous or hilly region."[258] But when it comes to making the wordplay, Matthew has to use the less common *petros* in the first half because it is a masculine noun, for he would not refer to Peter with a feminine noun. But the use of the two different Greek words does not change the meaning of the wordplay, because *petros* and *petra* were at times used interchangeably.

▶ Herod Philip the Tetrarch and Caesarea Philippi

Philip was the son of Herod by his fifth wife, Cleopatra of Jerusalem, and half-brother of Archelaus and Antipas. When Caesar Augustus settled Herod's will, he gave to sixteen-year-old Philip the title of tetrarch over the region north-northeast of the Sea of Galilee.[A-73] Philip ruled for thirty-seven years (4 B.C.–A.D. 33/34) and was a conscientious ruler. Josephus says, "In his conduct of the government he showed a moderate and easy-going disposition."[A-74] He married Salome, the daughter of Herodias, who had married Herod Antipas. She was the one who had danced at the infamous scene in which Herod Antipas beheaded John the Baptist.[A-75]

Although Philip was not as ambitious a builder as was his father, he did rebuild and enlarge the cities of Bethsaida-Julias, on the northern shore of the sea of Galilee (cf. 11:21), and Panion (or Paneas, the modern city of Banias), a scenic town at the foot of Mount Hermon, twenty-five miles north of the Sea of Galilee and thirty miles inland from the Mediterranean Sea. This town originally may have been the Old Testament Baal-Gad or Baal-Hermon,[A-76] a place of worship to the pagan god Baal, near the tribal area of Dan, the northern boundary of ancient Israel. During the Hellenistic occupation following the conquest of the region by Alexander the Great, a sanctuary to the god Pan was built in a grotto on the main source of the Jordan River, with the nearby town taking the name Paneas, and the shrine being called Panion. Pan is the god of fields, forests, mountains, flocks, and shepherds, keeping watch over this lush setting looking over the northern Galilean valley countryside.

After the Roman conquest, Caesar Augustus gave the region to Herod the Great, who built near the site of the Pan sanctuary a white marble temple to honor his patron Augustus.[A-77] Later, Philip developed near the site a sizeable town, which he renamed Caesarea-Philippi[A-78] in honor of Caesar Augustus, but carrying his own name (Philippi, i.e., "of Philip") to distinguish it from the larger and more influential Caesarea Maritima on the Mediterranean coast (Acts 8:40).[A-79]

At the time Jesus and his disciples traveled there, Caesarea Philippi was an important Greco-Roman city, whose population was primarily pagan. This region becomes the site where Jesus calls for a decision about his own identity and where it is revealed by the Father to Peter that Jesus is truly the prophesied divine Messiah.

The wordplay points to Peter as a leader among the apostles, who will play a foundational role in the early church. Once he has fulfilled that role, he will pass off the scene. He does not hold a permanent position that is passed on to others.

I will build my church (16:18). Matthew is the only evangelist to use the word "church" (*ekklēsia*; cf. 18:18), which brings to mind the "community/assembly (*qāhāl*) of the LORD" (Deut. 23:3; cf. 5:22). In selecting the twelve disciples/apostles to go with his message of fulfillment to Israel (Matt. 10:1–6), who will judge the tribes of Israel (19:28), Jesus points ahead to the time when his disciples, his family of faith (12:48–50), will be called "my church." Jesus will build his church, but it will come about through the foundational activity of the apostles and prophets (Eph. 2:20).

The gates of Hades will not overcome it (16:18). Hades, or Sheol, is the realm of the dead. "Gates," which were essential to the security and might of a city, indicate power. So the expression "gates of Hades" in the Old Testament and later Jewish literature,[259] which is basically the same as the "gates of death,"[260] refer to the realm and power of death. "For a moment my soul was poured out to death; I was near the gates of Hades with the sinner. Thus my soul was drawn away from the Lord God of Israel, unless the Lord had come to my aid with his everlasting mercy" (*Pss. Sol.* 16:2). Jesus thus promises that death will not overpower the church, his own family of faith (cf. Matt. 12:48–50).

I will give you the keys of the kingdom of heaven (16:19). The metaphor points most clearly to the authority given to Peter to admit entrance into the kingdom. In this way Peter is contrasted to the teachers of the law and Pharisees, who shut off entrance to the kingdom and do not enter in themselves (23:13). Peter, as the representative disciple who gives the first personal declaration of the Messiah's identity, is the one in the book of Acts who opens the door of the kingdom to all peoples (Acts 1:8). On each of three occasions, it is Peter's authoritative preaching and presence that opens the door to the kingdom—first to Jews (ch. 2), then to Samaritans (ch. 8), and finally to Gentiles (ch. 10).

Whatever you bind on earth will be bound in heaven, and whatever you loose on earth will be loosed in heaven (16:19).

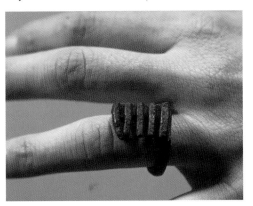

ANCIENT KEYS

(left) A key worn on the finger as a ring (discovered in Herodian-era Jerusalem).

(right) Door key to a house found in Tiberias (late Roman era).

Since the keys metaphor suggests that Peter is the one given authority to open the door to the kingdom of heaven, the binding and loosing metaphor continues that theme by indicating that Peter is the one who is given authority to declare the terms of forgiveness of sins under which God grants entrance to, and exclusion from, the kingdom. But Peter's role of binding and loosing is representative of what all disciples will experience, because all disciples share in the authority of "binding and loosing" (cf. 18:18; John 20:22b–23).

The Suffering Sacrifice (16:21–28)

Jesus began to explain to his disciples that he must go to Jerusalem and suffer many things (16:21). Martyrdom is the act of choosing death rather than renouncing one's religious principles.[261] Hebrews recounts the tragedies that befell many Old Testament heroes (Heb. 11:32–38), and Jewish literature abounds with stories of the gruesome treatment suffered by many who stood up for their faith. During the early stages of the Maccabean revolt the Jewish rebels refused to fight on the Sabbath day, even if attacked, choosing to die rather than to violate the commandment. When the enemy attacked, they said, "'Let us all die in our innocence; heaven and earth testify for us that you are killing us unjustly.' So they attacked them on the Sabbath, and they died, with their wives and children and livestock, to the number of a thousand persons" (1 Macc. 2:36–38).

Although others throughout Jewish history had experienced martyrdom, it was for them a *consequence* of their convictions. But for Jesus, his death is the *purpose* of his entrance to history (cf. 20:28). This is the first of four times that Jesus will predict his arrest and crucifixion (16:21; 17:22–23; 20:17–19; 26:2).

Suffer many things at the hands of the elders, chief priests and teachers of the law (16:21). The single article "the" with the three groups—the elders, chief priests, and teachers of the law—indicates the combined leadership of Jerusalem. "Elders" (*presbyteroi*) is a somewhat generic title for a person whose age, experience, and character have resulted in a position of leadership within groups such as the Pharisees and Sadducees. The "chief priests" (*archiereis*) were part of the ruling aristocracy over Judea during the reigns of the Hasmoneans, Herod, and the Roman governors. They came from four prominent families of chief priests who dominated Jewish affairs in Jerusalem at the time of Jesus up to A.D. 70, alternately supplying the offices of the high priest, captain, and treasurers of the temple and making up an intermediary layer of aristocracy above the general priestly line. The "teachers of the law" (*grammateis*) were professional interpreters of the law, especially associated with the Pharisees in the Gospels.[262]

Peter . . . began to rebuke him (16:22). Within Jewish master-disciple relationships, it was unthinkable for a disciple to correct his master, let alone "rebuke" him, as Peter does here.[263]

Get behind me, Satan! You are a stumbling block to me (16:23). "Satan" is not a proper name, but rather is a common Hebrew noun meaning "adversary." But when it occurs with the definite article, it means "the adversary." Satan had tried to tempt Jesus away from carrying out his

Father's will at the start of his earthly ministry (see comments on 4:1–11); he now uses a different strategy to accomplish the same goal: through Peter. A "stumbling block" (skandalon) was an obstacle in one's path, but it became a metaphor to indicate something that caused a person to sin or falter in his or her faith.[264]

If anyone would come after me, he must deny himself and take up his cross and follow me (16:24). In the first century, crucifixion was one of the most feared forms of execution, used effectively by the Romans as one of the strongest forms of deterrence against insurrection or rebellion. It was a dreadful way to die. Condemned victims were often forced to carry a cross-beam to the scene of crucifixion.[265] There they were nailed to it, which in turn was nailed to the upright beam, which was then hoisted into place. The horror of the cross will be Jesus' own tragic fate, but in what must have been to the disciples a shocking shift of emphasis, Jesus uses the cross and crucifixion as an image of discipleship. Although the image is often understood as bearing up under some personal hardship or life's cruel fate, as used here by Jesus the cross has a much more profound significance: One must die to his or her own will and take up God's will (cf. 16:25–26). Jesus' path of suffering and death on the cross is the ultimate example of obedience to the Father's will.[266]

What can a man give in exchange for his soul? (16:26). The word "exchange" (antallagma), found only in the New Testament here and in the parallel in Mark 8:37, occurs twice in Sirach, both times expressing something beyond comparative value: "Faithful friends are *beyond price* [antallagma]; no amount can balance their worth" (Sir. 6:15); "a wife's charm delights her husband, and her skill puts flesh on his bones. A silent wife is a gift from the Lord, and *nothing is so precious* [antallagma] as her self-discipline" (26:13–14).

For the Son of Man is going to come in his Father's glory with his angels, and then he will reward each person according to what he has done (16:27). Whether at the end of one's life or at the unexpected time of the return of the Son of Man in glory, each person must give an accounting of the choices made with his or her life. Although he will die (v. 21), the Son of Man will also come in glory, an allusion to the prophecy of Daniel 7:13–14, a theme Jesus takes up more fully later (cf. 19:28; 24:30–31; 25:31). The juxtaposition of dying and coming in glory provoked misunderstanding in at least some of the disciples (cf. 20:17–22).

Some who are standing here will not taste death before they see the Son of Man coming in his kingdom (16:28).

REFLECTIONS

PETER HAD HIS OWN IDEAS ABOUT THE PATH OF the Messiah, but he needed to know God's plans. God's ways are often different from our human ways. Peter partially understands Jesus' messiahship, but when it comes to an aspect of God's program that he does not understand, he tries to force it into his own understanding. He tries to stop Jesus from going to the cross, whereupon Jesus refers to Peter as a stumbling block. The word "stumbling block" is sadly significant, because it shows that without consistency of character, Peter the rock becomes Peter the stumbling stone. This disciple has perhaps been carried away with his importance as the "rock-man" and oversteps his responsibilities. We can each display a rock-like consistency in our lifestyle if we will know who we are as created by God (and no more!!), and if we will then commit ourselves to maximizing all God wants to do through us as his uniquely gifted vessels.

The expression "taste death" was an idiom for "die." The most natural reading of context concludes that Jesus refers to the Transfiguration that follows. Taking up the cross in discipleship is not something a person can put off, because death or the coming of the Son of Man will bring with it certain accountability and judgment.

The Transfiguration of Jesus (17:1–8)

Jesus took with him Peter, James and John the brother of James, and led them up a high mountain by themselves (17:1). The inner circle of disciples sometimes included the three found here (cf. 26:37; Mark 5:37), while other times Andrew was included (e.g., Mark 13:3).

There he was transfigured before them (17:2). Jesus was transfigured (*metemorphōthē*), a word Paul uses to describe the spiritual transformation that believers experience as a result of regeneration (Rom. 12:2; 2 Cor. 3:18). Here this word points to a physical transformation visible to the disciples that is a reminder of Jesus' preincarnate glory (John 1:14; 17:5; Phil. 2:6–7) and a preview of his coming exaltation (2 Peter 1:16–18; Rev. 1:16), revealing his divine nature and glory as God. Those in the presence of God often experience a radiant countenance, like Moses on Mount Sinai,[267] but here Jesus radiates from his own glory. In Scripture clothes that are "white as the light" indicate purity, like the angel at Jesus' resurrection (Matt. 28:3).

▶The "High Mountain" of Jesus' Transfiguration

The "high mountain" (17:1) of Jesus' transfiguration is not identified, but since Jesus and the disciples have been in the region of Caesarea Philippi (16:13), many scholars suggest nearby Mount Hermon. It is the most majestic summit in the region and is snow-capped much of the year. Its primary peak rises 9,166 feet above sea level, with a series of two other peaks rising somewhat less in altitude. If this is the location, Jesus and the disciples probably do not ascend to the top, but go up the mountainside to a secluded spot. The primary difficulty of identifying Mount Hermon as the site of the Transfiguration is that the following scene favors, although does not demand, a Jewish setting.

Mount Tabor is the site most favored by church tradition. It is a relatively small summit, only 1,800 feet above sea level, but rising prominently 1,200 feet above the northeast corner of the plain of Jezreel. It is only six miles from Nazareth and twelve miles from the Sea of Galilee. As early as Emperor Constantine in A.D. 326, a church was built there, with three small sanctuaries later erected in honor

of Jesus, Moses, and Elijah. But a fortress had been occupying the relatively flat summit for centuries prior to Jesus' time, since it was located at one of the most important crossroads of travel in the region. Consequently, it seems unlikely that Jesus would be on this mountain for the Transfiguration; moreover, it would have required an unusually roundabout route from Caesarea Philippi. Few today contend for Mount Tabor as the Mount of Transfiguration.

Another possible location is Mount Meiron (or Meron; *Jebel Jarmak*) in the upper Galilee region, eight miles northwest of the Sea of Galilee but still within the ancient boundaries of Israel. It is the highest peak within Palestine proper, at an altitude of approximately 3,960 feet; the towns at its base were Jewish. It is located on an easily accessible route back to Capernaum from Caesarea Philippi, yet in a more remote area than Mount Tabor. Matthew seems to suggest that the Transfiguration occurs outside Galilee (cf. 17:22), which Mount Meiron isn't. If so, Mount Hermon is the most likely spot.

Moses and Elijah (17:3). The arrival of two of the greatest Old Testament figures, Moses and Elijah, probably represents how Jesus is the fulfillment of the Law and the Prophets (5:17), and how Moses, the model prophet (Deut. 18:18), and Elijah, the forerunner of the Messiah (Mal. 4:5–6; cf. Matt. 3:1–3; 11:7–10), are witnesses to Jesus' eschatological role of initiating the kingdom of heaven. Both Moses and Elijah had unique endings: Elijah was taken directly to heaven (2 Kings 2:11–12), and Moses, whose grave was never found (Deut. 34:6), was said by rabbinic tradition to also have been taken directly to heaven.[268]

Peter said to Jesus, "Lord . . . if you wish, I will put up three shelters—one for you, one for Moses and one for Elijah." (17:4). This is the fourth of five incidents found only in Matthew in which Peter figures prominently.[269] He may here be indicating the tremendous privilege for the three disciples to witness the event, although "good" seems rather weak. Or is he here perhaps posing a question: "Is it good for us to be here?" voicing their fear at this frightening event? The offer to build three "shelters" may recall the tabernacle, since the same word (*skēnē*) is used in the LXX for the tabernacle (Ex. 25:9), though the same word is also used for the shelters erected during the Old Testament Feast of Tabernacles (Lev. 23:42). Peter, trying to make sense of this overwhelming transfiguration of Jesus and the appearance of these great Old Testament figures, apparently wishes to make some sort of memorial.

A bright cloud enveloped them (17:5). The bright cloud is reminiscent of the way God often appeared in the Old Testament—to Moses on Mount Sinai (Ex. 34:29–35); God's Shekinah glory filling the tabernacle (40:34–35); the cloud guiding the Israelites during their wandering in the desert (13: 21–22; 40:36–38); the cloud of the glory of the Lord filling Solomon's temple (1 Kings 8:10–13); and the Branch of the Lord bringing restoration to Jerusalem, as the cloud of the glory of the Lord shelters Zion (Isa. 4:1–6). Jewish literature recognized the cloud of God's glory as the time when the Lord would gather his people and reveal the location of the ark of the covenant (2 Macc. 2:4–8).

This is my Son, whom I love; with him I am well pleased. Listen to him! (17:5). The voice of God from the cloud gives the same public endorsement of Jesus as was given at his baptism (3:17), combining elements prophesied in Psalm 2:7

("this is my Son") and Isaiah 42:1 ("with whom I am well pleased"). Jesus is both Son and Suffering Servant. He is superior to both Moses and Elijah, so the disciples must listen to him to understand his messianic mission, which directs him to the cross.

The disciples ... fell facedown to the ground, terrified (17:6). To experience the awesome reality of God's presence God commonly produced fear, whether by observing a cloud or hearing his voice.[270]

Elijah Has Come (17:9–13)

Don't tell anyone what you have seen, until the Son of Man has been raised from the dead (17:9). The disciples (and the crowd) could think that Jesus' transfiguration and the meeting with Moses and Elijah indicate that the time has come to effect national and military liberation, but this would misunderstand his mission. Thus, once again Jesus directs them to be silent (cf. 8:4; 9:30; 12:16; 16:20). Jesus' message must be understood to focus on forgiveness of sins through his suffering on the cross. It will be at the resurrection that Jesus will clearly be declared to be Son of God (cf. Rom. 1:3); then they will finally understand who Jesus is, and what he had come to accomplish (for Son of Man, see "Son of Man" at 8:20).

Why then do the teachers of the law say that Elijah must come first? (17:10). The need for silence is immediately illustrated in the question the disciples ask. After having seen Elijah and Jesus transfigured, they don't understand how Malachi's prophecy of Elijah as the forerunner can be fulfilled in Jesus if he truly is the Messiah who has inaugurated the messianic age. The Jewish teachers of the law at

that time variously interpreted Malachi's prophecy, as is reflected in later rabbinic passages: "Elijah will not come to declare unclean or clean, to remove afar or to bring nigh, but to remove afar those [families] that were brought nigh by violence and to bring nigh those [families] that were removed afar by violence."[271]

Elijah has already come, and they did not recognize him, but have done to him everything they wished (17:12). John the Baptist was a partial fulfillment of Malachi's Elijah prophecy. He came "in the spirit and power of Elijah" (Luke 1:17), but he was not a reincarnated Elijah, as some of the religious leaders may have expected (John 1:19–27). John prepared the way for Jesus Messiah (Matt. 3:1–3), and if the people and religious leadership would have repented fully and accepted Jesus' message of the gospel of the kingdom, John would have been the complete fulfillment of Malachi's prophecy (11:14). But since the people rejected John and he was executed, and will reject Jesus, who will also be executed, another Elijah-type figure will yet have to come in the future (17:11), again preparing the way—but then for the final consummation of the wrathful Day of the Lord prophesied in Malachi.[272]

The Healing and Exorcism of an Epileptic Boy (17:14–23)

He has seizures and is suffering greatly. He often falls into the fire or into the water (17:15). "Seizures" is most likely the word for epilepsy (*selēniazomai*; lit. "moonstruck"), which occurred for the only other time in Matthew at the beginning of Jesus' ministry (4:24), when he also healed the demon-possessed and paralytics. The lack of control over motor skills causes the boy to suffer greatly.

REFLECTIONS

FAITH IS EITHER EXISTENT OR nonexistent, but it can also either function effectively or be defective. Jesus says that even the littlest faith (like a mustard seed, the smallest of seeds) can move a mountain. It is not the *amount* of faith that is in question, but rather the *focus* of faith. Faith is not a particular substance, so that the more we have of it the more we can accomplish. Rather, faith is confidence that God will do through us what he calls us to do—"taking God at his word." Jesus' point is that anyone with any amount of faith can do the most unthinkable things if that is what God has called him or her to do. Therefore, we should not place confidence in what we have, but rather have confidence that if God calls us to do something, we can do it in his strength, even the most absurdly impossible sounding things from the world's point of view.

Because you have so little faith (17:20). The people of Israel who have witnessed Jesus' miracles and heard his message should have believed on him as the long-anticipated Messiah, but instead he calls this generation "unbelieving" (*apistos*; 17:17). By contrast, he refers to his disciples who could not heal the boy as having "little faith" (*oligopistia*). That is, the crowd does not have faith in Jesus as Messiah; the disciples do have faith, but it is defective.

Paying the Temple Tax (17:24–27)

Doesn't your teacher pay the temple tax? (17:24). The Old Testament gave a directive that at the annual census each person over the age of twenty was to give a half-shekel (*beka*^{c}) offering to the Lord for the support of the tabernacle (Ex. 30:11–16). A half-shekel was approximately one-fifth of an ounce of silver (cf. Ex. 38:26), which after the Exile, with devaluation, equaled one-third of a shekel for temple support (Neh. 10:32). The half-shekel is the equivalent of two days of work wages.[273] At first the shekel was likely not a coin but a measure of weight, usually silver.[274] By Jesus' day, coins minted among the Romans, Greeks, and Phoenicians were used interchangeably. The half-shekel temple tax was the

◄

SHEKELS

(left) A horde of silver shekels dated to A.D. 66–70 with an oil lamp.

(right) Silver shekels *(top)* and half shekels *(bottom)*, which were used for the temple tax.

equivalent of the Greek silver *didrachma*, a "two-drachma" coin. But the most common coin used among the people was the *denarius*, equivalent to a day's wage, so a person would pay two denarii, the equivalent of the *didrachma*, since the latter was seldom minted (see "Equivalence Table of Weights and Coinage at the Time of Jesus" at 18:25).

These collectors of the temple tax are not "tax collectors" as Matthew had been, who had worked for the Roman occupying forces (cf. 9:9); rather, they are representatives of the Jewish religious establishment in Jerusalem overseeing the temple. The high priest was usually in charge of collecting the temple offering. In the Diaspora on the 15th of Adar, local community leaders collected the half-shekel tax by installing in conspicuous community centers containers similar to those found in the temple, shaped like trumpets.[275] In Palestine, representatives of the Jerusalem priesthood went throughout the land collecting the temple tax.[276]

The grammatical structure of the question indicates that these temple tax agents are attempting to elicit an affirmative response: "He does pay the tax, doesn't he?"[277] This may mask an attempt to embroil Jesus in a contemporary debate among the religious leaders about who should pay the tax. Some within the Qumran community declared that the census tax needed to be paid only once in a person's lifetime (4QOrdinances 1.6–7). Within the developing rabbinic tradition were some who questioned who exactly was liable for the tax (cf. *m. Šeqal.* 1:3–7). These representatives from the temple establishment may have been attempting, with duplicity, to confirm charges of Jesus' disloyalty to the temple.

From whom do the kings of the earth collect duty and taxes—from their own sons or from others? (17:25). The "duty and tax" are civil tolls and poll taxes that a ruler exacted from his subjects, not from his own sons.

Then the sons are exempt (17:26). Jesus is the Son of God, which makes him exempt from the tax, and Jesus' disciples, who are now part of the Father's family (12:48–50), are likewise exempt. This is a profound Christological statement, indicating not only Jesus' relationship by analogy to his Father, the ultimate King, but also the way in which he is the fulfillment of the law. As there will be no temple sacrifice in the heavenly kingdom because of Jesus' sacrifice (cf. Heb. 7:26–28), so there will be no temple tax for Jesus' disciples.

Go to the lake and throw out your line (17:27). All other references to fishing in the New Testament indicate the use of a net, not a hook. Interestingly, fishhooks were found beneath one of the upper pavements in the floor at the site of the ancient excavation believed to be Peter's home in Capernaum (see "Excavating the House of Simon Peter" at 8:14).[278] Although line and hook were used regularly for fishing on the Sea of Galilee, nets were the most effective means of commercial fishing (see comments on 4:18–22).

Take the first fish you catch (17:27). The miracle is both of foreknowledge (cf. 21:2) and of divine provision. God may have arranged providentially for a fish to swallow a shiny coin at the lake's bottom, which is not an unknown phenomenon, or this may have been a uniquely arranged miracle. The fish known popularly, but probably inaccurately, as "Saint Peter's Fish" is the *musht*. The reason why it probably is not the type of fish Peter caught is that it feeds only on plankton and is not attracted by bait on a hook. More likely Peter caught the *barbel*, a voracious predator of the carp family that feeds on small fry like sardines, but also on mollusks and snails at the lake bottom. Peter may have baited the hook with a *sardine*, the most numerous fish in the Sea of Galilee, to which the *barbel* would have readily been attracted[279] (see "Common Fish in the Sea of Galilee").

Open its mouth and you will find a four-drachma coin. Take it and give it to them for my tax and yours (17:27). The coin found in the fish's mouth was the *statēr*, a common coin minted in Tyre or Antioch. It was the equivalent of the *tetradrachma* or two *didrachma*, hence, one shekel (see "Equivalence Table of Weights and Coinage at the Time of Jesus" at 18:25). A treasure jar found at Qumran dating to around 10 B.C. was filled with Tyrian *staters* (*shekels*), which

bore the laureate head of Baal Melkart portrayed as a Grecian Heracles; on the other side the Seleucid eagle strode fiercely toward the left with a palm of victory and the Greek legend: "Of Tyre the Holy City-of-Refuge." This is one of many indications that Herod the Great originally had these coins minted in Jerusalem for use in paying the temple tax. It is estimated that the temple tax drew in silver alone the equivalent of 14.5 tons every year. Silver *statērs* were most likely the coins paid to Judas for his betrayal of Jesus (cf. 26:16).[280]

FISH FROM THE SEA OF GALILEE

(left) The Musht fish, also known as "Saint Peter's Fish."

(right) Various fish from the Sea of Galilee.

▼

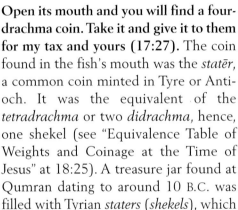

▶ Common Fish in the Sea of Galilee

- The Kinneret Sardine (*Acanthobrama terrae sanctae*) was the most important for commercial fishing on the lake.[A-80]
- The Barbel group of biny ("hair") Carp family (*Cyprinideae*) included three primary types, the first two of which were popular as fish dishes. (1) The Long-headed Barbel (*Barbus longiceps*), (2) the Kishri ("scaley") (*Barbus Canis*), and (3) the Hafafi (*Varicorhinus*) (a distasteful bottom feeder). One of the first two was probably caught by Peter with the line and hook.
- The Musht (*Tilapia Galilea*) means "comb" in Arabic, because of the long dorsal fin that looks

like a comb found on each of the species. It is a surface fish that moves in shoals, easily caught in nets. It has been named "Saint Peter's Fish," erroneously assuming that this was the fish Peter caught. The misnomer probably came from an attempt to capitalize on its tourism value because it is easily caught, fried, and sold at lakeside tourist sites.
- The Catfish (*Claries Lazera*) or *sfamnun* ("the mustached fish" in Hebrew) lack scales, so it was prohibited for consumption by Jews (Lev. 11:10; Deut. 14:11).

The Greatest in the Kingdom (18:1–9)

He called a little child and had him stand among them (18:2). Children in ancient society were often valued for the benefit that they brought to the family by enhancing the work force, adding to the defensive power, and guaranteeing the future glory of the house. In some cultures babies and young children were left exposed to the elements to die as a means of weeding out cripples and the unfit, often focusing on eliminating weak females.[281] Jewish tradition regarded children as a blessing and gift from God.[282] Josephus extols the joy and thankfulness that parents experience through the birth and upbringing of children, but he also emphasizes the necessity for children to be obedient and submissive to their parents in order to experience God's blessing. Rebellious children were subject to being stoned to death.[283]

Unless you change and become like little children, you will never enter the kingdom of heaven (18:3). Jesus does not commend an inherent innocence of children. The Old Testament has a balanced view of both the sinfulness and the value of children from birth. The psalmist acknowledges his sinfulness from conception (Ps. 51:5), yet he also knows that he is a wonderful creation of God (139:13–14). Children were without right or significance apart from their future value to the family and were among the most powerless in society. Yet Jesus celebrates the weakness, defenselessness, and humility of children in contrast to the self-advancement displayed in the Twelve. If persons wish to enter the kingdom, they must turn away from their own power, aggressiveness, and self-seeking and call on God's mercy to allow them to enter the kingdom of heaven.

The child thus becomes a metaphor of the values of discipleship.

Whoever humbles himself like this child is the greatest in the kingdom of heaven (18:4). The humility of a child consists of the inability to advance his or her own cause apart from the help, direction, and resources of a parent. The child who tries to take care of himself is destined for disaster. Childlikeness is a primary characteristic of discipleship, making for a reversal of the typical conception of "greatness."

Whoever welcomes a little child like this in my name welcomes me (18:5). Although the rabbis fell prey to the common human condition of seeking their

REFLECTIONS

CHILDLIKENESS IS A CHARACTERISTIC of all true disciples. Some of those who called themselves Jesus' disciples attached themselves to him according to their own agendas, not Jesus'—most noticeably Judas among the Twelve and many others who did not truly believe in his true identity and mission (cf. John 6:60–66). This encounter between Jesus and his disciples is an important time for them to check themselves. If they do not truly believe, even though they may be "disciples" in name, they must repent, be converted, and enter the kingdom of heaven. This is an important reminder for us as well. Not all who call themselves disciples of Jesus are so truly. The proof will be, at least in part, in our character of childlike discipleship, which is solely a product of the new life produced through entrance to new life in Christ.

own advancement (cf. Jesus' condemnation in 23:5–7), humility toward others, including children, was highly valued. "R. Ishmael says: Be swift to do service to a superior, and kindly to the young, and receive men cheerfully" (*m. ʾAbot* 3:13). For Jesus, the "child" is anyone who has humbled himself or herself to receive God's enabling mercy to enter the kingdom of heaven and become Jesus' disciple.

It would be better for him to have a large millstone hung around his neck and to be drowned in the depths of the sea (18:6). The normal millstone that people used in everyday life was the "hand mill" (*mylos*; cf. 24:41), which refers to the stones found in the home for grinding smaller portions of grain. This type of common millstone weighed from a few ounces to a few pounds and wouldn't be much of an anchor. Instead, Jesus refers here to the "large millstone" (*mylos onikos*), which means "donkey-driven millstone," the large stone rotary quern turned by donkeys or by prisoners (e.g., Samson in Judg. 16:21). This type of millstone, weighing dozens, if not hundreds of pounds, rotated in a cone-shaped interior piece of stone socket, propelled by a donkey walking in circles on a track and often guided by two men. It was used in areas where large amounts of grain were ground to make flour. The fires of the hell of Gehenna await those who receive God's judgment (cf. 3:12; 5:32; 25:42).

The Parable of the Lost Sheep (18:10–14)

Their angels in heaven always see the face of my Father in heaven (18:10). "Little ones" are disciples who have humbled themselves to be like powerless children (cf. 18:2–6). Angels are known to be active in the affairs of humans, but in a

strikingly personal way, Jesus refers to "*their* angels." Scripture speaks of angelic care for individual persons (Gen. 48:16; cf. Ps. 34:7; 91:11), individual churches (Rev. 1:20), and nations (Dan. 10:13), while Jewish literature has a fairly consistent emphasis on angels who are guardians of individual persons.[284] The Old Testament story of Jacob, who had angelic protection, is often picked up in later Jewish literature as an example of an individual with a guardian angel: "So the angel said to him, 'Do not fear, O Jacob; I am the angel who has been walking with you and guarding you from your infancy'" (*T. Jac.* 2:5–6).

Whether or not Jesus' statement should be interpreted to imply guardian angels who watch over individual believers on an ongoing basis, it nonetheless confirms that the heavenly Father uses angels to care for childlike disciples. The thought is similar to the role of angels mentioned in Hebrews 1:14, "Are not all angels ministering spirits sent to serve those who will inherit salvation?" Although some Jewish literature pictures only the higher echelons of the angelic orders who can approach God (cf. *1 En.* 14:21; 40:1–10), Jesus' statement "always see the face of my Father" speaks of the

constant access and communication of the disciples' angels with God, which implies the access of all angels to the Father.

If a man owns a hundred sheep, and one of them wanders away (18:12). The secure image of God's people as his sheep is replete throughout the Old Testament,[285] as is the distressful image of some who stray.[286] Since shepherds often worked with one another while their sheep grazed the hillsides, to leave the ninety-nine was of no real concern, since other shepherds would keep an eye on them. A hundred sheep is an average size for a flock, easily cared for by a shepherd.[287]

Discipline of a Sinning Brother (18:15–20)

If your brother sins against you, go and show him his fault, just between the two of you (18:15). "Brother" harks back to the scene where Jesus emphasizes that his disciples, who have obeyed the will of the Father by following him, are his mother and brother and sister (cf. 12:46–50). Jesus addresses in a practical manner what the community of disciples must do if one in the family commits a sin. The ultimate objective of the encounter is not punishment but *restoration*, winning over a brother so that he would be restored to the faithful path of discipleship. The basis of the process is rooted in Leviticus 19:15–18. This passage also stands behind a three-stage process of discipline found in the Qumran community, which includes individual confrontation, witnesses, and if necessary, final judgment by the leaders.[288]

But if he will not listen, take one or two others along (18:16). Deuteronomy 19:15 says, "One witness is not enough to convict a man accused of any crime or offense he may have committed. A matter must be established by the testimony of two or three witnesses."

If he refuses to listen to them, tell it to the church (18:17). This is the second time that the word "church" (*ekklēsia*) occurs in Matthew's Gospel, both times used by Jesus (see comments on 16:18). Jesus looks to the future functioning of his family of faithful disciples.

Treat him as you would a pagan or a tax collector (18:17). The fourth step of discipline is to treat the sinning brother like a pagan (lit., "Gentile," *ethnikos*) or a tax collector, the common titles for those who are consciously rebellious against God and his people. The Old Testament prescriptions for exercising punishment (Deut. 25:1–3) were later applied by Judaism to the responsibility of the synagogue. The synagogue was not only the place of worship, instruction, and fellowship, but also the place of discipline. Extreme discipline included flogging and expulsion (*m. Makk.* 3:1–2; cf. Matt. 10:17). Jesus does not reiterate physical punishment but instead focuses on spiritual exclusion from the fellowship of the church, which is symbolic of spiritual death.

Whatever you bind on earth will be bound in heaven, and whatever you loose on earth will be loosed in heaven (18:18). The same authority earlier given to Peter is here given to the church (see comments on 16:19).

If two of you on earth agree about anything you ask for, it will be done for you by my Father in heaven (18:19). Jewish councils required a minimum of three judges to come to a decision regarding minor cases in the local community, assuming that the Shekinah remains with a just court.[289] Likewise, when two men gathered to discuss the law, the Shekinah was present: "But if two sit together and words of the Law are spoken between them, the Divine Presence rests between them" (m. *Abot* 3:2). Jesus assumes the place of the divine presence among his disciples, guaranteeing that when his followers have consensus when asking in prayer for guidance in matters of discipline, his Father in heaven will guide them as they carry it out.

Parable of the Unforgiving Servant (18:21–35)

Lord, how many times shall I forgive my brother when he sins against me? Up to seven times? (18:21). Forgiveness in the Old Testament came from the God of grace, who instituted sacrifices that gave benefit only because he had given the means of making atonement through the shedding of blood (Lev. 17:11). But the same God of grace "does not leave the guilty unpunished; he punishes the children and their children for the sin of the fathers to the third and fourth generation" (Ex. 34:6–7). Judaism recognized that repeat offenders might not be repenting at all and drew the line at how many times a person could seek restoration and forgiveness: "If a man commits a transgression, the first, second and third time he is forgiven, the fourth time he is not" (b. *Yoma* 86b, 87a). Another case is even less forgiving: "If a man said, 'I will sin and repent, and sin again and repent,' he will be given no chance to repent . . . for transgressions that are between a man and his fellow the Day of Atonement effects atonement only if he has appeased his fellow" (m. *Yoma* 8:9). Peter's offer to forgive a person seven times is magnanimous, reflecting a desire for completeness that the number seven usually evokes. But he wonders where the limit should be drawn on his generosity of spirit.

I tell you, not seven times, but seventy-seven times (18:22). Whether one reads "seventy-seven times," which is the same wording found in the LXX of Genesis 4:24, or the less likely "seventy times seven,"[290] the meaning is that the number doesn't matter.

A man who owed him ten thousand talents was brought to him (18:24). The man must have been a significant figure since he owed the king ten thousand talents. The word for "ten thousand" is *myrioi*, "countless" (cf. Heb. 12:22; Jude 14). Perhaps in view is a governor of a region who collected taxes for the king but who had squandered the amount. The *talanton* was not a coin but a unit of monetary reckoning, valued at approximately seventy-five pounds or six thousand denarii. Today's equivalent would be at least two and a half billion dollars.

Josephus recounts the taxes that were collected at the death of Herod the Great by his sons. Antipas collected two hundred talents from Perea and Galilee, Philip received an income of one hundred talents from Batanaea, Trachonitis, and Auranitis, and Archelaus received

SILVER DENARIUS

A denarius from Tyre with an image of Alexander the Great.

from Judea, Idumea, and Samaria six hundred talents.[291] The total collected from the region was nine hundred talents (over two hundred twenty million dollars in modern currency). The man in the parable owed over ten times as much, an unthinkable amount. The hyperbole of the parable is dramatic.

The master ordered that he and his wife and his children and all that he had be sold to repay the debt (18:25). Debtors were often forced to sell their children as slaves, or their children were seized as slaves by the creditor (cf. 1 Kings 4:1; Neh. 5:4–8). A Hebrew slave had to work for six years as an attempt to recoup the loss.[292] Debtor's slavery was designed as much for punishment as for rerepayment. The rabbinic tradition forbad selling a woman into slavery (e.g., *m. Soṭah* 3.8), but the situation of the parable may assume a pagan king, who would have ignored these kinds of sensitivities.

He grabbed him and began to choke him. "Pay back what you owe me!" he demanded (18:28). Using the same fig-ures to compare the amount owed, the second slave owed just a little over four thousand dollars, a pittance in comparison to the billions owed by the first slave (see "Equivalence Table of Weights and Coinage at the Time of Jesus").

In anger his master turned him over to the jailers to be tortured, until he should pay back all he owed (18:34). Until modern times, prisons were commonly used for the confinement of debtors who could not meet their obligations. Debtor-prisoners were required to perform hard labor until the debt was repaid. Retribution in the form of corporal punishment was common among pagan nations (2 Kings 17:3–5; 25:7), although not unknown in Israel (Deut. 25:1–3; *m. Makk.* 3:1–2).[293] Since it was impossible for the servant in this parable to repay the vast amounts he owed, the scene concludes with the grim certainty that he will experience that punishment forever, a harsh allusion to his eternal destiny (cf. Matt. 8:12; 10:28; 13:42, 49–50; 18:34; 22:13; 24:51).

Equivalence Table of Weights and Coinage at the Time of Jesus[A-81]				
Jewish weight	**Greek coin or equivalent**	**Roman coin or equivalent**	**Phoenician (Tyrian) coin**	**Modern U.S. approximate equivalent**
	Drachma (Luke 15:8-9)	*Denarius* (Matt. 18:28; 20:2, 9, 13; 22:19; et al.)		Approximately $41.20[A-82]
Half-Shekel	*Diadrachma* (seldom minted) (Matt. 17:24)	Equivalent to two *Denarii*	*Diadrachma* (seldom minted) (Matt. 17:24)	Approximately $84.20
Shekel	*Tetradrachma* (not in the New Testament)	Equivalent to four *Denarii*	*Stater* or Shekels (Matt. 17:27; cf. 26:16)	Approximately $164.80
	Talent (Matt. 18:24; 25:15-28)	Equivalent to approximately 6,000 *Denarii*		Approximately $247,200.00

◀

This is how my heavenly Father will treat each of you unless you forgive your brother from your heart (18:35). "Mercy" is *not giving* to a person what *he deserves*, while "grace" is *giving* to a person what *he doesn't deserve*. A person who has truly experienced the mercy and grace of God by responding to the presence of the kingdom of God will be transformed into Jesus' disciple, which, in a most fundamental way, means to experience a transformed heart that produces a changed life of mercy and grace (cf. Isa. 40:2).

Marriage and Divorce (19:1–15)

Is it lawful for a man to divorce his wife for any and every reason? (19:3). A hotbed of discussion surrounded the various interpretations of Moses' divorce regulations. The leading Pharisaic scholars of Jesus' day debated the grounds for divorce that Moses established, who allowed a man to divorce his wife because he "finds something indecent about her" (Deut. 24:1). The debate focused on the meaning of "indecent." The Mishnah tractate *Gittin* ("Bills of Divorce") reflects back on the debate between different schools of thought among the Pharisees at Jesus' time and records the differing interpretations (*m. Git̲. 9:10*). The more conservative school of Shammai held to the letter of the Mosaic law and said, "A man may not divorce his wife unless he has found unchastity in her." The more liberal school of Hillel interpreted "indecency" to mean that "he may divorce her even if she spoiled a dish for him." The esteemed Rabbi Akiba, who belonged to the school of Hillel, later added, "Even if he found another fairer than she," demonstrating that divorce be granted for even the most superficial reasons (see also comments on Matt. 5:31–32).

"For this reason a man will leave his father and mother and be united to his wife, and the two will become one flesh" (19:5). God designed his human creatures to be male and female, with marriage to be a permanent union of a man and woman into one new, lasting union (Gen. 2:24). God "hates" divorce because it tears apart what should have been considered permanent (cf. Mal. 2:16).

Moses permitted you to divorce your wives because your hearts were hard. But it was not this way from the beginning (19:8). Since sinful abuse of a marriage partner was a harsh reality in the ancient world, Moses instituted a regulation designed to do three things (cf. Deut. 24:1): (1) protect the sanctity of marriage from something "indecent" defiling the relationship; (2) protect the woman from a husband who might simply send her away without any cause; (3) document her status as a legitimately divorced woman, so that she was not thought to be a prostitute or a runaway adulteress. Although this was allowed, divorce had never been God's intention.

GALILEE AND THE AREA EAST OF THE JORDAN ▼

Anyone who divorces his wife, except for marital unfaithfulness, and marries another woman commits adultery (19:9).

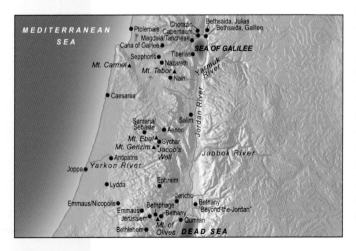

As did Moses, Jesus allows for an exception to protect the non-offending partner and the institution of marriage from being an indecent sham. Such an occasion is when a person has committed *porneia*, "marital unfaithfulness" (NIV). The semantic range of *porneia* includes whatever intentionally divides the marital relationship, possibly including, but not limited to, sexual sins such as incest, homosexuality, prostitution, molestation, or indecent exposure. Later rabbis declared that divorce was the requirement when adultery was committed, because adultery produced a state of impurity that, as a matter of legal fact, dissolved the marriage.[294]

For some are eunuchs (19:12). Singleness is an appropriate exception for those for whom it has been given as their lot in life, whether they are literal (either born or man-made; *m. Zabim* 2:1) or figurative eunuchs. Some eunuchs have been born impotent, especially those without the capacity for sexual relations, such as those born without properly developed genitalia, like hermaphrodites. Others have been castrated for official functions, especially those in some cultures, like the Ethiopian eunuch, who was castrated because he was an official in a court among royal women (e.g., Acts 8:27ff.). Others adopted abstinence because God made an exception for their particular work in the kingdom of heaven, such as John the Baptist and Jesus himself (cf. 1 Cor. 7:7–9). Some groups in Judaism went to the extreme of saying that celibacy was a higher spiritual order. There is fairly substantial evidence that at least some groups of Essenes practiced celibacy as a part of the ritual order.[295] On the other extreme, some excluded literal eunuchs from their worship assemblies as being unclean.[296]

Celibacy *is* an acceptable position, although it is the exception, and it is certainly not a higher calling than God's original order for men and women.

Let the little children come to me, and do not hinder them, for the kingdom of heaven belongs to such as these (19:14). Placing hands on children for blessing had a long history in Israel, primarily when passing on a blessing from one generation to another (cf. Gen. 48:14; Num. 27:18). Bringing children to Jesus for his blessing was an irritation to the disciples, probably because they had an insignificant societal status. Jesus once again turns prevailing societal values on their head (see comments on 18:1–5; also on Mark 10:13–16).

Valuing the Kingdom: The Tragedy of the Rich Young Man (19:16–22)

A man came up to Jesus (19:16). This young man (*neaniskos* in v. 22, which indicates that he is somewhere between twenty and forty years of age) is some kind of religious layleader, possibly a Pharisee (note his scrupulous adherence to the law), among the religious elite in the land. Such people often were well off because they were among the retainer class, well above the common people. In the political situation in first-century Palestine, the Roman occupiers allowed a form of self-rule, and within Judaism the religious leaders exercised much of that leadership.

Teacher, what good thing must I do to get eternal life? (19:16). Addressing Jesus with a title of respect that acknowledges the help he could receive from his learning and mastery of Scripture, the young man has evidently experienced a need in his life to perform some kind of righteous deed in order to assure him of having eternal life.

There is only One who is good (19:17). Among the many ways a person should bless God, Jewish writings exhorted each person to bless God as the truly Good: "For rain and good tidings he should say, 'Blessed is he, the good and the doer of good'" (*m. Ber.* 9:3). By looking at God as Good, Jesus takes the young back to obeying the law as the expression of the truly Good One. The truly Good God's law is the written good will of God for his people. The law is also equated with good in the rabbinic writings: "It is written, *The wise shall inherit honour*, and *The perfect shall inherit good*; and 'good' is naught else than 'the Law'" (*m. *Abot* 6:3).

Do not murder . . . (19:18–19). Jesus gives a representative listing of the law, including five of the ten commandments that come primarily from the second table of the Decalogue (sixth, seventh, eighth, ninth, and then fifth; cf. Ex. 20:1–17; Deut. 5:7–21) and the second of the two greatest commandments (Lev. 19:18; cf. Matt. 22:36–40).

All these I have kept (19:20). Although the man may seem presumptuous to say he has kept all the commandments, he was not alone in Israel. When Sirach calls his readers to acknowledge their responsibility for obedience to the law and the power of their own free choice, he challenges them, "If you choose, you can keep the commandments, and to act faithfully is a matter of your own choice" (Sir. 15:15). When the apostle Paul recounted his former life as a Pharisee, he said that, when viewing himself then

right ▶

**EXCAVATED
SEWING NEEDLES**

The needles and
two rings were
found in Jerusalem
and date to the
Roman period.

R E F L E C T I O N S

THE "GOD" OF A PERSON'S LIFE

is whatever rules his or her values, priorities, and ambitions. The lack this young man sensed could not be filled with his wealth or his own religious efforts. It could only be filled with the perfection that comes through entering the kingdom of heaven and experiencing the inner transformation of heart; those two things will set him on the path to be perfect as the heavenly Father is perfect (see comments on 5:48). The inner change will produce a transformation from the inside out.

and his obedience to the law, he considered himself, "as to righteousness under the law, blameless" (Phil. 3:6 NRSV).

If you want to be perfect, go, sell your possessions and give to the poor, and you will have treasure in heaven. Then come, follow me (19:21). The young man has almost certainly given to the poor in the past, because giving alms was one of the pillars of piety within Judaism, especially among the Pharisees (see comments on 6:1–4). But giving to the poor can be done out of the abundance of a person's life. It can give a person an even greater sense of power and pride.

He went away sad, because he had great wealth (19:22). The young man knows that Jesus has correctly pinpointed what is lacking in his life. His "great wealth" (lit., "many possessions"), which include money, but also his houses, land, animals, and so on, has captivated his heart, and he cannot exchange this god of his life for Jesus (cf. 6:21–24). So he goes away with great distress (cf. 26:22, 37), because he

knows deep in his heart that he has made a decision that will have eternal consequences.

Grace and Reward in the Kingdom for Those Who Follow Jesus (19:23–30)

It is easier for a camel to go through the eye of a needle than for a rich man to enter the kingdom of God (19:24). To illustrate the difficulty of a rich person entering the kingdom of God, Jesus draws on an analogy using a camel, the largest land animal in Palestine, and the eye of a needle, the smallest aperture found in the home. This may have been drawn from a pool of similar circulating analogies, for an illustration of "an elephant passing through a needle's eye" is found in the Talmud from Babylon, where elephants were the largest land-animal.[297] If not for the seriousness of the issue, the analogy would bring a chuckle to Jesus' listeners as they envision the impossibility of the huge, humped, hairy, snorting, spitting beast squeezing through the tiny eye of a common sewing needle.

Who then can be saved? (19:25). Wealth was often equated with the blessing of divine favor (Deut. 28:1–14). Abraham's wealth is assumed to be a reward for his obedience as a God-fearing man (Gen. 13:2), and the psalmist declares of the person who fears the Lord, "His children

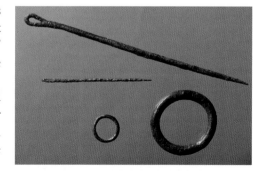

will be mighty in the land; the generation of the upright will be blessed. Wealth and riches are in his house, and his righteousness endures forever (Ps. 112:2–3). If those who seemingly are the most blessed of God cannot be saved, then who can be? Note that the disciples understand that "entering the kingdom of heaven/God" (19:23–24) is equivalent to being "saved" (19:25), which in turn is equivalent to entering life and obtaining eternal life (19:16–17).

With man this is impossible, but with God all things are possible (19:26). Other rich persons, like Joseph of Arimathea (27:57), found salvation by becoming Jesus' disciple. Even the despicable little tax collector Zacchaeus, who had accumulated great wealth at the expense of his fellow Jews, found salvation at Jesus' invitation (Luke 19:9–10). It is possible when one opens oneself to God.

At the renewal of all things, when the Son of Man sits on his glorious throne, you ... will also sit on twelve thrones, judging the twelve tribes of Israel (19:28). The word "renewal" or "regeneration" renders the Greek noun *palingenesia*, which occurs in the New Testament only here and in Titus 3:5. Here Jesus refers to the future time of renewal, a hope basic to the Jewish expectation of Israel's future national restoration. Although "judging" can indicate condemnation of Israel for rejecting Jesus as national Messiah, the idea of ruling or governing is paramount (cf. Rev. 3:21; 20:6). Jesus indicates a time of renewal when the Twelve will participate in the final establishment of God's kingdom on the earth, that is, when Israel is restored to the land and the Twelve will rule with Jesus Messiah over all things.

The Parable of the Workers (20:1–16)

For the kingdom of heaven is like a landowner who went out early in the morning to hire men to work in his vineyard (20:1). Grapes were one of the most important crops in ancient Israel, leading to one of the most important metaphors to describe Israel as the "vine" or "vineyard" of God (e.g., Jer. 2:21; Hos. 10:1).[298] Jesus pictures harvest time, when a landowner hired seasonal workers to help with an abundant harvest. In the parable, he goes early to the marketplace (20:3), where laborers have gathered waiting for landowners to hire daily laborers. The agreed-on sum of a denarius was expected, because a denarius was the equivalent of a day's wage for a common laborer.[299]

About the third hour he went out and saw others standing in the marketplace (20:3). The work day was typically divided into three-hour increments, running from approximately 6:00 A.M. to 6:00 P.M. The landowner hired the first workers at the beginning of the day, probably at about 6:00 A.M., to work in the vineyard at the coolest time of the day. Families in the ancient world usually went day to day, often earning only enough for the food for that particular day (cf. 6:11). If they didn't find work, they wouldn't have enough to eat, so these workers continued to wait in the marketplace for someone to hire them. In the parable, the laborers agree to work for the landowner for "whatever is right," expecting most likely to receive a proportional reduction from the day's regular denarius. The abundance of the harvest was such that he went again at the third (9:00 A.M.), sixth (noon), and the ninth hours (3:00 P.M.).

About the eleventh hour he went out and found still others standing around (20:6). Needing still more laborers, the landowner goes back to the town marketplace and finds workers who are desperate enough to remain waiting for work. It is the eleventh hour (i.e., 5:00 P.M.), close to the end of the work day. They would expect only one-twelfth of the amount of those who worked for the denarius, or only about $3.50 in modern equivalents, which probably indicates their desperate need.

Call the workers and pay them their wages (20:8–12). At the end of the day when the foreman or steward of his property[300] gives the day's wages, a shocking development unfolds. The laborers hired last are paid a full denarius, the wages expected for a full day's work. This builds up the expectation that those who worked longer would receive a proportional increase in their wages. But, no! Those who worked the entire long, hot day receive the same wage as those who worked only an hour, which quite expectedly causes the laborers hired first to protest that the others don't deserve equal treatment.

Are you envious because I am generous? (20:15). The expression "are you envi-ous" (20:14) can be rendered literally, "Is your eye evil?" (cf. 6:23), indicating that the laborer cannot be thankful because he is so blinded with self-centered envy.

So the last will be first, and the first will be last (20:16). The parable is a lesson on gratitude and motivation in service, not about salvation or gaining eternal life, because salvation is not earned by works (Eph. 2:8–9; Titus 3:5–6). That would be more similar to a saying found in the rabbinic literature: "Some obtain and enter the kingdom in an hour, while others reach it only after an lifetime" (b. ʿAbod. Zar. 17a). Nor is the parable about rewards for service, because God will reward believers differently according to their service (John 4:36; 1 Cor. 3:8).

Suffering and Service (20:17–28)

We are going up to Jerusalem, and the Son of Man will be betrayed to the chief priests and the teachers of the law (20:18). This is the third of four times that Jesus predicts his arrest and crucifixion, but the drama is heightened by the reference to Jerusalem for the first time, the religious leaders' condemnation of Jesus to death, and the Gentiles' carrying out the execution (see further details at 16:21; cf. 17:22–23; 20:17–19; 26:2).

Then the mother of Zebedee's sons came to Jesus with her sons and . . . asked a favor of him (20:20). The sons of Zebedee, James and John, were one of two sets of brothers called to follow Jesus (4:19–20). Their mother was a faithful follower of Jesus, but also evidently a relative of Jesus. She was among the women who attended Jesus at the cross and later witnessed the empty tomb, which would

VINEYARD

A view of a vineyard from the remains of an ancient gate at Lachish.

▼

identify her as Salome (cf. 27:56; Mark 15:40; 16:1), the sister of Mary, Jesus' mother. Therefore, Jesus is the cousin of James and John on his mother's side. The mother apparently comes to exercise her kinship advantage. A mother seeking the advancement of her sons through direct petition to a person in authority was a fairly well-known phenomenon, such as Bathsheba's seeking the throne for her son Solomon from the aging King David (1 Kings 1:15–21; cf. 2 Sam. 14:2–20).

Grant that one of these two sons of mine may sit at your right and the other at your left in your kingdom (20:21). Since "judging" indicates ruling more than condemnation, the mother desires for her sons to have the highest positions of importance when Jesus inaugurates his kingdom reign. Seated at the right hand side is the most typical place of honor, whether the king's mother at the king's right side (Judg. 2:19), King David at God's right hand side (Ps. 16:11), or the Messiah at God's right side (Ps. 110:1, 5; cf. Matt. 22:44). The left side is reserved for the second highest position of importance to the monarch. Josephus records that King Saul reserved those two places for his son and general: "The next day, which was the new moon, the king, after purifying himself as the custom was, came to the feast; and . . . his son Jonathan had seated himself on his right side and Abener, the commander of the army, on his left."[301] Relegating a person to the left hand side instead of the right side can be a place of disfavor symbolically (e.g., Matt. 25:33ff.), but typically it is a place of high importance.

Can you drink the cup I am going to drink? (20:22). The "cup" throughout Scripture refers figuratively to one's divinely appointed destiny, whether it was one of blessing and salvation (Ps. 16:5; 116:13) or of wrath and disaster (Isa. 51:17; Jer. 25:15–29). Jesus is referring to his forthcoming cup of suffering of the cross (Matt. 26:39), to which he has just given his third prediction (20:17–19).

"We can," they answered (20:22). Perhaps the brothers think of other heroes in Israel's history who boldly stepped forward in times of crisis and volunteered to fight for God. David had volunteered to fight Goliath to defend the honor of the living God, though he knew the one who killed Goliath was to be rewarded with wealth and the king's daughter in marriage (1 Sam. 17:25–37).

You will indeed drink from my cup (20:23). Jesus has seen down the corridor of time to when the brothers will suffer for the kingdom of heaven. James became a martyr (Acts 12:2), and John experienced persecution and exile (Rev. 1:9), although apparently not martyrdom.

The ten . . . were indignant with the two brothers (20:24). The other disciples are probably indignant not so much because of the immodesty of the request, but because Salome, James, and John have attempted to use the family relationship to Jesus as an unfair advantage to get what they themselves wanted. The disciples had already been arguing about who would be the greatest in the kingdom of heaven (cf. 18:1), and they had already been promised to sit on thrones in Jesus' eschatological rule over Israel (19:28).

You know that the rulers of the Gentiles lord it over them (20:25). Greatness among the Gentiles was measured by being able to be in a position to "lord it over" others and "exercise authority over" them. What may have first come to the minds of the disciples was the harsh Roman occupation under which Israel had suffered for decades, which meant repressive government, exploitive taxation, and tyrannical military rule. For oppressed people who have experienced such hardships, capturing positions of power and authority is the only way they can think of gaining any measure of self-respect and significance in their lives.

Whoever wants to become great among you must be your servant (20:26–27). The prevailing dictum in the ancient world was that ruling, not serving, is proper to the status of a human. The ancient Greek Sophists declared, "How can a man be happy when he has to serve someone?"[302] The servant (*diakonos*) worked for hire to maintain the master's home and property, and the slave (*doulos*) had been forced into service. These were two of the lowest positions in society's scale. The ideal servant or slave lived to care for, protect, and make better the lives of those over him or her.

Jesus' disciples have the ambition to be great (18:1), to be in the first and highest positions (20:21). Thus, Jesus gives them the means by which they can do so according to the values of the kingdom of God, not the kingdoms of the world. They must arrange their lives with the ambition to give themselves for the benefit of others. It is no coincidence that Paul adopts these titles to describe himself[303] and others[304] who would give their lives for the welfare of humanity and the church. John will later call himself a slave of Jesus (Rev. 1:1), as will Peter (2 Peter 1:1) and Jesus' own brothers, James (James 1:1) and Jude (Jude 1).

The Son of Man did not come to be served, but to serve, and to give his life as a ransom for many (20:28). Jesus gives for the first time an indication of his self-understanding of the purpose of the crucifixion that he has been predicting he will soon suffer (16:21; 17:22–23; 20:17–19). Jesus will give his life as a "ransom" (*lytron*), which means "the price of release,"[305] often used of the money paid for the release of slaves, but in the New Testament means "redemption" or "release" as a theological concept based on the experience of Israel's release from the slavery of Egypt. The term may also

REFLECTIONS

SACRIFICE IS A READILY UNDER-stood concept when we think of it in terms of our own benefit. "No pain, no gain" is an old adage that communicates a well-known and appreciated value among those who must sacrifice the present pleasure for personal gain, whether that means experiencing the pain of exercise for the gain of a healthy physical heart or the pain of sacrificing a periodic night at the movies to save enough for that long-anticipated skiing vacation.

Jesus would not overturn that principle completely, but he would reverse the focus to say, "My pain, others' gain." Jesus' sacrificial servanthood was not directed toward his own personal gain, but for the gain of all those who would believe on his atoning work on the cross and gain forgiveness of their sins. As such his servanthood provides us with the example we now must display toward one another. We sacrifice for the sake of empowering others.

contain an allusion to the Suffering Servant passage of Isaiah 53 (esp. v. 6b: "The LORD has laid on him the iniquity of us all"). The phrase "for many," which does not mean "on behalf of many" but "in place of many," signifies the notion of exchange substitution for all those who will accept his payment for their sins. This saying of Jesus is the basis of the doctrine of substitutionary atonement as the work of his sacrifice on the cross, which involves the greatest cost of all, the life of the Son of Man.[306]

Healing Two Blind Men (20:29–34)

As Jesus and his disciples were leaving Jericho, a large crowd followed him (20:29). Jesus leaves Jericho for the final approach to Jerusalem, which lies ahead on a winding road for fifteen miles as it ascends three thousand feet through dry desert. It would take some six to eight hours of uphill walking, so he and the dis-

ciples are naturally eager to make it to their destination before nightfall, because the road was infamous for highway robberies (cf. Luke 10:30ff.).

Two blind men . . . shouted, "Lord, Son of David, have mercy on us!" (20:30). The blind men understand Jesus to be the "Son of David," a reference to the promise of the messianic deliverer from the line of David whose kingdom would

---

▶ Jericho: Ancient and Herodian

In New Testament times the city of Jericho was not the ancient city of Old Testament fame (e.g., Josh. 5:13ff.), which was still inhabited, but whose days of glory were long past. It survived primarily because of the fresh water from the nearby spring, making it to this day perhaps "the oldest continually inhabited oasis in the world."[A-83]

The more prominent Jericho in Jesus' day refers to the developments surrounding a huge palace complex first built by the Hasmoneans on a three-acre site about a mile south of the ancient city mound. Much of this palace was destroyed in 31 B.C. by the same earthquake that destroyed much of the original Qumran community's buildings. The Hasmonean palace was greatly expanded by Herod the Great to include three contiguous palaces on an area of twenty-five acres. One part of the final palace had gardens, porticos, and a swimming pool, connected to the main building by a flight of stairs and a bridge across the Wadi Qelt, where there was a reception hall, colonnaded courtyards, and a large, lavish bathhouse.

On the spacious grounds, Herod also built a complex that was unique in the ancient world, consisting of an integrated horse- and chariot-racing course, a huge theater, and a large building that served either as a reception hall or gymnasium. The combined building project accommodated horse races, athletics, boxing, theater, and musical shows. Herod and later governors escaped the cold Jerusalem winters to this extravagant desert oasis.[A-84]

have no end (2 Sam. 7:12–16; cf. *Pss. Sol.* 17:23). The messianic age promised to bring healing to the blind (Isa. 29:18; 35:5; 42:7), which Jesus told John the Baptist was one of the signs that he indeed was the Expected One (Matt. 11:2–6), so these blind men ask for the gift of messianic mercy that will heal their blindness.

The Climactic Entry into Jerusalem (21:1–11)

The crescendo of Jesus' messianic ministry occurs as he enters Jerusalem, the city of the great King (Ps. 48:1–2), the center of Israel's spiritual life and messianic hope. This initiates the "Holy Week" or "Passion Week." "Passion" comes from the Latin *passio* ("suffering"), which originally meant the suffering of a martyr. Early Latin translations of the New Testament adopted the term *passio* to point to the Gospel narratives of Jesus' suffering and its attending events. The earliest message about Jesus given by the apostolic band was the Passion, as we can see from the earliest preaching accounts in Acts. If we look at percentages of the Gospels given over to the Passion Week, it comprises from 25–48 percent of their materials.

As they approached Jerusalem (21:1). On the road from Jericho to Jerusalem, see comments on 20:29. Close to Jerusalem, the road approached the back (east) side of the Mount of Olives, passing through Bethany, the place where Jesus stayed during his final week,[307] about two miles (3 km.) southeast of Jerusalem (John 11:18). The road continued over the Mount of Olives, down through the Kidron Valley, and entered Jerusalem.

Bethphage (21:1). Near Bethany was the town of Bethphage, today called el-Azariyeh, named in honor of Lazarus, who was raised in this proximity (cf. John 11:1, 17ff.). The traditional site of the village is on the southeast slope of the Mount of Olives, less than a mile east of Jerusalem. The name Bethphage (Heb. *bet pagê*) means "house of unripe young figs" (cf. linked with Bethany in Mark 11:1; Luke 19:29).[308] The name is men-

tioned in a number of rabbinic passages, sometimes as a village on its own and sometimes as part of Jerusalem, since Bethphage marked the limit of the confines of Jerusalem.[309]

On the Mount of Olives (21:1). Rising 2,660 feet above sea level, the Mount of Olives lies to the east of Jerusalem, directly overlooking the temple area. It is a flattened, rounded ridge with four identifiable summits. The name derived from the olive groves that covered it in ancient times. The traditional site of the Garden of Gethsemane lies near the foot of the Mount of Olives, on the western slope above the Kidron Valley.

The Lord needs them (21:3). The term "Lord" (*kyrios*) can be taken in a common

Walking With Jesus Through the Holy (Passion) Week	
A Harmony of the Events of the Week[A-85]	
Modern Calendar Days	**Event**
	• Arrival in Bethany (John 12:1)
Saturday	• Evening celebration, Mary anoints Jesus (Matt. 26:6-13; John 12:2-8)
Sunday	• Triumphal entry into Jerusalem (Matt. 21:1-9; John 12:12-18) • Jesus surveys the temple area (Mark 11:11) • Return to Bethany (Mark 11:11)
Monday	• Cursing the fig tree on the way to Jerusalem (Mark 11:12-14; cf. Matt. 21:18-22) • Cleansing the temple (Matt. 21:12-13; Mark 11:15-17) • Return to Bethany (Mark 11:19)
Tuesday	• Debates with religious leaders in Jerusalem and teaching in the temple (Matt. 21:23–23:39; Mark 11:27–12:44) • Olivet Discourse (Matt. 24:1–25:46; Mark 13:1-37)
Wednesday	• "Silent Wednesday"—Jesus and his disciples remain in Bethany • Judas makes arrangements for the betrayal (Matt. 26:14-16; Mark 14:10-11)
Thursday	• Preparations for Passover (Matt. 26:17-19; Mark 14:12-16) • Passover meal and Last Supper (Matt. 26:20-25; Mark 12:17-25) • Upper Room discourses (John 13–17) • Prayers in Garden of Gethsemane (Matt. 26:36-46; Mark 14:32-42)

Friday	• Betrayal and arrest (Matt. 26:47-56; Mark 14:43-50)
	• Jewish trial
	    Annas—John 18:13-24
	    Caiaphas—Matt. 26:57-68; Mark 14:53-65
	    Sanhedrin—Matt. 27:1-2; Mark 15:1
	• Roman trial (three phases)
	    Pilate—Matt. 27:2-14; Mark 15:2-5
	    Herod Antipas—Luke 23:6-12
	    Pilate—Matt. 27:15-23; Mark 15:6-14
	• Crucifixion (approx. 9:00 A.M. to 3:00 P.M.; Matt. 27:27-54; Mark 15:16-39)

Sunday	• Resurrection witnesses (Matt. 28:1-8; Mark 16:1-8; Luke 24:1-12) • Jesus' resurrection appearances (Matt. 28:9-20; Luke 24:13-53; John 20-21)

sense to mean one's earthly "master," or it can be taken to refer to deity. Jesus, at this climactic time of his earthly ministry, reveals himself with increasing clarity.[310]

"Your king comes to you, gentle and riding on a donkey" (21:5). The prophecy of Zechariah 9:9 indicates the nature of Jesus' arrival: He comes as the righteous one who offers salvation, not as a conquering military leader, and with reconciliation, as did rulers who sometimes rode a donkey in times of peace (Judg. 5:10; 1 Kings 1:33).

They brought the donkey and the colt (21:7). Zechariah's prophecy specified in synonymous parallelism that a young colt, the unbroken foal of a donkey, was the animal on which the peace-bringing king of Israel would enter Jerusalem. Matthew alone mentions two animals (cf. Mark 11:4, 7; Luke 19:33, 35), which adds a touch of historical reminiscence. An unbroken young colt would be controlled best by having its mother ride alongside to calm it in the midst of the tumult of entering Jerusalem.[311]

right ▶

COIN WITH PALM BRANCHES

Jewish coin minted during the Bar-Kochba revolt against Rome.

▶

DONKEY

Egyptian boy riding on a donkey.

Spread their cloaks on the road, while others cut branches from the trees and spread them on the road (21:8). Throw-

ing garments in the path of a king to walk on was a symbol of submission (cf. 2 Kings 9:13). Palms symbolized Jewish nationalism and victory, such as when Judas Maccabeus and his followers recovered Jerusalem and the temple was desecrated by Antiochus: "Therefore, carrying ivy-wreathed wands and beautiful branches and also fronds of palm, they offered hymns of thanksgiving to him who had given success to the purifying of his own holy place" (2 Macc. 10:7; cf. 1 Macc. 13:51). Palms are seen on many coins of that time, expressive of nationalism generally, both Jewish and Roman.

Hosanna to the Son of David! (21:9). "Hosanna" is the transliteration of a Hebrew expression that means "O save."[312] This draws the crowd to make a connection to the Egyptian Hallel (Ps. 113–118) sung during the Passover season, especially expressing the messianic hopes of Israel as voiced in Psalm 118:19–29 (see esp. v. 25). Linked with Hosanna, "Son of David" is unmistakably messianic. The crowd acknowledges what Jesus has already stated in his fulfillment of Zechariah 9:9: He is the Davidic Messiah (see comments on 1:1), whom they call on to save them out of their oppression.

This is Jesus, the prophet from Nazareth in Galilee (21:11). Some in the crowd preceding Jesus call him a prophet, which

◀

**JERUSALEM
TEMPLE**

The East Gate of
the temple viewed
from the east (the
model of the Tem-
ple at the Holyland
Hotel).

many in his ministry saw him to be (16:14; 21:46). This does not seem to imply that they understand Jesus to be *the* eschatological Prophet of Moses' prophecy (Deut. 18:15–18),[313] but rather the prophet who had been creating such a stir in Galilee, whose hometown was Nazareth. Others who call out "Hosanna" seem to expect Jesus to bring liberation, as had the kings of ancient Israel and the Maccabees of more recent times.

Jesus Challenges the Temple Establishment (21:12–17)

Jesus goes to the temple and drives out those selling and buying and overturns the money changers' tables. This has often been called a "cleansing" of the temple, implying that he is trying to purify the temple from corrupt practices and restore it to proper usage as intended by God. While corrupt practices are certainly being rebuked, Jesus goes beyond cleansing to perform intentionally a symbolic act of judgment against the religious leadership of Israel.

Jesus entered the temple area (21:12). Climbing the imposing steps on the southern end of the temple mount, Jesus enters the temple through the Huldah Gates located on the southern wall. The Huldah Gates, named after the prophetess Huldah (2 Kings 22:14; 2 Chron. 34:22) were a double and triple gate.[314] He then climbs another series of steps to enter the Royal Stoa, a long hall with four rows of forty thick columns each. The northern side opened into the temple courts, but within the Stoa was a market where commercial activity enabled pilgrims from the Diaspora to participate in temple activities. Here they exchanged their currency for temple currency, the Tyrian shekel, which was used to pay the required temple tax (17:24–27; cf. Ex. 30:11–16) and purchase animals and other products for their sacrifices.[315]

Drove out all who were buying and selling there (21:12). Both those buying and selling, as well as the money changers, were making this simply a commercial operation, and the temptation for abuse was real, since surplus tax was consigned to the temple fund (*m. Šeqal.* 2:5). Doves were the sacrifice made by the poor, who could not afford animal sacrifices, and by those making a variety of types of personal offerings (cf. Lev. 5:7; 12:6; 15:14, 29). Temple commerce was at times notorious for exploiting the disadvantaged (*m. Ker.* 1:7). As a spokesman for God, a prophet sometimes performed acts that were pronouncements of judgment, even in the temple precincts (cf. Jeremiah's smashing the clay pot; Jer. 19).

"My house will be called a house of prayer, but you are making it a 'den of robbers'" (21:13). The religious leaders were treating the temple as robbers do their dens—a place of refuge for both accumulating illicitly gained wealth and for plotting future illegal activities. Caves in Palestine were regularly used as robbers' dens, so the metaphor was clear to Jesus' hearers.[316] The temple's primary purpose, as a house for communing with God, was lost in the frenzy of temple activity.

The blind and the lame came to him at the temple, and he healed them (21:14). The blind and lame were restricted from full access to temple activities, to symbolize purity in those approaching God (cf. Lev. 21:18–19). The Qumran community employed these restrictions for admission to their covenantal fellowship.

And no-one stupid or deranged should enter; and anyone feeble [-minded and insane,] those with sightless [eyes, the lame or one who stumbles, or a deaf person, or an under-age boy, none of these] should enter [the con-

gregation, since the holy angels are in its midst]. (CD 15:15–17)

He . . . went out of the city to Bethany (21:17). Jesus first arrived in Bethany prior to his climactic entry to Jerusalem (cf. John 12:1) and returned to Bethany throughout the week. His close association with Lazarus, whom he raised from the dead, and with Lazarus's sisters, Mary and Martha (Luke 10:38–42; John 11:1–44), leads many to assume Jesus spends each night at their home.

Cursing the Fig Tree: Judgment of the Nation (21:18–22)

Seeing a fig tree by the road (21:19). Known for its abundant produce of early figs (Bethphage means "house of the early fig"), the appearance of leaves on a fig tree in this region was a promise of the especially sweet early fig, which also was a promise of later fruitfulness when the normal crop of figs was produced. The fig tree without the early fig was an appropriate object for Jesus to use to indicate that Israel, which should have been producing the sweetest of all figs, was unproductive and so was being judged. This had just been demonstrated by Jesus in the temple (cf. Hos. 9:10).[317]

You can say to this mountain, "Go, throw yourself into the sea," and it will be done (21:21). Using the handy object of either

the Mount of Olives or perhaps even the temple mount across the Kidron Valley, Jesus says that one with faith could throw the mountain into the sea. If they are on the western slope of the Mount of Olives moving into the city, it is doubtful that they could see the Dead Sea. Jesus is more likely using a general figure of speech.

Controversies in the Temple Court over Jesus' "Authority" (21:23–27)

Jesus now enters into a series of interactions with the religious leaders. After they question his authority, he gives three extended parables (21:28–22:14) that reveal God's judgment on them for not fulfilling their responsibility among the people to respond to his invitation to the kingdom of God. Then there is a series of four interactions with the religious leaders (22:15–46) as they attempt to entrap him, in which he turns the tables to reveal his true identity as the Son of God.

The chief priests and the elders of the people came to him (21:23). The "chief priests" were high-ranking members of the priestly line who joined the high priest in giving oversight to the temple activities, treasury, and priestly orders (cf. 2:4). Linked here with the "elders" (so

also in 26:3, 47; 27:1), they were members of the Sanhedrin, the ruling body (although Matthew doesn't refer to this body; cf. 26:57; Mark 14:53). The elders were representatives from the Sadducees and Pharisees.

By what authority are you doing these things? (21:23). The religious leaders question Jesus' "authority" to do "these things," most likely referring to his cleansing the temple on the day before (21:12–13), but also questioning his authority to heal (21:14–16) and to preach and teach in the temple (21:23). Jesus was, after all, neither an official priest nor a scribal authority. He engages in a series of rabbinic-type debates that follow a typical pattern: a hostile question, a counterquestion, admission, and final rejoinder.[318]

John's baptism—where did it come from? Was it from heaven, or from men? (21:25). Jesus counters by asking whether

◀ *left*

A WELL-KNOWN MOUNTAIN

The Herodion, location of a citadel built by Herod the Great.

REFLECTIONS

THE FIG TREE PROVIDED A STRIKING LESSON FOR the disciples. Just as its fruitfulness was a sign of its health, so fruitfulness was a sign of Israel's faithfulness to the covenantal standards. Now that Israel, especially represented by its religious leadership, had perverted temple practices and had not repented at the appearance of Jesus Messiah proclaiming the arrival of the kingdom of heaven, Israel was being judged by God.

Jesus' cursing the fig tree was not a fit of temper but a symbolic act, demonstrating that God's creatures must produce that for which they were created. Even so we humans have been created by God to carry out his will, which means first of all entering into a relationship with him, which will then allow us to bear the fruit of that relationship, found especially in the fruit of the Spirit produced in our lives (cf. Gal. 4:6–7; 5:13–26). With the empowering of God's Spirit, whatever he calls for us to do we can accomplish in his power, if we only will submit to his will.

▶

the religious leaders think John the Baptist had divine or human authority. By shifting the questioning back to the religious leaders, Jesus lays a logical trap (21:25b–26). They cannot alienate the people by saying that the highly popular John's prophetic ministry was not from God, but they cannot endorse the prophet who had condemned them for not repenting (cf. 3:7–10).

The Parable of the Two Sons (21:28–32)

Son, go and work today in the vineyard (21:28). The grapevine and the vineyard were one of the most important crops in ancient Israel and became one of the most important metaphors to describe Israel, God's vineyard (e.g., Jer. 2:21; Hos. 10:1; cf. *2 Bar.* 36–40).[319]

Which of the two did what his father wanted? (21:31). The son that originally refused but then obeyed is like those in Israel who were disobedient to the law, such as the tax collectors and prostitutes. But when John came with the message of

true righteousness through the announcement of the arrival of the kingdom of God, they obeyed God's call and repented. By contrast, the religious leaders are like the son who agreed but did nothing. They were externally obedient to the law, but when God sent his messenger John the Baptist, they did not obey God's message through him.

The Parable of the Wicked Tenants (21:33–46)

A landowner ... planted a vineyard (21:33). Clearly alluding to Isaiah 5:1–7, Jesus intensifies his rebuke of the religious leadership by pronouncing God's judgment. Stone walls were built around vineyards to protect them from thieves and wild animals, and some larger vineyards had watchtowers built for added security. It was common to have large farming estates in Palestine, which were owned either by foreigners or wealthy Jews and rented out to poor Jewish farmers. A wealthy landowner might employ a farmer or rent out his vineyard to tenants, if he had other preoccupations.[320]

The tenants seized his servants; they beat one, killed another, and stoned a third (21:35). Many absentee landowners were notorious for harsh treatment of their tenants. Here, the scene is reversed, and the landowner's servants are abused when they come to collect a portion of the harvest. The treatment of these "servants" calls to mind the same fate that befell God's prophets throughout Old Testament history (e.g., 1 Kings 18:4; Jer. 20:1–2).

Last of all, he sent his son to them (21:37). This is an unmistakable allusion to the Father's sending his Son, Jesus (cf. 10:40–41; cf. 3:17; 11:27; 15:24; 17:5), which is further evidence of Jesus' self-consciousness of his identity as God's unique Son (cf. 3:17; 11:27).

They . . . threw him out of the vineyard and killed him (21:39). Jesus has been telling his disciples of his crucifixion at the hands of the religious leaders for several months (16:21; 17:23; 20:18), and now he tells the rulers themselves in parabolic form.

"The stone the builders rejected has become the capstone" (21:42). The crowds at Jesus' entrance into Jerusalem had sung out a portion of the last of the Egyptian Hallel psalms, "O Lord, save us," a quotation of Psalm 118:25 (cf. Matt. 21:9). Now Jesus draws on Psalm 118:22 to point to his rejection and future vindication. God has given prominence to his suffering servant like a "capstone" (lit., "head of the corner"), either the stone that held two rows of stones together in a corner ("cornerstone") or the wedge-shaped stone placed at the pinnacle of an arch that locked the ascending stones together. The suffering of the Son will be turned into the position of ultimate prominence and importance.

The kingdom of God will be taken away from you and given to a people who will produce its fruit (21:43). In the context of the parable this means that the privileged role of the religious leaders in caring for God's "vineyard" is now being taken away. But this is also a hint that Israel's privileged role in the establishment of God's kingdom will be taken away and given to another people. "People" is the singular *ethnos*, which prepares for the time when the church, a nation of gathered people, will include both Jew and Gentile in the outworking of God's kingdom in the present age (cf. 1 Peter 2:9).

He who falls on this stone will be broken to pieces, but he on whom it falls will be crushed (21:44). Not only will the

rulers' privileged position and role in the outworking of the kingdom of God be taken away, but judgment also will come on those rejecting the Son. Those who stumble over the stone and try to destroy it, such as the religious leaders who reject Jesus and will later condemn him, will be destroyed. In the end Jesus will come as judge and fall on those who have rejected him (cf. chs. 24–25).

The Parable of the Wedding Banquet (22:1–14)

The kingdom of heaven is like a king who prepared a wedding banquet for his son (22:2). A Jewish wedding (Heb. ḥatunnâ) was a sacred affair, in which the wife was separated to the husband through the wedding ceremony (qiddušin, "sanctification"), which in later Talmudic times was formalized when the groom recited to the bride: "You are sanctified to me in accordance with the law of Moses and Israel (b. Qidd. 5b).[321] In the case of a king's son's wedding, this would be a country-wide celebration that would go on for several days.

He sent some more servants (22:4). Although one might overlook a first invitation, the refusal of the invitation from the king to the wedding would be unthinkable, a terrible and dangerous affront to the monarch. Yet his graciousness wins the day, and he reissues the invitation, elaborating on the bounty of the celebration.

The rest seized his servants, mistreated them and killed them (22:6). The allusion to the vineyard of Isaiah's prophecy in the preceding parables is continued, as Jesus points to the destruction of the vineyard and judgment on Israel for despising the Holy One of Israel (cf. Isa.

5:3–12; 24–25).[322] Not only do the invitees reject the king's second invitation with trivial substitutes of everyday affairs (e.g., farming and business); others actually abuse and kill the king's messengers. This is an unthinkable insult to the king, who now finally brings judgment on his insubordinate subjects for the most serious treason and revolt against the monarch. While this may predict the destruction of Jerusalem and the judgment of the religious establishment in A.D. 70, the destruction of the rebellious subjects and their city parallels other rebellions in Jewish history.[323]

Go to the street corners and invite to the banquet anyone you find (22:9). The second part of the parable draws on another unthinkable development. Instead of the privileged few, now the undeserving and unworthy many are invited to the wedding.

He noticed a man there who was not wearing wedding clothes (22:11). The third part of the parable focuses on one of the guests who has gained entrance to the wedding, but who did not have the appropriate wedding garment. Although the invitation was given to all, both good and bad, proper attire is expected. Drawing on some evidence for a king in the ancient world supplying festal garments for guests (Gen. 45:22; Est. 6:8–9), some have understood this as an allusion to the imputed righteousness that Jesus hinted at early in his ministry (Matt. 5:20), and which Paul will later enunciate (e.g., Rom. 3:21–31; 4:22–25). Others suggest this refers to clean garments as opposed to dirty ones, symbolizing not works meriting salvation but evidential works of righteousness.[324] In any case, since the individual is addressed as "friend" and is left speechless when confronted by the king (22:12), the implication is left that the guest had proper clothing available, but declined to wear it. This once again points to the culpability of both the privileged religious leaders, the populace in Israel, and even Jesus' professing disciples such as Judas (called "friend" in 26:50), which is the point of all these parables. The man is bound and cast into the outer place of weeping and gnashing of teeth—language that commonly refers to eternal judgment (cf. 8:12; 13:42, 50; 24:51; 25:26, 30).[325]

For many are invited (22:14). This pithy statement gives a concluding pronouncement to the parable of the wedding feast, but also to the preceding parable. "Many" (*polloi*) without the article is a common Semitic universalizing expression, which is normally translated "everyone" or "all" (cf. 20:28). This is seen in the use of the Hebrew *rabbim* in Psalm 109:30, which the LXX translates with the Greek *pollōn*, indicating an inclusive reference for "all" in the congregation. The Hebrew parallel also occurs in the Qumran literature, especially in 1QS as a fixed inclusive title for "the many," whether all those in the Congregation (1QS 6:8–11) or all those who exercise jurisdiction as leaders in the Congregation (e.g., 1QS 6:1).[326] By the expression "many are invited," Jesus points to a universal invitation to the kingdom of heaven.

But few are chosen (22:14). The counterbalancing point in the second half of the saying emphasizes that not all those who are called are chosen. This does not specify the actual amount, but rather points to the divine perspective of the preceding parables. Those chosen are "the

elect," which for Jesus is an alternative expression for his true disciples (cf. 11:27; 24:22, 24, 31). Israel and her leadership had been known as the "chosen," but even their privilege is lost through unresponsiveness to Jesus' invitation to the kingdom of heaven.

Tribute in the Kingdom: Paying Taxes to Caesar (22:15–22)

They sent their disciples to him (22:16). As the controversies continue to unfold between Jesus and Israel's religious leadership, the Pharisees send their disciples to entrap Jesus.[327] The "disciples" of the Pharisees are mentioned in the New Testament only here and in Mark 2:18. Josephus refers to John Hyrcanus, the Jewish Hasmonean high priest and prince, as a disciple of the Pharisees, indicating that he was an adherent of the sect's way of life and thinking. The disciples of the Pharisees are most likely those in training to become full initiates to their brotherhood and would be fully engaged in the Pharisaic commitment of the oral law and rigorous practice of their traditions.

The Herodians (22:16). The Herodians are noted only here, in the parallel (Mark 12:13), and in an earlier incident where they also join the Pharisees in an attempt to destroy Jesus (Mark 3:6).

The Herodians were supporters of the Herodian family—most immediately Herod Antipas, the Roman client tetrarch—and they were unhappy that he had not gained control over all of his father's former territory. Thus, the Herodians joined Antipas in an attempt to regain Judea, which Pilate now governed for Rome. Although the Herodians and the Pharisees were normally at odds on many political and religious issues, here they combine to combat the common threat to their respective power bases.

Teacher . . . we know you are a man of integrity (22:16). "Teacher" (*didaskalos*) is a title of respect, equivalent to the Hebrew title "rabbi." "Teacher" can be used generically (13:52; 23:8) or it can be used positively to refer to Jesus (10:24–25; 23:10; 26:18; cf. 8:19). In Matthew it is the normal title used when non-disciples approach Jesus.[328]

Is it right to pay taxes to Caesar or not? (22:17). Either answer Jesus might give could be used against him. At question was the legal requirement of paying taxes to Caesar, the family name of Julius Caesar, which had become a title for the Roman emperors who followed him. Currently, Tiberius Claudius Caesar Augustus was emperor of Rome.

The tax mentioned here was the *kēnsos* (Lat. *census*), which was either the annual head tax or one of the more general taxes, such as the poll-tax.[329] The people of Israel, indeed all of Rome's subjects, labored under heavy taxation that kept the empire operating. The Herods had long collected taxes in the name of Rome to support their own military ventures, building projects, and lavish lifestyles. The Herods paid a tribute to Rome directly, so they exacted heavier taxes to compensate. The prefect of Judea and Samaria collected the land and poll

The Roman Emperors Called "Caesar" During New Testament Times and Later	
Caesar was the family name of Julius Caesar (assassinated in 44 B.C.), which became a title for the Roman emperors who followed him.[A-86]	
Roman Emperor	**New Testament Reference or Incident**
Augustus (31 B.C.—A.D.14)	Birth of Jesus (Luke 2:1).
Tiberius (A.D. 14-37)	Jesus' public ministry; birth of the church (Luke 3:1; cf. Matt. 22:17, 21, par.; Luke 23:2).
Gaius (Caligula) (A.D. 37-41)	Not mentioned in the New Testament. Demanded worship of himself, ordered a statue of himself placed in the temple in Jerusalem, but died before carried out.
Claudius (A.D. 41-54)	Expelled Jews from Rome (Acts 17:7; 18:2; cf. 11:28).
Nero (A.D. 54-68)	First major persecution of Christians. Peter and Paul martyred. (Acts 25:8-12, 21; 28:18; Phil. 4:22)
Galba (A.D. 68)	
Otho (A.D. 69)	
Vitellius (A.D. 69)	Siege of Jerusalem (civil war in Rome).
Vespasian (A.D. 69-79)	Siege of Jerusalem (ended civil war in Rome).

taxes directly for Rome. The Jewish religious authorities exacted their own taxes for the temple and their other institutional expenses (cf. 17:24–27), so the people were seething at the exhausting taxation. Some estimate that a Jewish family paid approximately 49 percent of its annual income to these various taxes: 32 percent to the Romans (19 percent on crops; 13 percent on sales, income, and other taxes), 12 percent to Jewish taxes (8 percent on crops and 4 percent on temple and sacrifice taxes), and 5 percent on forced extractions from corrupt officials.[330]

Show me the coin used for paying the tax (22:19). The smallest silver coin of the day in circulation in Palestine was the denarius. It was the equivalent of a day's wage for an agricultural worker, so it was widely circulated and readily available in the pouches of those testing Jesus.

Whose portrait is this? And whose inscription? (22:20). On the obverse side of the silver denarius was a profile of the head of Tiberius Caesar, with the Latin inscription on the perimeter of the coin, "Tiberius Caesar, son of the divine Augustus." On the reverse of the coin was a picture of the seated Pax, the Roman goddess of peace, with the Latin inscription "High Priest." The coins were issued by Herod Antipas in Tiberius, his new capital on the Sea of Galilee named in honor of Tiberius Caesar, where Herod had established a mint.[331]

Give to Caesar what is Caesar's, and to God what is God's (22:21). Those who respond to the invitation to the kingdom of heaven will continue to have obligations to the governing authorities of this world, a fact that later New Testament writers emphasize while living under oppressive authorities (Rom. 13:1–7; 1 Peter 2:13–17). God as Creator has sovereign right over all creation and everything in it, however, which implies that even what belongs to Caesar is only his in a secondary way. Allegiance to God takes precedence over allegiance to Caesar, especially when Caesar attempts to usurp allegiance to God's will (cf. Acts 4:19; 5:29). Jesus may have implied further that while the "image" (*eikōn*) of Caesar was stamped on coins, humans bear the image of God from creation (Gen. 1:26–27), and therefore God has claim on all that any person has or is.

Marriage at the Resurrection (22:23–33)

The Sadducees, who say there is no resurrection (22:23). The Sadducees (see "Pharisees and Sadducees" at 3:7) did not believe in the resurrection since they drew only on the Pentateuch for doctrine. Resurrection as a doctrine is developed more clearly in the latter books of the Old Testament (Isa. 26:19; Dan. 12:2). It occurred regularly in Jewish literature[332] and became a central belief in later rabbinic thought[333] (see "The Resurrection of the Dead in Judaism and in Jesus" at 28:6–8).

Moses told us that if a man dies without having children, his brother must marry the widow and have children for him (22:24). The Sadducees cite the Old Testament law of "levirite marriage," in which the "levir," the surviving brother of a childless, deceased man, was required to marry his sister-in-law (also called the "rite of removing the shoe"). The law was designed to provide care for the widow as well as an attempt to preserve the deceased brother's genealogical line if they should bear children (Deut. 25:5–10).

At the resurrection people will neither marry nor be given in marriage (22:30). Jesus accuses the Sadducees of developing faulty doctrine, such as denying the resurrection, because "you do not know the Scriptures or the power of God" (22:29). They should recognize that the rest of the Old Testament is also truly Scripture, where the doctrine of resurrection is clearer. He also chides them for denying the reality of the resurrection, because what lies behind any thought of resurrection is the power of God to do so.

They will be like the angels in heaven (22:30). Jesus draws a parallel to angels to note that resurrected humans will not continue the practice of marriage. This line of argumentation holds a double edge, since the Sadducees also denied the existence of angels (cf. Acts 23:8).

He is not the God of the dead but of the living (22:32). Drawing on the present tense in Exodus 3:6, "I *am* the God of Abraham, the God of Isaac, and the God of Jacob" (LXX, *eimi*, "I am"), Jesus states that the logical implication is that even though the patriarchs died physically, they were still alive at the writing of the book of Exodus, since God continues in a relationship with them as their God, which could not be sustained with them if they were dead. If they were still alive, and if the rest of Scripture points to resurrection, the Sadducees should believe the power of God to raise them to enjoy his continued purposes for humanity.[334]

The Greatest Commandment (22:34–40)

One of them, an expert in the law, tested him (22:35). This "expert in the law" (*nomikos*), another expression for the scribe of the Pharisees, also "tests" Jesus

(*peirazō*; cf. 22:18). But Mark tells us that at the end of the interchange Jesus commends him (Mark 12:34), which may indicate that he approaches Jesus with more sincerity than the previous questioners.

Love the Lord your God with all your heart and with all your soul and with all your mind (22:37). The twice-daily repeated Shema was well-known as an overarching obligation of each individual Jew, which included the duty of obedience to the other commandments given by God (see the similar logic in 5:16–20). Love for God was not understood as simply emotion, but as the entire person—heart, soul, and mind—given over to God.

The second is like it: "Love your neighbor as yourself" (22:39). The venerable Rabbi Akibah declared Leviticus 19:18 to be a "great principle in the Torah" (*Gen. Rab.* 24:7), an opinion that was likely expressed also in Jesus' day, with which this expert in the law would be familiar. "Love" indicates a concrete responsibility, the act of being useful and beneficial to God and to one's neighbors, both Jew and Gentile (cf. Lev. 19:18, 34).[335] In this light, these commandments are similar to the responsibility of the Golden Rule, which Jesus said is a summary of the Law and the Prophets (7:12).

The Son of David (22:41–46)

The Christ . . .whose son is he? (22:42). This must have seemed like a simple question to the Pharisees. The automatic reply is that the Messiah is the Son of David, based on common knowledge that the prophesied Messiah was from the line of David.[336] This is confirmed by common practice, with the recurring declarations of Jesus' messianic identity as "Son of David."[337]

If then David calls him "Lord," how can he be his son? (22:45). Jesus takes the Pharisees to Psalm 110:1, the most quoted Old Testament passage in the New Testament, which they recognized as a messianic prophecy by David under the inspiration of the Holy Spirit. David refers to the coming messianic ruler, his son, as *kyrios*, "lord." The LXX has *kyrios* in both instances of the word "Lord." The underlying Hebrew has *Yahweh* for the first and *Adon* for the second occurrence of "Lord." Jews would not read the term *Yahweh*, but instead would substitute *Adonai* when they read it, thus making Psalm 110:1 read, "The *Adonai* says to my *Adon*...."[338] Familial respect would not expect an older person, such as David, to refer to his offspring as "lord"; rather the offspring, "son," would refer to David, his "father," as "lord." The coming Messiah is not just his descendant, but his "Lord."

REFLECTIONS

IF JESUS IS TRULY WHO HE DECLARES himself to be, then we have a most unique message to proclaim. Jesus is unlike any figure ever to walk the earth, because he claims not to be simply a messenger of God, but the unique Son of God. The religious leaders' silence (22:46) is outspoken testimony that the straightforward implication of the text cannot be avoided. Their silence is also outspoken testimony of their own hypocritical avoidance of the implications for themselves. They should acknowledge Jesus as their own Lord and Messiah. But ultimately, none of us, Christian or non-Christian, can ignore the implications of Jesus for our personal lives.

Judgment on the Teachers of the Law and Pharisees (23:1–12)

The series of "woes" Jesus pronounces on the religious leadership of Israel follow closely from the preceding parables and debates that have revealed the culpability of these Jewish authorities for not leading the nation in repentance with the arrival of the kingdom of heaven.

So you must obey them and do everything they tell you (23:3). Jesus' statement follows from the religious leaders' position as expounders of Moses' teaching (23:1). He gives a scathing denunciation of the teachers of the law and the Pharisees, yet he recognized their official capacity when exercised in the proper manner.

They tie up heavy loads and put them on men's shoulders (23:4). "Heavy loads" denotes the rabbinic oral tradition that was a distinctive feature of the Pharisaic branch of Judaism. It was intended as a means of making the Old Testament relevant to life situations where it seemed irrelevant, such as the complex sacrificial system in life contexts removed from the temple, both in time and in locale (for more on this, see "The Tradition of the Elders" at 15:2). Since the oral law was considered to be of divine origin, its massive obligations became far more burdensome than Scripture itself, and with the passing of years and the addition of more and more prescriptions, the rabbis could not lessen the burden without overthrowing the whole system.

They make their phylacteries wide (23:5). Phylacteries (only here in the New Testament) or *tefillin* (from the Heb. *tefillah*, "prayer") are small leather cubical cases containing passages of Scripture written on parchment. They were worn as an attempt to obey literally the Old Testament admonition, "Fix these words of mine in your hearts and minds; tie them as symbols on your hands and bind them on your foreheads" (Deut. 11:18; cf. Ex. 13:9, 13; Deut. 6:8). The phylacteries were fastened to the left arm and forehead and worn by adult males in the morning service.

Tassels on their garments long (23:5). On the four corners of a garment worn by men were attached "tassels" (*kraspeda*) that had a blue cord, conforming to the

THE SEAT OF MOSES

(left) From the synagogue at Chorazin.

(right) From the synagogue on the island of Delos.

▶The Seat of Moses

Jesus' allusion to the "seat [*kathedra*] of Moses" in Matthew 23:2 is the earliest known reference to this expression.[A-87] A later Jewish midrash (c. 5th to 6th century) also refers to a "seat of Moses" (*Pesiqta de-Rab Kahana* 1:7). Other references in rabbinic literature speak more generally of a synagogue chair on which an esteemed rabbi sits when teaching (e.g., "R. Huna in the name of R. Yose said: 'Everywhere that this Jerusalemite goes they offer him a cathedra and they seat him on it so that they can listen to his wisdom'"; *t. Sukkah* 4:6).

This "seat" was often viewed as a figurative expression, referring to the authority of Moses. However, recent archaeological evidence points to a literal chair found in early synagogues. A magnificent marble chair was excavated in a synagogue dating to as early as the first century B.C. on the Aegean island of Delos. A stone chair was found attached to the synagogue structure at Dura Europas in western Syria (c. 3d cent. A.D.). Stone chairs, dating to the third or fourth centuries A.D. have been found at excavations of synagogues in Palestine, at Hammat Tiberias, Chorazim, and En Gedi.

The purpose of the seat has been debated. Some view it as the place where the Torah scroll was placed after being read. Most scholars, however, view it as the seat for a leader in the synagogue, although the role of that leader is questioned. Some suggest it was the place from which the ruler of the synagogue presided, others suggest it was the place from which the person interpreting would sit after reading a portion of Scripture, while still others suggest that it was a place where an honored guest or speaker would sit.[A-88] Jesus' statement confirms the use of the "seat of Moses" as a place from which experts in the law would teach.

▶ Phylacteries at Qumran

Two intact phylactery cases of leather and parts of others were found in Qumran Cave 1 (1Q). One type was about two centimeters long (approximately one inch), with four small inner compartments for holding four tiny scrolls on which would have been written in tiny script, Exodus 13:9, 16; Deuteronomy 6:8; 11:18, respectively. This type was worn on the forehead. The second type of phylactery discovered measured nine by seven millimeters (approximately 1/3 inch) and had only one compartment formed of a single piece of leather folded in half to contain a single minute scroll with all four verses. This type was worn on the left arm.[A-89]

The rabbis had regulations about wearing phylacteries because of the temptation to wear them too large or inappropriately to draw attention to one's piety: "If a man made his phylacteries round, it is a danger and is no fulfilling of the commandment. If he put them on his forehead [too low down] or on the palm of his hand [instead of above the inside of the elbow], this is the way of heresy. If he overlaid them with gold or put them over his sleeve [to make conspicuous], this is the way of the sectaries" (m. Meg. 4:8).

admonitions of Numbers 15:37–42 (ṣîṣît; LXX kraspeda) and Deuteronomy 22:12 (gedilim; LXX kraspeda). Tassels were to be a reminder to obey God's commandment and to be holy to God (Num. 15:40). Jesus himself wore these tassels on his garment (Matt. 9:20; 14:36), although the term in these contexts could refer to the outer fringe (decorated or plain) of the garment. Jesus chides these religious leaders for extending the tassels as a display of their piety, another way to try to gain the admiration of the people.

They love the place of honor at banquets (23:6). Seating at special occasions such as banquets required that the most honored guests were on either side of the host. The other guests were seated in descending order of importance.[339]

The most important seats in the synagogues (23:6). Seating in the synagogue varied from location to location, with some synagogues having stone benches along one, two, three or four of the walls, with removable benches or mats brought in for the majority of the congregation. There is ample evidence that the elders and other synagogue leaders, including the ḥazzan (the synagogue administrator), had places of prominence. A later rabbinic passage may be representative: "How did the elders sit? Facing the congregation and with their backs to the holy [i.e., Jerusalem and the temple] . . . the ḥazzan of the synagogue faces the holy and the entire congregation faces the holy" (e.g., t. Meg. 3:21). Benches or chairs may have been reserved on special occasions for important personages, and if a regular part of each synagogue, the seat of Moses (Matt. 23:2) was reserved for the one expounding on Scripture.[340]

They love to be greeted in the marketplaces and to have men call them "Rabbi" (23:7). The rabbi was generally a master of the Torah, and the title was used most frequently to refer to the head of a rabbinical school (*bet midrash*), such as the leader of the school of Shammai or Hillel. Association with these schools tended to set a person aside somewhat from the populace. The school was a holy community, and the people regarded the members with great deference.[341] The rabbinic tradition indicates that these academic institutions were distinguished from the synagogue, with the academy a place to promote Torah study and the synagogue a place to promote prayer (e.g., *b. Meg.* 27a).[342]

But you are not to be called "Rabbi," for you have only one Master and you are all brothers (23:8). The ultimate goal of a disciple of a rabbi was to become a rabbi himself at the end of his course of study and initiation. Later rabbinic literature is insightful to the aspirations of students, who would traverse the levels from the basic "disciple" (*talmîd*), to "distinguished student" (*talmîd watîq*), to "disciple associate" (*talmîd hāber*), to "disciple of the wise" (*talmîd hākām*). At the later stages a disciple became a rabbi himself, the ultimate goal being to become a master of Torah with disciples studying under him.[343] With Jesus a new form of discipleship emerged. A disciple of his would always and forever be only a disciple, because Jesus alone is Teacher (*didaskalos*; "Master" is better for 23:10, where *kathēgētēs* occurs; see comments).

Do not call anyone on earth "father" (23:9). "Fathers" is a term used to refer to esteemed patriarchs, such as in the Mishnah tractate *Pirqe ʾAbot*, the "Sayings or Chapters of the Fathers." *ʾAbba* was used regularly in rabbinic sources as a title for esteemed scholars and rabbis, such as

Rabbi Abba Arikha (cf. *b. Ketub.* 8a; *t. Beṣah* 1:7).[344] The expression "father of the synagogue" (*patēr synagōgēs*) was used in rabbinic times of an individual holding a place of honor and leadership within the synagogue affairs generally. This continuation of the use of the term "father" as a title of honor, respect, and authority had deep roots in ancient Judaism, including its use by Elisha to cry to Elijah who was ascending to heaven (2 Kings 2:12; 6:21), its reference to the Maccabean martyr Razis as "father of his people" (2 Macc. 14:37), and its later use to denote the head of a rabbinic court (*ʾab bet din*).[345]

You have one Father, and he is in heaven (23:9). The motif of the heavenly "Father," occurring throughout the Old Testament,[346] grew increasingly popular during the Second Temple period in prayers for protection and forgiveness.[347] Jesus brought his disciples into a unique relationship with God as Father, since he is the unique Son of God and they are his brothers and sisters (cf. 6:9; 12:48–50).

Nor are you to be called "teacher," for you have one Teacher, the Christ (23:10). Matthew uses a word found only here in the New Testament to describe the third title that Jesus' disciples are to avoid. The word is *kathēgētēs*, which is a near synonym for *didaskalos* (23:8), but it carries an additional sense of "leader" (NASB). Some have suggested that Jesus may have originally used the term *môreh*, "guide," which was used to refer to the Teacher of Righteousness at Qumran,[348] although a direct allusion by Jesus to the sect is unlikely.[349] The term *kathēgētēs* does not occur in the LXX, but does occur in Greek literature to designate a teacher, especially a private tutor.[350] Since Jesus seems to be alluding to various titles that one might take, perhaps a better rendering might be "master."[351] Jesus' disciples are not to seek out personal authority as "master" over other disciples, because as "the Christ," Jesus alone is Master.

The Seven Woes (23:13–36)

Woe to you, teachers of the law and Pharisees, you hypocrites! (23:13). Now begin a series of seven woes on the religious leaders, which flesh out the condemnation Jesus has directed to them throughout his ministry. The first "woe" establishes the strong language, "Woe to you" that is reminiscent of Old Testament prophetic series of pronouncements of judgment.[352]

You travel over land and sea to win a single convert (23:15). In the second woe, Jesus addresses the extent of Jewish activity of making proselytes. Jewish history records an active propaganda that was directed toward gaining proselytes, because some of the rabbis declared that this was actually the divine purpose for the dispersion of the Jewish people (cf. *b. Pesaḥ.* 87b).[353] Josephus indicates that immediately before and after the destruction of the Second Temple many proselytes were made both among the masses and the upper classes in the Gentile cities surrounding Israel. He states that the men of Damascus set out to kill the Jews among them, because their own wives "had all become converts to the Jewish religion."[354] Josephus also tells of Queen Helena and her son King Izates of Adiabene (possibly a region on the Armenian border east of the sources of the Tigris River), who were converted independently to Judaism.[355]

Some advocate that the extant evidence does not indicate that Judaism was a proselytizing religion.[356] Others, however, while recognizing that Judaism never had professional missionaries, counter that the evidence in Josephus and the strong Gentile criticism of conversions to Judaism[357] suggest that common Jews zealous for their faith carried out an active attempt at bringing Gentiles to their faith through their everyday occupations and lifestyles.[358]

You make him twice as much a son of hell as you are (23:15). Jesus criticizes the way in which the Pharisees, zealous to win people (whether pagan Gentiles or "God-fearers") to their ways succeed only in placing them under their particular burdensome code of conduct in the oral law (cf. 23:4). On "son of hell" (lit., "child of Gehenna"), see comments on 5:22.

If anyone swears by the temple (23:16). The Pharisees developed a complicated

Matthew

REFLECTIONS

THREE TIMES IN 23:8–10 JESUS GIVES AN ADMONITION to his disciples that they are not to be called by a certain title. The warning is not so simple as to suggest that titles are always inappropriate. No, the warning is directed against three issues that can stifle our discipleship to Jesus.

- *Rabbi* (23:8)—In our desire to teach and provide others with insight into the Word of God, we should be careful to avoid *academic arrogance.* We should never seek to supplant Jesus as the Teacher who will guide his disciples into all truth through the Spirit-guided Word of God (cf. John 16:13–14).
- *Father* (23:9)—In our desire to protect and nurture others, we should be careful to avoid *religious elitism.* All Jesus' disciples are his brothers and sisters, and we should never elevate ourselves to where we supplant our heavenly Father.
- *Master* (23:10)—In our desire to guide and lead others into the fullness of discipleship, we should be careful to avoid *authoritarian dominance.* Jesus is the Master, the one with all authority, the Lord and Head of the church.

series of rulings regarding vows and oaths (see comments on 15:5). The Pharisees distinguished between oaths made "by the temple" and those made "by the gold of the temple," and oaths made "by the altar" and those made "by the gift on it" (23:18). A person who lives in moment-by-moment accountability to the presence of the living God will need only to give a simple "yes" or "no" as a binding oath (cf. 5:23, 34–37).

You give a tenth of your spices—mint, dill and cummin (23:23). The Mosaic law specified that a tenth of all that one had was to be given to the Lord for the ongoing work of God through the Levites and the priests.[359] The Pharisees were so scrupulous about attending to this requirement that they measured out the smallest of crops—such as the spices mint, dill (cf. *b. ʿAbod. Zar.* 7b), and cummin (cf. *Demai* 2:1)—and paid a tenth out of these.

You blind guides! You strain out a gnat but swallow a camel (23:24). With sardonic humor Jesus shows through what may have been a well-known proverbial saying that the Pharisees and teachers of the law have indeed overlooked the obviously important issues while focusing on minute regulations. The law declared that

many winged creatures were unclean (Lev. 11:23, 41), which the rabbis applied by straining wine to keep out small insects that made wine unclean (cf. *m. Šabb.* 20:2; *b. Ḥul.* 67a). While attending to the minutia of legal matters, they overlooked the largest land animal in Palestine, the camel, which was also ceremonially unclean (Lev. 11:4).

You are like whitewashed tombs (23:27). The term for tomb (*taphos*) probably indicates a burial ground rather than an individual monument or coffin. It was the custom to mark tombs with white chalk to make them publicly conspicuous so that passersby unfamiliar with the terrain would not come in contact with a tomb and so be rendered unclean for seven days (Num. 19:16; cf. Luke 11:44). This whitewashing practice was especially carried out in Jerusalem on the 15th of Adar, lest those pilgrims who

right ▶

WHITEWASHED TOMB

A tomb with ossuaries on the grounds of the Dominus Flevit chapel.

▶

CUPS AND DISHES

Pottery excavated east of Jerusalem at the Monastery of St. Martyrius.

made the trek to the holy land inadvertently walked over tombs and so incurred pollution before the Passover (cf. John 11:55; 18:28).[360]

You build tombs for the prophets and decorate the graves of the righteous (23:29). Matthew alternates here between the "tombs" (*taphoi*) of the prophets and the "graves" (*mnēmeia*) of the righteous. This may indicate a difference between these two terms, the former indicating "burial grounds" for prophets, the latter indicating "monuments" (RSV) adorned for "righteous" religious leaders. The "prophets" and the "righteous" are linked elsewhere (10:41; 13:17), indicating Old Testament prophets and others renowned for their righteous lives lived out before God. During the second century B.C., Simon Macabbee built an elaborate memorial in Modin for his family that was well-known for its uniqueness (1 Macc. 13:27–30). In the first century A.D., burial customs underwent a transformation. Secondary burials were commonly practiced, in which a person's decomposed bones were removed from a burial tomb and placed in ossuaries (cf. comments on 27:57–61). Funerary art became rich and varied, with widespread ornamentation of tomb facades, ossuaries, and sarcophagi, as well as wall paintings and graffiti.[361] The well-known tombs of esteemed figures from Israel's history (cf. Acts 2:29) benefited from this development of funerary beautification.

Final Invective and Lament Over Jerusalem (23:33–36)

You snakes! You brood of vipers! (23:33). The wording is reminiscent of John the Baptist's pronouncement against the religious leaders earlier (see comments on 3:7), as well as Jesus' (see comments on 12:34). Snakes (*opheis*; only here in Matthew) and "brood of vipers" are virtually synonymous, thus heaping up the culpability of these religious leaders.

Some of them you will kill and crucify (23:34). The Jewish leaders could not take on capital punishment without support from the Roman occupying forces, so with their backing they were able to unfurl their wrath first on Stephen (Acts 7:54–60). Crucifixion of Christians would have been at the hands of the Romans but likely instigated by jealous Jewish officials.

From the blood of righteous Abel to the blood of Zechariah son of Berekiah (23:35). The first righteous person in human history to be killed was Abel, slain by his brother Cain in an act of unrighteous jealousy, whose innocent blood cried out from the ground (cf. Gen. 4:8–11). The last murder recorded in the Old Testament in the canonical order of the Hebrew Bible (Law, Prophets, Writings) was Zechariah, a son of the high priest (2 Chron. 24:20–22). The language there fits closely with Jesus' statement, because he was murdered in the courtyard of the temple. Like Abel, his death called for revenge from the Lord. Zechariah's death was either identified by a developing tradition with the prophet Zechariah,[362] or he was named in Chronicles from his grandfather rather than his father, a common practice (see comments on Matt. 1:1–16).[363]

O Jerusalem, Jerusalem (23:37). Jerusalem has stood for the leadership of the nation (cf. 2:3), but the lament now seems to include a reference to the whole nation of Israel for whom Jesus was deeply burdened.

He is especially burdened in light of her coming judgment.

"Blessed is he who comes in the name of the Lord" (23:39). The Christological implications of Jesus' quotation of Psalm 118:26 are profound. The same words were cited in 21:9 at Jesus' entrance to Jerusalem, shouted by those identifying him as the messianic Son of David. Now as Jesus cites the same passage, he iden- tifies himself with God, Israel's Savior, the Coming One, who will once again come to his people after a time of great judgment, when they will have no other choice but to acknowledge him as Lord, either in great joy or in great sorrow.

The Setting of the Olivet Discourse (24:1–3)

The series of "woes" Jesus has pro- nounced on the religious leadership of Israel stem from their culpability for not leading the nation in repentance with the arrival of the kingdom of heaven. The woes transition Jesus' attention to the events of judgment that will befall the nation with the destruction of the tem- ple, but also beyond that to prepare them for the interval before his return in glory and triumph. This is the fifth and final major discourse in Matthew's Gospel.

His disciples came up to him to call his attention to its buildings (24:1). The rabbinic saying, "Whoever has not beheld Herod's building [i.e., the temple] has not seen anything beautiful in his life,"[364] attests to the magnificence of the temple as rebuilt by Herod the Great. Josephus likewise gushes,

The exterior of the building wanted nothing that could astound either mind or eye. For, being covered on all sides with massive plates of gold, the sun was no sooner up than it radiated so fiery a flash that persons straining to look at it were compelled to avert their eyes, as from the solar rays. To approaching strangers it appeared from a distance like a snow-clad mountain; for all that was not overlaid with gold was of purest white.[365]

Not one stone here will be left on another (24:2). Herod the Great had ascended to power in 37 B.C. when he recaptured Jerusalem from the Hasmoneans and took over ruling for the Romans. He began the rebuilding of the temple in 20/19 B.C., and most of the major renovations were completed within a decade. However, additional details and ornamentation continued to be added to it up to the outbreak of the Jewish revolt in A.D. 66 (cf. John 2:20).[366] Now Jesus is giving a prophecy of its destruction, which will occur in A.D. 70!

The Birth Pains (24:4–14)

Many will come in my name, claiming, "I am the Christ" (24:5). Prophetic figures and messianic deliverers had long attempted to incite revolution against occupying forces in the Second Temple period, and they continued into the years after the foundation of the church. Simon Bar Kokhba ("son of a star") was so named by Rabbi Akiba, proclaiming

him Messiah on the basis of the star from Jacob in Numbers 24:17. Later rabbis rejected this identification and referred to him as Bar Kosiba ("son of a lie"), a pejorative epithet reflecting the rabbinic rejection of him as Messiah.[367] Throughout the ages since Christ, many have attempted to claim messianic identity.

You will hear of wars and rumors of wars . . . but the end is still to come (24:6). The Old Testament linked wars, cosmic battles, famines, earthquakes, and other catastrophic events with the end of the age, as did the apocalyptic vision of *4 Ezra* 9:1–6. Note also the catastrophic events recorded in Revelation. But Jesus emphasizes that throughout this age these activities will be a regular and recurring part of the suffering of this life until the coming of Christ begins the redemption of all creation. The end is not near even though calamities may seem to indicate it is.

◀

EARTHQUAKES
Ground deformation following a major quake

All these are the beginning of birth pains (24:8). "Birth pains" is a common metaphor from the Old Testament prophets to depict terrible human suffering generally,[368] but it also points to the suffering that Israel specifically will endure prior to her deliverance.[369] The imagery points to an expected time of suffering that would characterize the period prior to the messianic age.

Then you will be handed over to be persecuted and put to death (24:9). The disciples will be handed over to *thlipsis* ("persecution, distress, tribulation"), a word that occurs four times in Matthew, three of which are found in this chapter (13:21; 24:9, 21, 29). In 24:21, 29, *thlipsis* points to a specific future period of unparalleled "distress" (NIV) or "tribulation" (NASB); here, as in 13:21, the use of the term indicates a general kind of trouble or persecution.

He who stands firm to the end will be saved (24:13). The disciple who endures to the end, which points to the end of the persecution with the advent of the Parousia, or perhaps to the end of a person's life, will be saved. "Saved" does not speak of rescue from death, because many true disciples have experienced martyrdom, but to the full blessing and peace of salvation with Jesus' arrival.

This gospel of the kingdom will be preached in the whole world . . . then the end will come (24:14). Although the increase of events in 24:9–13 are some indication that the Parousia is near, the only explicit condition to be met is the proclamation of the gospel of the kingdom to all the nations. After this proclamation has occurred, the end will come.

The Abomination that Causes Desolation (24:15–28)

"The abomination that causes desolation," spoken of through the prophet Daniel (24:15). The prophecy in Daniel refers to a period of "seven," during which in the middle of the seven a ruler will set

up "an abomination that causes desolation."[370] During the days of the Maccabees this expression was used to describe the sacrilege of Antiochus IV Epiphanes, the Seleucid king who decreed that an altar to Olympian Zeus and perhaps a statue of himself were to be erected in the temple on 15 Chislev, 167 B.C.: "They erected a desolating sacrilege on the altar of burnt offering. They also built altars in the surrounding towns of Judah."[371] Antiochus further decreed that the Sabbath and other festal observances were to be profaned, that circumcision was to be abolished, and that swine and other unclean animals were to be sacrificed in the temple (cf. 1 Macc. 1:41–50). This was one of the lowest points of Jewish history and was considered by many the primary focus of Daniel's prophecy.

But the Daniel references were also brought to mind in A.D. 26 when Pontius Pilate arrived as prefect in Judea and

right ▶

STANDARD OF THE 10TH ROMAN LEGION

This legion attacked and destroyed Jerusalem in the Jewish War (A.D. 70).

introduced to Jerusalem military standards bearing idolatrous symbols of the emperor.[372] Others believed Daniel's prophecy was about to be fulfilled when Emperor Gaius (Caligula) ordered a gigantic statue of himself be set up in the temple, although he was dissuaded by King Herod Agrippa I and died in A.D. 41 before the order could be carried out.[373]

Jesus now quotes Daniel directly to clarify that the fulfillment of the "abomination that causes desolation" is yet future.[374] Paul harks back to Jesus' and Daniel's prophecy as he gives his own prophetic statement of the Antichrist who is yet to come (2 Thess. 2:3–4), which prefigures the Antichrist (the first beast) who will be set up by the false prophet (the second beast) as a god in the temple (Rev. 13:11–18).

Let the reader understand (24:15). This phrase is an aside intended to get the reader of Matthew to see that in Jesus' words one will find the true fulfillment of Daniel's prophecy. With the onset of the abomination of desolation as spoken of by Daniel (Dan. 9:27), the period of "great tribulation" begins (Matt. 24:21). This desolating sacrilege is the predominant event of the period of tribulation, which corresponds to Daniel's period of "seven" (see previous comment). When we look closely at Daniel (esp. Dan. 9:25–27) and the events recorded in Revelation (see the 1,260 days, Rev. 12:6 = 3-1/2 years), this marks the second half of the seven years of tribulation, the time of "great tribulation." Apparently the first three and a half years is a time of relative peace and quiet.

Let those who are in Judea flee to the mountains (24:16). The Christian historian Eusebius reported that Jesus' warning to flee to the mountains was fulfilled during the Jewish revolt when Christians fled to Pella.[375] But Jesus' warning is more general, for mountains have always been a place of refuge for those beleaguered by invading armies; thus, they must find refuge there at this future time of great danger.

One on the roof (24:17). Likewise, there will not be time to gather provisions in the home. The flat rooftops on many homes in Israel were places to find a cool breeze in the evening and were considered part of the living quarters.

One in the field (24:18). The outer coat was an essential garment for traveling, often used as a blanket when sleeping outdoors, and only those in the greatest hurry would think of leaving it behind.

How dreadful it will be in those days for pregnant women and nursing mothers! (24:19). The danger of travel in this perilous time is greatest for those most at risk, especially pregnant mothers and their infants. Jesus describes their fate with a cry of "woe," emphasizing that those who are most vulnerable and who normally can rely on the help of others, may not find any help and thus will suffer the most.

Pray that your flight will not take place in winter or on the Sabbath (24:20). Flight in winter, when roads are washed out and rivers are swollen, presents even more difficulty for those fleeing the horrors of the coming desolation. In prayer the disciples must cling to God's presence and ever-ready help, even though they may have to disrupt even the most devoutly held religious traditions, such as the Jewish Sabbath.

Great distress, unequaled from the beginning of the world until now—and never to be equaled again (24:21). In his *Jewish War* 5–6, Josephus describes in great detail the horrors that fell on Jerusalem during the siege of A.D. 70. But the description here in Matthew indicates a time of tribulation that did not occur during the fall of Jerusalem. The horrors that fell on the Jewish people and on the entire world with the two World Wars of the twentieth century are a somber warning that the desolation that comes from humanity's unleashed depravity will yet be unequaled. The vision Jesus paints must yet be ahead (e.g., Rev. 7–19).

For the sake of the elect those days will be shortened (24:22). This is not a shortening of twenty-four hours, but rather is a proverbial way of indicating that God is in control even of these days of horror. If the wickedness of humanity and the wrath of God were allowed to run unchecked, there would be no end to the horror and no one would survive. This is a promise that the time of tribulation will not last indefinitely, because God is in control. The people of Israel are often referred to as "the elect" (e.g., Isa. 45:4; *1 En.* 1:1), but in the New Testament it refers to believing Christians (e.g., Rom. 11:7). In the time of future great tribulation, when Israel will once again be used of God for witness (e.g., Rev. 7:3–8) to bring in a multitude of believers from all the nations who worship God and the Lamb (7:9–12), the expression "the elect" includes all those who believe on Christ during this period (cf. Matt. 24:22, 24, 31).

If anyone tells you, "There he is, out in the desert," do not go out (24:26). The desert had messianic overtones for diverse groups within Israel, who associated the desert with God's forthcoming deliverance (e.g., Essenes of the Qumran community), and messianic pretenders often gathered their followers in the desert prior to their public appearance.[376] Josephus narrates the story of Simon, son of Gioras, who joined the brigands of Masada in the desert, but then withdrew to the hills of the desert where, "by proclaiming liberty for slaves and rewards for the free, he gathered around him the villains from every quarter." As his success and reputation grew, many other men of higher standing went to the desert to join him, "and his was no longer an army of mere serfs or brigands, but one including numerous citizen recruits, subservient to his command as to a king." Josephus calculates Simon's army at over 20,000 men.[377]

"Here he is, in the inner rooms," do not believe it (24:26). Josephus also recounts how John of Gischala, with an army of six thousand men, seized the temple during the Jewish rebellion, and how 2,400 Zealots joined him there in the inner quarters of the temple.[378]

Wherever there is a carcass, there the vultures will gather (24:28). The term *aetos* can be used to refer to an "eagle" (Rev. 4:7; 8:13), but where a carcass is mentioned, it is best to render it as "vultures" (NIV; contra RSV, KJV) since eagles do not gather as a group and do not normally feed on dead meat. This saying is proverbial, either quoted by Jesus or created by him to make a macabre point (cf. Luke 17:37; cf. Job 39:26–30). This saying either connects with the appearance of false messiahs and prophets or else illustrates the coming of the Son of Man.

Description of the Coming of the Son of Man (24:29–31)

Immediately after the distress of those days (24:29). Here "distress" (*thlipsis*) connects with 24:21 to point to a specific period of great tribulation, not with 24:9, where it is used to point to general distress. Once again, the mixture of prophecy referring to both the fall of Jerusalem and the end of the age must be acknowledged. Although the judgment that was to fall on Israel in A.D. 70 with the destruction of Jerusalem does seem to be in Jesus' mind (cf. 23:37–39; Luke 21:20–24), the primary emphasis must rest on the end of the age, when he will come as the Son of Man in great universal power.

"The sun will be darkened, and the moon will not give its light; the stars will fall from the sky, and the heavenly bodies will be shaken" (24:29). Jesus uses typical apocalyptic imagery as he alludes to passages such as Isaiah 13:10 and 34:4[379] to describe his coming with a mixture of literal and figurative language. God will cause the skies to be darkened and the heavenly bodies to be disturbed. Such language may point both to physical phenomena and to political and spiritual disruptions. The darkness at Jesus' crucifixion indicated that Jesus had conquered the forces of evil on the cross, and the darkness during the second coming of the Son of Man is an indication that he will now exert his rule over all forces, especially those of the demonic prince of the powers of the air.

The sign of the Son of Man will appear in the sky (24:30). Many have connected the "sign" with the "banner" that the Messiah will raise as he gathers the nations and Israel (Isa. 11:10–12; 18:3), or the type of "banners" noted in the War Scroll that the battle formations of the congregation at Qumran will raise at the final battle (cf. 1QM 3:13–4:17). However, since the rest of the verse points to the coming of the Son of Man himself as that which promotes mourning, the apparent reference to Daniel 7:13 ("one like the son of man") indicates that Christ himself is the sign of the eschatological consummation of the age (see Matt. 16:27; 26:64).

All the nations of the earth will mourn (24:30). This language would have held special meaning to a Jewish audience, since the prophecy of Zechariah 12:10 speaks of the people of Israel mourning when they look on the one whom they have pierced. The apostle John applies this prophecy to those Jews who mourned the crucifixion (John 19:37), and he quotes the prophecy at the beginning of his revelation of the end times (Rev. 1:7). Those events had great import for the people of Israel, and John uses the same term for "nations" (*phylē*) as he does to refer to each individual tribe of the twelve of Israel (Rev. 7:4–8).

The Son of Man coming on the clouds of the sky, with power and great glory (24:30). Jesus completes his self-identity

◀

COMING OF THE SON OF MAN

The return of Christ will be accompanied by signs in the heavens.

through the use of the relatively ambiguous title "Son of Man" (see "Jesus as the 'Son of Man'" at 8:20). He is the Son of Man who displays humiliation with nowhere to lay his head (8:20), who experiences suffering as the Servant who gives his life for many (20:17–19, 28), and who is now revealed as the One who will come in glorious power as the majestic sovereign designated by the Ancient of Days to receive worship as the divine King of the kingdom of God (cf. Dan. 7:13–14).

He will send his angels with a loud trumpet call (24:31). Both banners and trumpets were associated in Jewish eschatological thought with the majestic arrival of the Messiah.[380]

They will gather his elect from the four winds, from one end of the heavens to the other (24:31). This gathering has been taken to refer to the four points of the compass (cf. Ezek 37:9; Dan. 8:8; 11:4) to indicate the gathering of all believers who are on the entire earth at the time. Others have taken the expression "from one end of the heavens to the other" to refer to Jesus' angels gathering and bringing with him all of the redeemed already in heaven to join living believers on the earth (cf. Rev. 19:11–16). It probably should include both, so that as Jesus returns, he both brings with him those who have died and are with him in heaven (e.g., 1 Thess. 4:14) and

gathers those believers alive on the earth (e.g., 1 Thess. 4:17).

The Lesson of the Fig Tree (24:32–35)

Jesus now deals with attitudes that should characterize those who live during this age and await his coming. He gives several lessons in order to equip people during this age in preparation for the end: The first is the parabolic lesson from the fig tree.

As soon as its twigs get tender and its leaves come out (24:32). In the winter months figs lose their leaves, so even as the buds on a branch and new leaves in spring indicate that summer is near, so also when the events in the preceding context occur, the disciples are to be prepared for the coming of the Son of Man. Jesus stated in 24:1–8 that the general distressful events of this age must not be interpreted to mean that the Lord is near. However, as the end does grow nearer, subtle increases of difficulty begin to mark the end (24:9–14).

This generation will certainly not pass away until all these things have happened (24:34). The identity of "this generation" has vexed interpreters. Perhaps it is easiest to see a twofold reference, as Jesus has done throughout the discourse. The disciples to whom Jesus is speaking on the Mount of Olives is most naturally "this generation" who sees the events of the destruction of the temple, which shows the applicability of the discourse to A.D. 70. Yet within the context of Jesus' statements about the coming of the Son of Man at the end of the age, there must be primary applicability to those at the end of the age who see the events surrounding the abomination of desolation occurring. When these signs of the end of the age appear, those waiting for his arrival are to recognize that their redemption is drawing near (Luke 21:28). The generation that sees these things occurring will be the generation that sees the Lord appear.

The "Time" of Jesus' Coming (24:36–41)

No one knows about that day or hour, not even the angels in heaven (24:36). Now Jesus gives a direct answer to the question about the time of his coming: No one knows! The expression "day or hour" is used throughout Scripture to indicate a general reference to time (cf. 7:22; 10:19; 24:42, etc.). This includes not only a literal day or time of day, but also the year or month.

As it was in the days of Noah, so it will be at the coming of the Son of Man (24:37). The people in the days of Noah did not heed the warnings given. They continued to carry along their activities as normal. They were caught off-guard because they were so wrapped up in the everyday events of life that they had no concern for the warnings Noah had given about spiritual realities. By contrast, Noah and his family went about with preparations for the future deluge even

though they saw no specific signs of its coming and did not know the time of its arrival until it came.

Two women will be grinding with a hand mill (24:41). For "hand mill" see comments on 18:6.

One will be taken and the other left (24:40, 41). The "taking" and "leaving" probably indicates that one is taken away to safety to enjoy the blessing of the arrival of the Son of Man (like Noah and his family in the ark) and the other is left to experience the wrath of the Son of Man (like those who died with the arrival of the Flood). This view has in its favor that it corresponds in some sense with the angels who gather the elect at the coming of the Son of Man (24:31) and seems to be more consistent with the following parables.

The Homeowner and the Thief (24:42–44)

Jesus has stressed the deep division between those who are prepared and those who are not. He now tells four parables that give variations on the theme, each teaching a particular point about how and why people should be prepared: the homeowner and the thief in the night (24:43–44), the good and wicked servant (24:45–51), the ten virgins (25:1–13), and the talents (25:14–30).

Keep watch, because you do not know on what day your Lord will come (24:42). "Watch" implies not only looking out, but also includes the active dimension of being prepared.

If the owner of the house had known at what time of night the thief was coming (24:43). Jesus used the image of a thief digging through to break in, in the Sermon on the Mount (see comments on 6:19–20). This parable is consistent with the roofing materials and clay walls of common homes.

He would have kept watch and would not have let his house be broken into (24:43). The responsibility for the safety of each home lay on the master of the house, since modern conceptions of police force were nonexistent. Some protection was provided by military forces for rulers and for the upper classes, but not for individual homes. If a homeowner knew that a thief was coming, he would do whatever was necessary to be prepared, whether that meant staying up all night, or patrolling each opening, or even enlisting the help of neighbors.

So you also must be ready, because the Son of Man will come at an hour when you do not expect him (24:44). The point of comparison between the thief and the Son of Man is the unexpectedness of his coming (cf. 1 Thess. 5:2;

2 Peter 3:10; Rev. 3:3; 16:15); it will be at an unknown hour. Thus, they are to watch all through the age because he can come at any time.

The Two Servants (24:45–51)

Who then is the faithful and wise servant, whom the master has put in charge of the servants in his household? (24:45). The servant placed in a position of responsibility to oversee and care for other servants in the master's household was often called a "steward" (*oikonomos*), which is the term used in a similar parable in Luke 12:41–46. He was the chief servant, head over the master's household affairs and staff, and he was often responsible for caring for the master's personal affairs. The more responsibly the chief servant carried out those affairs, the more responsibility he was given.

He will cut him to pieces and assign him a place with the hypocrites, where there will be weeping and gnashing of teeth (24:51). The wickedness of the chief servant comes because the master's long absence allows him to abuse his authority, mistreat his fellow servants, and consort drunkenly with bad acquaintances— all activities characteristic of idolaters, pagans, and unbelievers.[381] When the master does return, the servant is caught unawares. He is therefore cut in pieces and given treatment that is proverbial for hell (cf. 8:12).

The Ten Virgins (25:1–13)

The kingdom of heaven will be like ten virgins who took their lamps and went out to meet the bridegroom (25:1). "Virgins" is *parthenoi*, the same term used of Mary, Jesus' mother, at the time when she was discovered to be with child (1:23). These ten virgins are bridesmaids,

---

R E F L E C T I O N S

ACTIONS REVEAL OUR NATURE. IN THE PARABLE OF the two servants, Jesus indicates that a person's faithfulness is the external evidence of whether or not he or she is truly one of Jesus' own. We should therefore examine ourselves to determine whether we are true believers, which will be evidenced by the way we think, the way we treat others, and our righteousness or unrighteousness. We must be careful not to imply that one can earn one's salvation by watchfulness or preparedness, but rather that a person who truly is a disciple of Jesus will watch and be prepared, because it is their good new nature to do so. The point for non-disciples is that they should not delay repenting too long, thinking they will have time. Rather, their own death or Jesus' return may find them to be unrepentant sinners.

in 25:8 has more of the connotation of a torch. It was a larger dome-shaped container with rags soaked in the oil to light the way while a person was walking outside.[384] These outdoor torches could last for several hours when extra containers of oil were brought for replenishing the lamp (25:2), as the wise virgins had done.

The virgins who were ready went in with him to the wedding banquet. And the door was shut (25:10). The previous parable (24:50–51) and the following one (25:29–30) both speak of hell as the destiny for those who do not "watch" correctly by being properly "prepared" with salvation. Therefore, the shut door would appear to point to hell here as well, especially with the comment from the bridegroom: "I tell you the truth, I don't know you" (25:12), a stark, straightforward statement of rejection of a person who does not have a true relationship with Jesus (7:23). Throughout the Old Testament God is said to "know" those whom he has chosen to be his people (Jer. 1:5; Hos. 13:5; Amos 3:2), a theme reiterated throughout the New Testament to speak of a saving relationship found with God through Jesus Christ (cf. Gal. 4:8–9; 2 Tim. 2:19).

◀ *left*

OIL LAMP

and the description of them as virgins emphasizes that they also have not yet married. Following typical Jewish marriage customs[382] (see also comments on 1:18), the groom left his parents' home with a contingent of friends to go to the home of his bride, where nuptial ceremonies were carried out. After this the entire wedding party formed a processional to a wedding banquet at the home of the bridegroom. The wedding feast was usually held at the house of the groom (22:1–10; John 2:9) and often at night (Matt. 22:13; 25:6), although sometimes the banquet was held at the home of the bride following the nuptial ceremonies. The Old Testament portrayed Yahweh as the "husband" of his people Israel,[383] which paves the way for Jesus as the messianic Son of Man to be pictured as a bridegroom (cf. 9:14–17).

The foolish ones said to the wise, "Give us some of your oil; our lamps are going out" (25:8). The word for lamp is *lampas*, different from the lamp in 5:15 (*lychnos*), which was used in a typical Palestinian home. Both lamps were similar in makeup, basically a clay basin filled with oil with a wick attached, but the *lampas*

The Talents (25:14–30)

A man going on a journey . . . called his servants and entrusted his property to them (25:14). Wealthy landowners often entrusted their property and affairs to trustworthy servants (*doulos*, as in 24:45) when they went away on business or for personal dealings.

To one he gave five talents of money, to another two talents, and to another one talent (25:15). The landowner in the parable is portrayed as wealthy, for he has liquid disposability of eight talents. The exact monetary value is difficult to determine, because the *talanton* was not a coin but a unit of monetary reckoning. Silver was the most common precious metal available in Palestine, so a talent was usually of silver—which is confirmed here by the use of the term *argyrion* ("silver, silver coin") in 25:18. A silver talent weighed approximately seventy-five pounds and had a value of six thousand denarii. It therefore was worth approximately $247,200 (see chart at 18:24). Altogether, the landowner dispersed nearly two million dollars to the three servants. Comparisons are difficult to appreciate, however, because such a sum in first-century Palestine would have been far more disproportionate to the average worker than in modern times.

The man who had received the five talents ... put his money to work and gained five more (25:16). The first and second servants "at once" made effective use of their entrusted amounts, probably setting up some kind of business and making a capital return on the original investment.

Well done, good and faithful servant! (25:21, 23). The identical statement of praise to both servants, even though they received different amounts of talents and earned different amounts, indicates that the point of the parable is not on amount earned, but on faithful responsibility in living up to one's potential and giftedness.

You wicked, lazy servant! (25:26). The wickedness of the third servant primarily stems from his attitude about his master, which in turn led to laziness and bad stewardship. The way he conceives of him ("you are a hard man") causes him to

fear him and then to hide away the talent and not seek to advance the master's capital. The servant's misperception of the master produces alienation, mistrust, fear, and then personal sloth. Had he truly loved his master, he would not have attempted to place the blame on the master, but would have operated out of love.

You should have put my money on deposit with the bankers (25:27). The word "banker" comes from *trapeza* ("table"), most often used to refer to the money changer's table (cf. 21:12). The reference here is most likely to money changers who charged a fee for their services. Investment houses or banks as we know them, in the sense of an establishment for the safekeeping of private money or the granting of commercial credit, were basically nonexistent in Judaism. For safe-keeping a private person would either bury valuables (see 13:44; cf. Josh. 7:21) or entrust them with a neighbor (Ex. 22:7).

So that when I returned I would have received it back with interest (25:27). The Old Testament prohibited charging interest from other Jews,[385] but not from Gentiles (Deut. 23:20). While contemporary usage distinguishes interest from usury, which is a higher rate of interest charged for a loan than is allowed by law or common practice, ancient Judaism and later rabbinic practice made no such distinction and consistently avoided all appearance of charging interest from each other.[386] Jesus may be referring to the investment of the talent with money changers who performed a valuable service of exchanging a variety of forms of currency for those traveling through Palestine from the Diaspora. This is different from the money changers who were perverting temple practice (see comments on 21:12).

Judgment at the End (25:31–46)

Each of the preceding four parables included statements of judgment, but the emphasis has been on getting one's life prepared. Now the emphasis is squarely on the judgment of those who are excluded and on the reward for those who are admitted to the kingdom (25:34).

All the nations will be gathered before him (25:32). All the nations are gathered before the ruling Son of Man. This debated expression has been interpreted to mean the church, all humanity, and all unbelievers, among other things, but within the Matthean context it is most likely intended to mean both Jews and Gentiles, who throughout this age are the combined object of the Great Commission (see comments on 24:14; 28:18–20).

He will separate the people one from another as a shepherd separates the sheep from the goats (25:32). The nations as entities are not judged, but rather the people within them, who are separated one from another. The shepherd metaphor softens the judgment image, but does not diminish the foreboding consequences of separating the sheep from the goats. "Sheep" is a consistent image of God's people, whether the reference is specifically to Israel[387] or to Jesus' disciples.[388] Goats do not occur often in the New Testament,[389] but in the Old Testament seventy percent of the references concern their use as animals for sacrifice, such as the goat offered for sin sacrifice and the scapegoat, where in a symbolic way sin was removed from the community and sent to the region of desert or death (Lev. 16:8–10, 26).

In most areas of the world the problem of separating the sheep from the goats would never arise, since such flocks are unlikely to mix. But in the lands surrounding Palestine they often run together, and native breeds can look alike in size, color, and shape.[390] There does not appear to be any significant reason why the goat was selected to contrast with the sheep, except for the symbolism that will be attached to both in a surprising manner.

He will put the sheep on his right and the goats on his left (25:33). For the significance of the right hand side, see comments on 20:21. The left hand side is not typically a place of disfavor (cf. 20:21, 23), although the context signifies it to be so here.

The King will say to those on his right, "Come, you who are blessed by my Father; take your inheritance, the kingdom" (25:34). The King is understood to be the Son of Man sitting on the throne (25:31), bringing to mind Daniel 7:13–14, where the Son of Man receives the kingdom from the Ancient of Days. This is one of the rare times that Jesus refers to himself as King, although the theme

GOATS AND SHEEP

has been there throughout Matthew's Gospel. The King addresses the sheep on his right as "blessed by my Father." The blessing consists of their inheritance, which is the kingdom that they now receive, not because they have earned it through their own efforts, but because it is a gift of their relationship with the Father and the Son.

I was hungry and you gave me something to eat (25:35). The explanation for why the sheep receive the inheritance of the kingdom is that they cared for Jesus when he was hungry, thirsty, a stranger, naked, sick, or imprisoned. The precedent is found in those Old Testament admonitions where God rejects Israel's external displays of religiosity (e.g., fasting) as a sham and declares that true righteousness is displayed in caring for the needy (e.g., Isa. 58:6–10).

Whatever you did for one of the least of these brothers of mine, you did for me (25:40). Solving the question of the identification of these "brothers" is important, and four primary solutions have been offered: all needy persons in humanity, all Christians, Jewish Christians, Christian missionaries. The use of "brothers" by Jesus in Matthew's narrative to refer to his disciples is the most convincing argument, suggesting that Jesus is referring to his disciples. But the expression "least of these my brothers" points to needy disciples. This helps make some distinction from the sheep (disciples generally), to emphasize that needy disciples are often the ones excluded from care, while attention is given to prominent members of the discipleship community.

Then they will go away to eternal punishment, but the righteous to eternal life (25:46). Daniel's prophecy of a future time of great tribulation that will come on the earth leads to a prophecy of eternal life and punishment: "Multitudes who sleep in the dust of the earth will awake: some to everlasting life, others to shame and everlasting contempt. Those who are wise will shine like the brightness of the heavens, and those who lead many to righteousness, like the stars for ever and ever" (Dan. 12:2–3; cf. *2 Bar.* 51:5–6). Daniel's prophecy is echoed here in the final words of Jesus' discourse. As has been the emphasis throughout this discourse and ultimately throughout this Gospel, there are only two types of people: Those who have not followed Jesus are actually against him and will endure separation from him in their eternal punishment, while his disciples are with him and will enjoy with him life that is eternal.

REFLECTIONS

THOSE ON JESUS' LEFT ARE AS surprised as the others. The five foolish virgins and the wicked servant who did not invest his talent in the preceding parables (25:1–30) were condemned to eternal punishment, not for some externally heinous sin but for their failure to do the right thing. Here too "sins of omission" are also worthy of eternal damnation because they are an evidence that a person has not been made righteous by the work of the Spirit. Righteous acts spring from a heart made righteous by the Spirit of God, while unrighteous acts, even of omission, indicate a heart lacking in the Spirit's work of transformation (cf. 15:19; Titus 3:1–8).

Jesus' Prediction and The Plot of the Religious Leaders (26:1–5)

The Passover is two days away (26:2). The Passover Feast was celebrated annually to commemorate Israel's escape from Egypt under Moses' leadership (Ex. 12). The month of Passover (Abib/Nisan) was to be the first month of the religious year for the Israelites (12:2), which corresponds to the current calendar of late March to the beginning of April (Neh. 2:1). The Passover lamb was selected on the tenth day of the month and sacrificed at twilight on the fourteenth day. "Twilight" was interpreted by the Pharisees to be between the decline of the sun (3:00–5:00 P.M.) and sunset.[391] By New Testament times the custom moved the time up so that the Levites could help the large crowds assembled at the temple with their sacrifices. After dark (Nisan 15) the Passover meal itself was eaten (Ex. 12:2–11), which commenced the seven-day Feast of Unleavened Bread.[392]

The NIV rightly follows the traditional order of the events, with the conclusion of the Olivet Discourse (26:1) and the plot to arrest Jesus (26:3–5) on late Tuesday afternoon, two days before the Passover. Jesus is pointing ahead to Thursday evening at sundown when he and the disciples will celebrate the Passover together, at which he initiates the "Lord's Supper."

The chief priests and the elders of the people (26:3). The chief priests and elders (cf. 21:23; 26:47; 27:1) are probably representatives of the Sanhedrin, the ruling body in Jerusalem, but not here the full assembly (see comments on 26:59).[393]

Assembled in the palace of the high priest, whose name was Caiaphas (26:3). The "palace" (Gk. *aulē*, "courtyard") in

◀
SITE OF THE HOME OF CAIAPHAS?

Some traditions suggest this location north of the church of Dormition on Mount Zion as the site of Caiaphas's home.

▶ The High Priest, Caiaphas

Caiaphas was appointed high priest in A.D. 18 by the Roman prefect Valerius Gratus, Pontius Pilate's predecessor.[A-90] He maintained the office until he was deposed in A.D. 36 by Vitellius, the Roman consular legate of Syria.[A-91] Because the Roman governor appointed and deposed the high priest, he made the office into a political office, which apparently Caiaphas knew how to manipulate well. He reigned as high priest for around eighteen years, whereas from the time he was deposed until the destruction of the temple in A.D. 70, Josephus counts no less than twenty-five high priests appointed and removed from office.[A-92] This points to the close cooperation between Caiaphas and the Roman government, especially at that time with the Roman prefect, Pontius Pilate. Because the high priest's office had been more of a political office than a place of religious leadership ever since the Hasmonean period, the reputation of the office was ruined (cf. the Dead Sea Scrolls in their criticism of the high priestly leadership, which they subsumed early under the title "Wicked Priest," declaring that the judgment of God would fall on the priesthood for plundering the people of Israel[A-93]).

this context must mean the private home of the high priest (see 27:56), Caiaphas, whom Josephus calls "Joseph surnamed Caiaphas."[394] "Caiaphas" is probably a family nickname that was passed on from generation to generation and may derive from a word meaning "basket" or "wooden rod." The original family patriarch who introduced the name may have been a basketmaker, a person who used pack-animals to move goods, or a person who worked in the vineyard business.

▶ OSSUARY OF CAIAPHAS

Not during the Feast . . . or there may be a riot among the people (26:5). Popular uprisings were increasingly common in first-century Palestine as the people grew weary under the oppression of the Romans and the duplicity of their own religious leaders. These religious leaders may well have remembered the uprising in the temple at Passover after the death of Herod the Great in 4 B.C. His son Archelaus quickly displayed the same

▶ The Ossuary of Caiaphas

In November 1990, while constructing a children's recreational water park in Jerusalem's Peace Park, workmen using bulldozers unearthed an ancient burial cave. When Israeli archaeologists arrived, they found a dozen ossuaries or burial bone boxes. The most elaborate ossuary had an exquisitely decorated façade featuring two large circles, each composed of five rosettes surrounding a center rosette. The sides and top were framed with stylized branches. On the back and on one side were slightly varied inscriptions that read, "Yehosef bar Qafa" ("Joseph son of Caiaphas"). Excavators discovered the bones of six different people inside the ossuary, which were determined to be the bones of two infants, a child between two and five years, a boy between thirteen and eighteen years, an adult woman, and a man about sixty years old. The remains of the man very well could be those of the high priest Caiaphas, who directed the Sanhedrin's trial of Jesus. The tomb therefore was determined to be the burial cave of Caiaphas's family or clan, typical of tombs that were reserved for temple aristocracy, landed gentry, and wealthy merchants. This

is a remarkable find, because, as Jewish scholar David Flusser remarks, "Caiaphas is the most prominent Jewish personality of the Second Temple period whose ossuary and remains have been discovered."[A-94]

The Jews for about a hundred years ending in A.D. 70 had developed a practice chiefly in Jerusalem of regathering from a burial chamber the bones of a decayed corpse and placing them with the bones of family members in a depository called an ossuary, a small, rectangular coffin-like box made of a single block of limestone (approx. two feet long, one foot wide, and a little more than one foot high). The ossuary lids varied, some flat, others triangular (gabled) or curved (vaulted). The ossuaries were often decorated with geometric designs; many were inscribed with graffiti-like inscriptions to commemorate and preserve the deceased.[A-95]

This discovery gives remarkable insight into burial practices of the Jewish aristocracy and offers an electrifying archaeological link to real-life persons involved in the events of Jesus' final days before going to the cross.

kind of cruelty that had marked his father when he sent in troops and cavalry who killed about three thousand pilgrims who had taken part in the riots.[395]

Jesus Anointed at Bethany (26:6–13)

Matthew (and Mark 14:3–9) recounts the story of Jesus' anointing thematically, placing it in the context of the conspiracy to arrest Jesus, whereas John (12:1–8) narrates the story chronologically, showing that it occurred on the Saturday night before the triumphal entry into Jerusalem. This sort of thematic arrangement is typical of Matthew's style (see comments on 8:1ff).

In the home of a man known as Simon the Leper (26:6). On Saturday evening, just after the end of the Sabbath at sunset, Jesus and the disciples attend a dinner at the home of Simon the leper in Bethany. Since Simon is hosting a meal in his own home, Jesus has probably healed him of his leprosy, since lepers were required to live away from the common population. John fills in important details when he tells us that Lazarus and his sisters, Mary and Martha, were there.

A woman . . . with an alabaster jar of very expensive perfume . . . poured on his head (26:7). At a Jewish banquet, small amounts of oil were poured on a guest's head, which would remain on the hair and clothing, enhancing the fragrance of the feast for the guest. At this dinner, Mary is the woman who brings an alabaster jar filled with very expensive perfume (John 12:3). The vessel is likely a long-necked flask made of translucent, finely carved stone standing some five to ten inches high. The perfume is pure nard (see Mark 14:3; John 12:3), an oil extracted from the root of the nard plant grown in India.[396] This is not a typical household oil for anointing, but an expensive perfume oil used for a solemn and special act of devotion. By breaking the flask Mary shows that she is not just pouring a few drops to enhance the aroma of the feast but is performing the highest act of consecration to Jesus, even to the anointing of his feet (cf. John 12:3).

The poor you will always have with you, but you will not always have me (26:11). The perfume had cost at least three hundred denarii (Mark 14:5), equivalent to about a year's wages for the average worker, or the equivalent of over $12,000 (cf. 18:28; 20:9). Jesus is not relieving the disciples of caring for the poor, but instead is drawing on the law, which emphasized that precisely because there are always the poor among them, giving to the poor is a duty of ideal conduct (cf. Deut. 15:11). The last scene of the preceding discourse has left the disciples with a dramatic scene of reward and punishment related to caring for the needy (25:31–46). In other words, Jesus is here emphasizing that the woman is performing an act of homage to him that can only be done at this time while he is with them.

She did it to prepare me for burial (26:12). Whatever her motivation, Jesus tells his disciples that unknowingly she

PERFUME JARS

Cosmetic jars and other instruments found in the excavations at Masada.

has begun the preparations for his burial, which will come sooner than any of them conceive possible.

Judas Arranges the Betrayal (26:14–16)

So they counted out for him thirty silver coins (26:15). The counting out of thirty silver coins calls to mind Zechariah 11:12. This amount was the price of a slave accidentally gored to death by an ox (Ex. 21:32). The identity of the coin is not specified, but a manuscript variant reading has *statēr*, the most common coin used for paying the temple tax (see com-

right ▶

SILVER COINS

A handful of silver Tyrean drachmas.

▶ The Day of the Lord's Supper and Crucifixion During the Passion Week

The traditional understanding of the day of the week on which the Passover and the celebration of the Lord's Supper occurs, and thereafter the day of the week of Jesus' death, derives from a basic comment from all the Gospels, namely, that Jesus was crucified on the "day of Preparation": "It was Preparation Day (that is, the day before the Sabbath)" (Mark 15:42).[A-96] This expression points to Friday, the day preceding the Sabbath, when the Jews would prepare everything for the beginning of the Sabbath. When Sabbath began, all work was to cease. This indicates that Jesus died on Friday afternoon.[A-97]

However, several passages in John's Gospel seem to indicate that when Jesus was led away to trial and crucifixion, the Passover meal had not yet been eaten by the Jews, which would imply that Jesus' final meal with his disciples was not a Passover meal.[A-98]

Explanations for the Differences between the Synoptics and John

There have been several attempted explanations of the differences between the Synoptics and John, but the two most promising are as follows:

1. One view suggests that Jesus and the disciples celebrated the Passover according to a solar calendar known from *Jubilees* and possibly used by the Qumran community.[A-99] The rationale for this position is as follows: (a) The Synoptic Gospels followed the method of the Galileans and the Pharisees, by whose reckoning the day was measured from sunrise to sunrise. Jesus and his disciples had their Paschal lamb slaughtered in the late afternoon of Thursday, Nisan 14, and ate the Passover with unleavened bread later that evening. (b) John's Gospel followed the method of the Judeans, especially the Jerusalem Sadducees, in reckoning the day from sunset to sunset. Therefore the Judean Jews had the Paschal lamb slaughtered in the late afternoon of Friday Nisan 14 and ate the Passover with the unleavened bread that night, which by then had become Nisan 15. (c) Thus, Jesus had eaten the Passover meal when his enemies, who had not yet celebrated the Passover, arrested him.[A-100]

2. Another view suggests that the passages in John that seem to contradict the Synoptics all point to a use of the expression "Passover" for the week-long series of events, not just the Passover meal itself. Therefore, Jesus and his disciples ate the Passover meal on Thursday, the beginning of Nisan 15, at the same time that the rest of those assembled in Jerusalem.[A-101]

ments on 17:27). It was the equivalent of four denarii, so that a total amount is equivalent to four months' wages, or about $5,000.

The Lord's Supper (26:17–30)

Where do you want us to make preparations for you to eat the Passover? (26:17). Since the Passover lamb was actually sacrificed on the afternoon of Nisan 14, just prior to the Passover meal after sundown, this seems to imply that the day of Unleavened Bread was prior to the Passover. However, although the lambs were slain on the afternoon of Nisan 14 and the Passover meal, initiating the Feast of Unleavened Bread, was eaten after sundown, initiating Nisan 15, popular usage viewed the slaughter of the lambs as initiating the Passover. This is in part attributable to the wording in Exodus 12:6, where animals were to be slaughtered at "twilight." Popular usage saw the beginning of Passover with the slaughtering of the animals, whereas technically the Passover itself was the meal, which began after sundown. Josephus uses this popular reckoning often when he refers to the Passover beginning on Nisan 14.[397]

I am going to celebrate the Passover with my disciples at your house (26:18). The famous Church of the Apostles, now incorporated within the Crusader Church of Saint Mary on Mount Zion, has a long tradition that claims it is the site of the home containing the Upper Room, in which Jesus celebrated the Last Supper with his disciples (Mark 14:15; Luke 22:11). The tradition further claims that this is the same home where the disciples gathered after Jesus' crucifixion when he appeared to them, where the apostles and other disciples gathered

after Jesus' ascension (Acts 1:13), and where the Spirit was poured out on Pentecost. Recent archaeological work has convinced many that after the destruction of Jerusalem in A.D. 70, Jewish-Christians returned to the city and built a Judeo-Christian house of worship on the site to commemorate the Last Supper and the headquarters of the early church. Although it has been enhanced, destroyed, and rebuilt several times throughout the centuries, it still marks the site revered by early Christians as the place of the home of the Upper Room.[398]

Jesus was reclining at the table with the Twelve (26:20). The most widespread style of formal dining in the Greco-Roman world was the *triclinium*, which is demonstrated in the "House of the Faun," an exquisite, luxurious home in the city of Pompeii, which was captured for later centuries' enlightenment in the violent eruption of Mount Vesuvius in A.D. 79.[399] Common also in the Jewish world, the *triclinium* was a dining room in which

UPPER ROOM

An historical tradition locates the last supper in the Cenacle on Mount Zion. This present structure was reconstructed by Franciscans in 1335.

the guests reclined on a couch that extended around three sides of the room. The host was seated in the center of the U-shaped series of tables, with the most honored guests on either side, their heads reclining toward the tables and their feet toward the wall.[400]

The one who has dipped his hand into the bowl with me will betray me (26:23). Each of those around the room dipped their bread into bowls that served the group around the table, so this saying implies no more than one of those who was at the meal, rather than specifying any one particular person.

"Surely not I, Lord?" . . . "Surely not I, Rabbi?" Jesus answered, "Yes, it is you" (26:22, 25). Although "Lord" (*kyrios*) can be used as a formal address (7:21), when addressing Jesus it has come to designate discipleship. It is interesting to note that Judas is never recorded to have addressed Jesus as "Lord," only as "Rabbi" (cf. 26:49), perhaps a clue to the fact that Jesus knew all along those who did not truly believe in him and who would betray him (cf. John 6:60–65).

The Institution of the Lord's Supper (26:26–30)

Jesus took bread, gave thanks and broke it, and gave it to his disciples, saying, "Take and eat; this is my body" (26:26). The "Haggadah of Passover" was the set form in which the Exodus story was told on the first two nights of Passover as part of the ritual *Seder* ("order"). The expression "Haggadah of Passover" then came to be used for the entire *Seder* ritual as well as for the book containing the liturgy and ritual narration of the events of Deuteronomy 26:5–9 (first referred to in *m. Pesah*. 10). Central to the meal were

three foods—unleavened bread, bitter herbs, and the Passover offering (lamb in temple days)—along with the four (traditional) cups of wine. Since the Old Testament prescribed that the paschal sacrifice was to be consumed by a company previously invited (Ex. 12:4), Jewish practice has always focused on the corporate character of the *Seder*.[401] Jesus uses the bread as a stunning illustration that his body will be the fulfillment of the ceremonies surrounding the Passover lamb, as he will become the sacrificial atonement for the "passing over" of the sins of the people.

He took the cup, gave thanks and offered it to them, saying, "Drink from it, all of you" (26:27). The traditional four cups of wine consumed at a Passover celebration each had special significance: (1) The first cup initiated the ceremony with the Kiddush, the cup of benediction, a blessing over wine that introduces all festivals. (2) The second cup just before the meal and after the Haggadah of the Passover concluded with the singing of the first part of the Hallel (Ps. 113–114). (3) The third cup was drunk after the meal and the saying of grace. (4) The fourth cup followed the conclusion of the Hallel (Ps. 115–118) (*m. Pesah* 10:1–7).[402]

This is my blood of the covenant, which is poured out for many for the forgiveness of sins (26:28). The traditional cups of the Passover celebration now offer another stunning illustration for Jesus to show that his sacrificial life is the fulfillment of all that for which the historical ritual had hoped. This is the new covenant that was promised to the people of Israel: " 'The time is coming,' declares the LORD, 'when I will make a new covenant with the house of Israel and with the house of Judah. . . . For I will forgive their wickedness and will remember their sins no more" (Jer. 31:31, 34).

I will not drink of this fruit of the vine from now on until that day when I drink it anew with you in my Father's kingdom (26:29). In later Judaism a dispute arose as to whether a fifth cup was obligatory during the Passover celebration. This led to the custom of filling, but not drinking, still another cup of wine, subsequently called the cup of Elijah. This is the cup kept in readiness for the advent of the prophet Elijah, who the Jews believed would come on the Festival of Redemption from Egypt to herald the messianic redemption of the future.[403]

Prediction of the Falling Away and Denial (26:31–35)

"I will strike the shepherd, and the sheep of the flock will be scattered" (26:31). The shepherd who is struck by the sword is the one described as pierced (Zech. 12:10; cf. Matt. 24:30) and rejected (Zech. 11). But the scene shifts in Zechariah 13:7, as this time Yahweh strikes the shepherd. This shepherd is identified as Yahweh's companion, who is side-by-side with Yahweh as his equal. As this messianic Shepherd is smitten, the sheep are scattered, which in the Zechariah context speaks to the dispersion of the Jews,[404] but as applied by Jesus refers to the hardship that will also fall on Jesus' disciples.

This very night, before the rooster crows, you will disown me three times (26:34). Roman military guards were organized around various "watches" (see comments on 14:25). The crowing of the rooster is proverbial for the arrival of the day. Thus, the denial will take place before the end of the fourth watch.

Gethsemane: Jesus' Agonizing Prayers (26:36–46)

Jesus went with his disciples to a place called Gethsemane (26:36). Gethsemane is only mentioned twice in the Bible— here and in Mark 14:32. Luke's parallel account only notes that they went to the Mount of Olives (Luke 22:39). In neither place is Gethsemane called a "garden," but John locates Jesus' arrest in a *kēpos* (John 18:1, 26), a term that indicates a cultivated area or garden.[405] The Greek word

Gethsemane (*Gethsēmani*) comes from the Hebrew/ Aramaic *gat šᵉmanîm*, which most likely means "oil-press." Therefore, Gethsemane was a garden area among the olive tree groves on the Mount of Olives where a place for the preparation of olive oil was located, which Jesus and his disciples often frequented (John 18:2).

▶

GARDEN OF GETHSEMANE

The traditional site of the garden on the Mount of Olives.

THE ROCK OF AGONY

The patch of bedrock in the chancel floor of the Church of All Nations next to the Franciscan Garden of Gethsemane is the traditional location of where Jesus sweat drops of blood as he prayed.

▼

Two primary sites for the actual location of Gethsemane have claimed scholars' attention.[406] The first site now houses the Church of All Nations (or the Franciscan Basilica of the Agony), which is adjacent to an olive grove about fifty-five yards square, with olive trees perhaps more than a thousand years old. Josephus indicates that Titus cut down the original trees in the siege of Jerusalem.[407] This site corresponds to the area specified by Eusebius and Jerome.

The second site is perhaps more promising, which is located a few hundred feet north of the traditional garden, slightly lower on the Mount of Olives. The cave is quite large, measuring approximately 36 by 60 feet (11 by 18 meters), with interior caves cut into the walls for locating oil presses. Some suggest that a cultivated garden area originally surrounded the cave within the olive groves on the hill. After an extensive archaeological reconstruction, one archaeologist suggests that the disciples went to the cultivated garden area to sleep in the cave that they had frequented on other occasions. Once there, Jesus asked the inner group of disciples to stay awake with him while he prayed. The soldiers came to the garden area and found Jesus praying there, with the disciples asleep in the cave.[408]

The Arrest (26:47–56)

A large crowd armed with swords and clubs, sent from the chief priests and the elders of the people (26:47). The most heavily armed would have been a contingent of Roman soldiers assigned by governor Pilate to the temple for security,[409] who were authorized to carry swords (*machaira*), the short double-edged sword preferred in hand-to-hand combat (cf. 26:51; Eph. 6:17). Levitical temple police and personal security of the chief priests and Sanhedrin carrying clubs would have made up another large detachment in the arresting crowd.

Judas said, "Greetings, Rabbi!" and kissed him (26:48–49). Men in ancient (and modern) Palestine customarily greeted one another with a kiss on the cheek. This was the customary way of greeting a venerable rabbi and would have seemed to the other disciples as a greeting of peace, but it was only shameless hypocrisy.[410]

One of Jesus' companions reached for his sword . . . and struck the servant of the high priest, cutting off his ear (26:51). It is likely that Judas brought such a heavily armed contingent because they expected Jesus' disciples to resist arrest, which indeed was the reaction of at least one, whom John tells us was Simon Peter (John 18:10–11). Peter tries to defend Jesus by taking the sword he is carrying and striking Malchus, the high priest's servant. At least some of the disciples regularly carried swords, most likely for self-defense from robbers as

they traveled (cf. Luke 22:36). Essenes were known to carry arms as protection against thieves.[411]

He will at once put at my disposal more than twelve legions of angels (26:53). A Roman legion had six thousand soldiers, which means Jesus could have called on 72,000 angels. The number may have symbolic value, but more importantly it points to the enormous resources at Jesus' disposal, should he desire. This is similar to the angelic host that surrounded Elisha, ready to come to his aide, even though his servant could not see them until his eyes were opened (1 Kings 6:17).

Jesus Before the Sanhedrin (26:57–68)

The courtyard of the high priest (26:58). The "courtyard of the high priest" harks back to the same phrase in 26:3, where it is rendered "palace of the high priest" in the NIV. Jesus is taken to the home of the high priest, Caiaphas, which was a large enough complex to be used for the business of the Sanhedrin.

The chief priests and the whole Sanhedrin were looking for false evidence against Jesus so that they could put him to death (26:59). "Sanhedrin" means a gathered council, rendered loosely in Judaism to indicate a local Jewish tribunal, but also, as here, the supreme ecclesiastical court of the Jews. Later, "Sanhedrin" became a title for the Mishnah tractate dedicated to the organization of the Israelite government and court system. Although the Sanhedrin had seventy members plus the high priest, cases concerning theft or personal injury could be decided by as few as three members. When a capital case was

◀ *left*

SWORD

A Roman soldier holding his sword.

THE HOUSE OF
CAIAPHAS?
(left) The Church of
St. Peter Gallicantu.
(top right) A wealthy
Herodian era home
discovered in exca-
vations of the Jewish
quarter in Jerusalem.
(bottom right) This
area north of the
Dormition Church
on Mount Zion is
another possible
location for
Caiaphas's home.
This is a portico of
an Armenian shrine
under restoration.

▶ The Trial of Jesus and the House of Caiaphas

Apparently Jesus is taken after his arrest at Gethsemane to the palatial mansion home of the high
priest, Caiaphas. Tradition has identified a site at
the Church of St. Peter Gallicantu (Latin for "Cock-
crow") as the home of Caiaphas, but most scholars
now reject that proposal. Archaeologists have
recently focused on a nearby area on the eastern
slope of the Upper City of Jerusalem, where large
homes of the upper class in the Herodian era were
located. This district, immediately overlooking the
temple mount across from the south end of the
western wall, was known to be the location of the
homes of the high priestly families[A-102] and accords
with some of the earliest known records.[A-103]

In this district a team of modern archaeologists
have excavated a large palatial type mansion that
covered an area of over six hundred square meters,
laid out with a large, central paved courtyard reach-
ing through a secluded gateway and forecourt.
Around the courtyard was a series of living quarters,
some with second floors, indicating that more than
one family occupied the quarters. There was also a
large room decorated with elaborate plaster design
and an elegantly adorned vaulted ceiling, as well as
rooms for ritual *mikveh* baths. By all standards this
was the home of a very wealthy family, matched in
size and affluence with the wealthiest of homes
uncovered at the ruins of Pompeii, Herculaneum,
Delos, and Ephesus.

All of this evidence has led many to postulate
that this is a home similar to the home (if not the
very one) that Caiaphas owned. His home was likely
the quarters for both Caiaphas's family and the
family of his father-in-law, Annas, the former high
priest. Jesus was shuffled through the complex,
appearing first to Annas, then to Caiaphas, then to
the assembled Sanhedrin (cf. 26:57–58; 27:1–2; John
18:12–28). Peter appears to have remained in the
same courtyard, moving from the entryway to the
main courtyard.[A-104]

involved, the sages required that twenty-three members made up a quorum (*m. Sanh.* 1:1). The composition of the Sanhedrin at the time of Jesus would have been a mixture of the priestly nobility, the aristocratic elders of Jerusalem, especially dominated by Sadducee influence, but with some elements of Pharisee influence through their scribal legal experts, the "teachers of the law" (26:57).[412]

I charge you under oath by the living God: Tell us if you are the Christ, the Son of God (26:63b). In the minds of the common people the title *Christ* (Heb. *Messiah*) probably implied the hope of a deliverer out of the house of David, who would liberate the people of Israel. By leading Jesus this way, Caiaphas is trying to get him to pit himself against the Roman rule, so that Caiaphas can rightly take Jesus to Pilate with charges of insurrection. "Messiah" and "Son of God" are basically equivalent expressions in this context, emphasizing that the expected Messiah is both Son of David and Son of God.[413] Caiaphas draws on the Jewish conception of the Messiah as the Davidic king, God's Anointed, who will rule his people forever (cf. Ps. 2:7).

In the future you will see the Son of Man sitting at the right hand of the Mighty One and coming on the clouds of heaven (26:64). Jesus declares that he is not just a human messianic deliverer, but he is the divine Son of Man foretold earlier in Daniel's prophecy (Dan. 7:13–14) and the object of the psalmist's reference to the divine figure who sits at the right hand of God (Ps. 110:1–2), cited earlier in his debates with the Pharisees (Matt. 22:41–46). The very title that Jesus has used throughout his ministry to clarify his identity, *Son of Man*, now unmistak-

ably clarifies for Caiaphas and the Sanhedrin that the next time they see him, he will come as the everlasting King, who will be worshiped and will reign for ever. He is the Messiah, the Son of God, but in an exalted way that they cannot possibly conceive. Jesus is making himself equal with God.

Then the high priest tore his clothes and said, "He has spoken blasphemy!" (26:65). Caiaphas does not miss Jesus' point. Blasphemy is to act or, more specifically, to speak contemptuously against God.[414] The Old Testament tells of the stoning of a man who "blasphemed the Name with a curse" (Lev. 24:11; cf. Dan. 3:29; 2 Macc. 15:22–24). The Mishnah gave guidelines for blasphemy, which specified that a person "is not culpable unless he pronounces the Name itself"; witnesses were needed to confirm the pronouncement. After confirmation, "the judges stand up on their feet and rend their garments, and they may not mend them again" (*m. Sanh.* 7.5). The culpable act of blasphemy in Jesus' case is not his claim to be the Messiah, but his assertion that he has divine status as the Son of Man. Caiaphas tears his clothing and pronounces that there are witnesses enough to the blasphemy. Later Barnabas and Paul will tear their clothes in horror when the people at Lystra try to assign them divine status (Acts 14:14).

He is worthy of death (26:66). From the standpoint of the law (Lev. 24:10–23), as interpreted by the rabbis as well (*m. Sanh.* 7:5), Jesus now deserves death because he has made himself to be of divine status by taking to himself the Name of God. But from the standpoint of Roman law blasphemy is not a crime deserving of death. Therefore, the Jewish leaders will have to manipulate the charges and focus on Jesus as a common messianic pretender, one who is dangerous to Rome as an insurrectionist, gathering around himself men whom he will lead in an uprising against the military government.

Peter's Denial of Jesus (26:69–75)

You also were with Jesus of Galilee (26:69). Peter's three denials are all compressed into one passage (26:69–75), which makes their impact on the reader all the more striking. At the same time, it supports the theory that the three phases of Jesus' Jewish trial (Annas, Caiaphas and partial Sanhedrin, the official Sanhedrin) take place in the palatial compound that is home to the familes of Caiaphas and Annas and also acts as the meeting place for the Sanhedrin.

Surely you are one of them, for your accent gives you away (26:73). The accent in the pronunciation of "shibboleth" by the Ephraimites gave them away to the men of Gilead (Judg. 12:1–6). There is some evidence that people from Galilee had difficulty distinguishing their gutturals. Judeans were contemptuous of the way Galileans pronounced certain words, not certain whether a Galilean meant "wool," "a lamb," "an ass," or "wine" (*b. ʿErub.* 53a, 53b).[415]

Judas's Remorse and Death (27:1–10)

Early in the morning, all the chief priests and the elders of the people came to the decision to put Jesus to death (27:1). At daybreak on Friday morning, probably a larger number of the Sanhedrin assemble to form a quorum so that they can give

▶

ST. PETER'S CHURCH IN GALLICANTU

The courtyard and various chambers. The rock cut structures, cellars, and chambers date to the Herodian period (37 B.C.- A.D. 70).

▶ Pilate, the Governor (A.D. 26–36)

Pilate was the Roman prefect and governor of Judea under Emperor Tiberius. He was a Roman equestrian (knight) of the Pontii clan (hence the name Pontius[A-105]). He was appointed prefect of Judea through the intervention of Lucius Aelius Sejanus, who was prefect of the emperor's household troops, the Praetorian Guard. Sejanus became one of the most powerful men in Rome, when he ruled as de facto emperor in Tiberius's absence.

Under the protection of Sejanus, Pilate was secure and carried out an attempt to impose Roman superiority throughout Israel. He hung worship images of the emperor throughout Jerusalem and had coins bearing pagan religious symbols minted. However, Sejanus's thirst for power caused him to fall under the suspicion of Tiberius, who had him arrested and executed (A.D. 31). During the time of his demise, Pilate was exposed to increasing criticism from the Jews. This may have encouraged the religious leaders to capitalize on Pilate's vulnerability, leading them to align themselves with him in his attempt to maintain peace. Their demand for a legal death sentence on Jesus, a falsely accused rival to Caesar (27:11–14; John 19:12), would have been a welcome way of putting down a popular uprising.

Several years later (A.D. 36), during a religious prophetic revival among the Samaritans on Mount Gerizim, Pilate's military forces suspected political and military insurgency, so they attacked the supposed uprising with great severity. Vitellius, legate of Syria, reported the attack to Tiberius, and Pilate was ordered back to Rome to give account for the actions of his soldiers. Pilate is not heard from again, but according to an uncertain fourth-century tradition, he killed himself on orders from Emperor Caligula in A.D. 39.

The New Testament, Josephus,[A-106] Philo,[A-107] and later historians[A-108] all record the rule of Pilate as prefect over Judea during the time of Jesus. In 1962 a stone slab was discovered at Caesarea Maritima that provides archaeological evidence as well. Caesarea Maritima was an architectural and engineering marvel built by Herod the Great (see discussion in Acts), which was used as the residence for the Roman governors in Palestine, including Pilate. When archaeologists excavated the ancient Roman theater that had been destroyed and rebuilt, a two-by-three foot stone slab was discovered that had been reused as one of the steps of a stairway. The stone bore an inscription, though several letters are obliterated or marred:

S TIBERIÉVM
NTIVS PILATVS
ECTVS IVDA E
É

The best reconstruction renders the basic words to be: "...this Tiberium, Pontius Pilate, prefect of Judea, did (or erected)." The full text and meaning of the inscription is still debated, but scholars are vitually unanimous that this stone is an authentic contemporary witness of Pilate's existence and the only extant archaeological evidence that he was prefect of Judea at the time of Jesus. This provides solid support for the consistent New Testament record.[A-109]

THE PONTIUS PILATE INSCRIPTION

▼

a more formal ratification of the earlier pronouncement (see comments on 26:59). The ruling is still not legal by Mishnaic criteria, but those are later idealized standards for the Jewish judicial system. They may not have been fully in force at this time.

They . . . handed him over to Pilate, the governor (27:2). Since the Jewish religious leaders at this time do not have the liberty under the Roman occupation to perform capital punishment at will, they take Jesus to Pilate to have the deed carried out. Handing over a Jewish citizen to a foreign power was considered a horrible deed in Jewish practice.[416] The Qumran *Temple Scroll* declares, "If there were to be a spy against his people who betrays his people to a foreign nation or causes evil against his people, you shall hang him from a tree and he will die."[417]

Returned the thirty silver coins to the chief priests and the elders (27:3). It is unlikely that Judas could have gotten near the inner sanctuary, so the scene may indicate his getting as near as he can to the restricted area of the priests, and he throws the coins over a separator.

He went away and hanged himself (27:5). This is the only example of suicide in the New Testament. The Old Testament records the cases of Saul and his armor-bearer (1 Sam. 31:4–5), Ahithophel (2 Sam.17:23), and Zimri (1 Kings 16:18). The death of Samson (Judg. 16:28–31) may be seen as either a heroic suicide or an acceptance of an inevitable consequence of his life's actions. Rabbinic Judaism considered suicide morally wrong, as a rebellion against God who gave life and who alone may choose to take it (*b. ʿAbod. Zar.* 18a).

The potter's field as a burial place for foreigners. That is why it has been called the Field of Blood to this day (27:7–8). As early as the third and fourth centuries, Christian travelers visiting Jerusalem identified the place to be about a half mile south of the Old City of Jerusalem—at the southeast end of the Hinnom Valley, near where it joins the Kidron Valley. This was based on the fact that the area contains about eighty burial caves, most of which date to the time of Jesus. However, most scholars consider this a faulty identification. This section is indeed an ancient burial ground, some dating to the First Temple era, but restored in its second phase as a tomb complex for the wealthy aristocracy of Jerusalem. One elegant tomb may well be the burial place of the family of Annas, who was high priest from A.D. 6–15 and who was the father-in-law of Caiaphas, the high priest at Jesus' trial. Later Christians mistakenly identified this tomb complex as the "field of blood," even though there is no evidence to link it to any prior "potter's field."[418]

The Roman Trial of Jesus (27:11–26)

Jesus stood before the governor (27:11). Pilate carried the title "procurator," which

POTTER'S FIELD

The traditional site of Hakeldama, the "field of blood," in the Hinnom Valley near the monastery of St. Onuphrius.

▼

in Roman imperial administration indicated the financial officer of a province, but it was also used as the title of the "governor" (27:11) of a Roman province of the third class, such as in Judea. A governor was a "legate" with control over the military legions. Pilate also originally carried the title "prefect," which is used to designate various high officials or magistrates of differing functions and ranks in ancient Rome. It carried with it administrative, financial, military, and judicial functions, and included responsibilities as final judge in a region, under the emperor, with power to pronounce death sentences. Tiberius had created a hybrid of responsibilities in Judea in Jesus' time, so that Pilate had a combination of responsibilities as prefect and procurator/governor.

Are you the king of the Jews? (27:11). Pilate's question probably reflects the change of charges brought to him, making it a more politically subversive allegation. Pilate would not be concerned with the religious implications of the Sanhedrin's charge of blasphemy, so the Jewish leaders focus their allegation on challenges to Roman rule.

It was the governor's custom at the Feast to release a prisoner chosen by the crowd (27:15). There is no extrabiblical historical verification for this Passover pardon custom, but there is evidence of widespread customs of prisoner releases at festivals in the ancient world. The Gospel account of such a custom echoes the practice of the ancient world. Some scholars find reflections of this custom in a rabbinic ruling on killing a paschal lamb for those in need, including an imprisoned person: "They may slaughter for one that mourns his near kindred, or for one that clears away a ruin; so, too, for one whom they have promised to bring out of prison, for a sick man, or for an aged man that is able to eat an olive's bulk" (*m. Pesaḥ.* 8:6). Apparently this custom originated in Judea with Pilate as a way of creating good will with the people.

A notorious prisoner, called Barabbas (27:16). Barabbas does not occur elsewhere in the New Testament, and there is no extrabiblical account of his activities leading up to the biblical account or of his subsequent history. An interesting

▶ Barabbas and the Thieves

Barabbas is called "one of those among the rebels who had committed murder in the insurrection,"[A-110] a "notorious prisoner" (Matt. 27:16), and a "bandit" (John 18:40 NRSV). These terms closely resemble the characteristics of social banditry common in first-century Palestine.[A-111] As a "bandit" (*lēstēs*), Barabbas may have belonged to one of the rural brigands who instigated social unrest. The two criminals between whom Jesus is crucified are also called by this same term.[A-112] These bandits were popular with the common people because they preyed on the wealthy establishment of Israel and created havoc for the Roman government.

Barabbas is being held prisoner by the Roman authorities at the time of Jesus' trial and is released by Pontius Pilate to carry out the customary Paschal pardon (27:15–26; Mark 15:6–15). The reason given for the crowd's choosing Barabbas over Jesus is said to be the instigation of the chief priests and elders (Matt. 27:20; Mark 15:11). Likely the Jerusalem crowds also have come to recognize that Jesus is not going to be the military and political liberator that they want, preferring Barabbas's active methods of Roman resistance to Jesus' way of nonresistance.[A-113]

manuscript variant occurs in 27:16–17, where he is called "Jesus Barabbas." While manuscript evidence is weak, Origen implies that most manuscripts in his day (c. A.D. 240) included the full name. Many scholars today accept this name as original and suggest that it was probably omitted by later scribes because of the repugnance of having Jesus Christ's name being shared by Barabbas.[419] It is not improbable for Barabbas to have the common name Jesus. Matthew's text reads more dramatically with two holders of the same name: "Which Jesus do you want; the son of Abba, or the self-styled Messiah?"[420]

While Pilate was sitting on the judge's seat (27:19). The judge's seat or tribunal is the *bēma* (Acts 18:12ff.), the platform on which a Roman magistrate sat, flanked by counselors, to administer justice. The *bēma* could be located in an auditorium (Acts 25:23), but was traditionally in some public place—as apparently is the case here, because Pilate is able to address the assembled crowd. The location where Pilate adjudicates Jesus' case is debated, but a good candidate is the magnificent palace of Herod the Great, built on the western edge of the Upper City, described by Josephus as "baffling all description: indeed, in extravagance and equipment no building surpassed it."[421] After the demise of Herod's son Archelaus, the palace was the Jerusalem residence of the Roman prefect. Therefore, when Pilate was in Jerusalem, he may have taken up residence there and held court there. The palace had been built to double as a fortress, so a large military contingent accompanied Pilate.

Others suggest that Pilate stayed at the old palace/fortress Antonia that is adjacent to the northwest corner of the outer temple, since this would put him in a more strategic location to keep an eye on the religious leaders of Jerusalem and to have his troops readily available for any uprisings.[422] Still others suggest that he resided at the old Hasmonean royal palace on the west slope of the Tyropoean Valley, opposite the southwest corner of the Temple.[423]

Don't have anything to do with that innocent man, for I have suffered a great deal today in a dream because of him (27:19). Dreams have figured prominently in Matthew's narrative, especially since supernatural dreams guided Joseph to protect the innocent infant Jesus from social rejection and from the cruelty of Herod the King (cf. chs. 1–2). It is possible that the dream of Pilate's wife is a supernatural dream used by God to make clear to Pilate that Jesus is innocent of any crime. On the other hand, the Romans often took dreams as omens. Dio Cassius tells the story of Caesar's wife, who, "the night before he was slain his wife dreamed that their house had fallen in ruins and that her husband had been wounded."[424] There is no indication that Pilate's wife is either a God-fearer or a

"ANTONIA PAVEMENT"

Roman period pavement where the Antonia Fortress once stood but now in the monastery of the Sisters of Zion.

▼

disciple of Jesus, which may lead to the conjecture that this is a natural, although profound premonition.

Pilate ... took water and washed his hands in front of the crowd. "I am innocent of this man's blood," he said (27:24). There is abundant background for the practice of washing one's hands as a way of showing public innocence,[425] not an attempt to purge oneself of sin, as is practiced elsewhere.[426] When asked why the Jewish translators of the LXX washed their hands in the sea while saying their prayers to God, the response was: "It is evidence that they have done no evil, for all activity takes place by means of the hands."[427]

All the people answered, "Let his blood be on us and on our children!" (27:25). The term "crowd" (*ochlos*) has been the normal word Matthew uses to designate the masses of people who have been witnessing the trial, and then ask for Jesus' crucifixion (27:20–24). But now Matthew switches to "people" (*laos*), the term normally used to designate Israel.[428] The Jewish leaders and the crowds whom they have manipulated are responsible for Jesus' death, as they now claim in the expression, "Let his blood be on us and on our children!" Blood on a person (or "on the head") is a common idiom to indicate responsibility for someone's death[429]; "on our children" indicates the familial solidarity of generations within Israel (e.g., Gen. 31:16).

Then he released Barabbas to them. But he had Jesus flogged (27:26). Flogging or scourging was a beating administered with a whip or rod, usually on the person's back. It was a common method of punishing criminals and preserving discipline. In the Old Testament, flogging was

a punishment for crime (Deut. 25:1–3), and later rabbinic tradition gave extensive prescriptions for flogging offenders in the synagogue[430] (cf. Matt. 10:17; 23:34, *mastigoō*). But the Roman flogging (*phragelloō*) mentioned here is quite different. It is a Latin loan word used to designate the Roman *verberatio*, a horrific

R E F L E C T I O N S

ANTI-SEMITISM IS A CANCER THAT HAS PLAGUED humanity for much of history. Unfortunately, Matthew's narration of the people's statement—"Let his blood be on us and on our children!"—has been wrongly interpreted to condone, and even promote, anti-Semitism. But we must clearly understand that Matthew's statement is not the invoking of a self-curse by the Jews, nor an oblique reference to God's curse on Israel. Matthew records the statement to show how the religious leaders and some of the people of Israel claimed responsibility for Jesus' death. They believe him to be a blasphemer and want him executed for it. The words reflect the same accusatory statements elsewhere in the narrative when Jesus places the blame squarely on the religious leaders for not receiving him as the Messiah of Israel, and for their role in turning the people away from him (e.g., 23:13ff.). But this certainly does not mean that later Jews should be labeled with racist titles like "Christ-killer," or that Christians should abuse Jews in the name of seeking revenge for God.

The sad and painful tragedy of this verse is that Israel has rejected its Messiah. But God's love for Israel continues, and he will remain loyal to the covenants with the nation (23:39; Rom. 11:25–32). Now each individual Jew must consider the claims of Jesus and the message the apostles bring. Thousands of Jews only days later will repent at Peter's preaching about the Jesus whom they have put to death (Acts 2:23, 37–41), and even many of the priests will become believers (6:7). Those who reject Jesus, whether Jew or Gentile, will suffer the consequences.

The responsibility of Christians today is to love Jews as God does, recognize the special place that they enjoy in God's plan for the ages, and share the gospel with them as they would any other people. No one can support racial bigotry toward Jews by appealing to Matthew's record.[A-114]

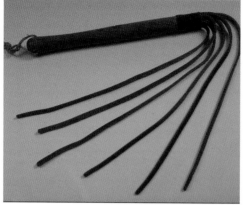

▶

**FORTRESS OF
ANTONIA**

A model of the
Roman fortress,
which was located
in the northwest
corner of the
temple mount.

▼

form of flogging. Roman law required that the *verberatio* always accompany a capital sentence, preceding the execution. Flogging in the Jewish synagogue was limited to forty lashes by the law (Deut. 25:3), but no such restrictions limited Roman flogging. In many cases the flogging itself was fatal. When the condemned man (women were not flogged) was tied to a post, he was flogged with the cruel *flagellum*, a leather strap interwoven with pieces of bone and metal that cut through the skin, leaving the skin hanging in shreds. The repeated flaying often left the bones and intestines showing, and the person was not infrequently near to the point of death when he was taken to be executed.

The Soldiers' Treatment of Jesus (27:27–31)

The governor's soldiers took Jesus into the Praetorium (27:27). The Praetorium was the official residence of the Roman governor, but the term was also used of the camp of the troops that served him. The location of Pilate's residence in Jerusalem is debated (see comments on 27:19). Each of the three possible palaces had been built to double as a fortress, so a large military contingent was right there at Pilate's residence.[431]

Gathered the whole company of soldiers around him (27:27). The "whole company of soldiers" probably indicates a Roman military cohort, from 420 to 600 soldiers, which is the tenth part of a legion. But the term was also used of a *maniple* (a third part of a cohort), which was from 120 to 200 soldiers. Josephus says that a large contingent (Gk. *tagma*, "cohort") of Roman soldiers was permanently quartered at the Antonia palace,[432] which would support Antonia being Pilate's residence. Yet the wording "the governor's soldiers" may indicate that in addition to the cohort at the Antonia, a smaller *maniple* was housed at Herod the Great's palace, which attended Pilate as his personal guard.[433]

They stripped him and put a scarlet robe on him (27:28). Roman soldiers in Jerusalem at the time were known to play a cruel game with condemned prisoners, especially revolu-

tionary bandits. The prisoner was dressed up like a burlesque king and used as a game piece. With each roll of "dice" the prisoner "king" was moved around a game board etched in the floor. All for the entertainment of the troops, they hurled verbal and physical abuse at the mock king.[434] One of the red cloaks worn by the Roman soldiers became a mock royal robe. Plaited branches with thorns became a mimic crown, perhaps inflicting wounds to his head, but certainly becoming a malicious imitation of a Roman emperor's crown. A common wooden staff was a nasty hoax for a ruler's scepter. This staff is used to beat Jesus again and again around the head, as they spit at him and mock him.

The Journey to Golgotha and the Mocking (27:32–44)

A man from Cyrene, named Simon, and they forced him to carry the cross (27:32). Criminals condemned to die were customarily required to carry to the scene of crucifixion the heavy wooden crosspiece (*patibulum*), on which they were to be nailed. Plutarch writes, "Every criminal condemned to death bears his own cross on his back."[435] The crosspiece was then secured to the vertical beam, and the entire cross was hoisted into the air with the victim attached to it. The *patibulum* usually weighed thirty or forty pounds and was strapped across the shoulders. The scourging and loss of blood had so weakened Jesus that he could hardly walk and carry the *patibulum*, because the skin and muscles of his back had been lacerated. Apparently at random the Roman soldiers forced Simon of Cyrene into service to carry Jesus' cross. Cyrene was a town in North Africa that had a large Jewish population. Simon is likely a Jew who had made a pilgrimage to Jerusalem for the Passover. Mark says that Simon was the father of Alexander and Rufus (Mark 15:21). Many suggest that Rufus is the one named in Romans 16:13 (cf. Alexander in Acts 19:33). The connection is strong when we consider that earliest tradition declares that Mark wrote his Gospel while in Rome, to the Roman church.

Golgotha (which means The Place of the Skull) (27:33). On the name "Golgotha," see "Golgotha." The common designation "Calvary" comes from the Latin word for skull, *calvaria*.

They offered Jesus wine to drink, mixed with gall; but after tasting it, he refused to drink it (27:34). A rabbinic tradition indicates that when a prisoner was led out to execution, he was to be given a goblet of wine containing a grain of frankincense to numb his senses.[436] The practice was done out of sympathy and was performed by Jewish sympathizers.

More likely the present drink is another attempt at cruelty by the Roman soldiers, who are hardly sympathetic. Feigning that they are offering Jesus a cup of refreshment, the wine has instead been mixed with "gall," a bitter herb that could even be poisonous. When Jesus tastes the bitter drink, he knows it is not for refreshment but is only another way of

▶ Golgotha

Golgotha is the name attached to the place where Jesus was crucified. The identity and location of the place has been given considerable attention throughout history.

Proposals for the name Golgotha: No known place in ancient Jerusalem has ever been found that is called Golgotha, but three primary reasons for the name have been proposed: (1) it was a place of execution; (2) it was an area known for having a number of tombs; or (3) the site in some way resembled a skull. That leads to the following discussion.

Clues to the location of Golgotha: The most important clues to the identity and location of Golgotha are as follows. (1) The place must have been outside of Jerusalem, because Roman law (and Jewish law, Lev. 24:14) directed crucifixion to take place outside the city. (2) It must have been a fairly conspicuous spot, probably not far from a city gate and a highway, because the Romans used crucifixion as a deterrent and wanted the gruesome scene to be witnessed by as many people as possible. (3) A garden containing a tomb was nearby. The tomb belongs to Joseph of Arimathea, who claims Jesus' body and places him there (John 19:41–42).

Two primary locations have been proposed:

(1) "Gordon's Hill" and the "Garden Tomb" are named after General Charles George Gordon, a renowned British military hero. During his brief service in Israel (1883) he identified a hill that looked similar to a skull. The hill was located north of the northern wall of the Old City of Jerusalem. Under-

neath the hill is a vast underground cemetery, including one tomb that he identified as Jesus' burial tomb. Scholars agree that this Garden Tomb was part of a vast series of tombs that date to the eighth or seventh centuries B.C.; it was reused for burial purposes in the Byzantine period (fifth to seventh centuries A.D.). Therefore, it cannot be identified as the newly hewn tomb of Joseph of Arimathea.[A-115]

(2) "The Church of the Holy Sepulchre" was built in the fourth century by Emperor Constantine as a memorial to Jesus' crucifixion and burial. Three Christian religious communities—Armenian, Greek, and Latin—have long traditions that point to this site, west of the city of Jerusalem, as both the place of Jesus' crucifixion and burial. Scholars agree with these traditions for the following reasons: (a) During the time of Jesus this location was located outside of the city walls. Another wall was built later by Herod Agrippa between A.D. 41 and 44, which enclosed the site within the city. (b) The area was likely near a thoroughfare, since it was adjacent to a working stone quarry. (c) The site is an ancient limestone quarry, which had been exhausted of its useable stone by the first century B.C. At that time the quarry was filled and used as a garden or orchard. The area also began to be used as a cemetery, and by the turn of the era contained a large burial ground. A number of tombs have been discovered that are consistent with the type of tombs long associated with Jesus' first-century burial.[A-116]

torturing him. The bitterness will only intensify his parched thirst, so he refuses (see Ps. 69:20–21).

The Crucifixion (27:35–44)

Crucified him (27:35). Recent historical and archaeological studies have helped bring a more realistic sense of crucifixion's horrors.[437] The bones of a crucified man named Jehohanan were discovered in Jerusalem in 1968 at Giv'at ha-Mivtar in a group of cave tombs. He had been crucified sometime between A.D. 7–66.[438] His arms were evidently tied to the crossbeam, and he had apparently straddled the upright beam with each foot nailed laterally to the beam. Likewise, once at the crucifixion site, the soldiers may have tied and nailed Jesus' hands to the crossbeam he carried[439] and nailed his ankles to the upright beam, possibly with a spike driven through the bones and into the beam between them (see comments on Mark 15:24; "Crucifixion" at Luke 23:33).

They divided up his clothes by casting lots (27:35). The readers know that as the soldiers divide up his clothing by casting lots, this fulfills what Scripture anticipated (Ps. 22:18). The lot was cast in the Old Testament to discover God's will on various matters, such as the goat to be sacrificed on the Day of Atonement (Lev. 16). But here the lot is used as a form of gambling by the Roman guards as they divide up whatever is left of Jesus' clothes. By so doing they take away his final external dignity and protection from the flies and elements that torture his beaten body.

Two robbers were crucified with him (27:38). The two robbers between whom Jesus is crucified likely were political insurrectionists like Barabbas, since the same term (*lēstēs*) is used of them and Barabbas (see "Barabbas and the Thieves" at 27:16).

Those who passed by hurled insults at him, shaking their heads (27:39). Golgotha must have been a fairly conspicuous spot, probably not far from a city gate and a highway (see "Golgotha" at 27:33). Quintilian states, "Whenever we crucify the guilty, the most crowded roads are chosen, where the most people can see and be moved by this fear. For penalties relate not so much to retribution as to their exemplary effect."[440]

The Death of Jesus (27:45–46)

From the sixth hour until the ninth hour (27:45). The most widely accepted method of calculating the time of the day throughout much of the ancient world began with sunrise, generally 6:00 A.M. (cf. *Let. Aris.* 303). Therefore, the sixth hour is 12:00 noon and the ninth hour is 3:00 P.M. According to Mark, Jesus has already been on the cross for about three hours, because he was crucified at the third hour (Mark 15:25).

CHURCH OF THE HOLY SEPULCHRE

A courtyard by the entrance of the church. Ancient tradition associates the location of this church with both the crucifixion and burial of Jesus.

Darkness came over all the land (27:45). If light symbolizes God, darkness evokes everything that is anti-God: the wicked, judgment, death.[441] Salvation brings light to those in darkness (Isa. 9:1; Matt. 4:16). The time of God's ultimate judgment, the Day of the Lord, is portrayed in both Old and New Testaments as a day of darkness.[442] While darkness often accompanies the concept of death in Scripture (cf. Job 10:21–22), darkness at the crucifixion scene displays the temporary power of Satan (cf. Luke 2:53), God's displeasure on humanity for crucifying his Son, and most importantly God's judgment on evil.[443] This was not an eclipse, for the Passover was at the full moon, but was some unknown act of God indicating his judgment on the sins of the world.

***"Eloi, Eloi, lama sabachthani?"*—which means, "My God, my God, why have you forsaken me?" (27:46).** Once again the crucifixion scene is reminiscent of Psalm 22.[444] Jesus is experiencing the separation from the Father that must accompany bearing the sin of his people (1:21; 20:28; 26:28). He now bears the divine retribution and punishment for sin, as the Father's cup of wrath is poured out on him in divine judgment of sin. In the apostle Paul's words, "God made him who had no sin to be sin for us, so that in him we might become the righteousness of God" (2 Cor. 5:21), and, "Christ redeemed us from the curse of the law by becoming a curse for us, for it is written: 'Cursed is everyone who is hung on a tree'" (Gal. 3:13).

The Bystanders Think of Elijah (27:47–50)

He's calling Elijah (27:47). Jesus' citation of Psalm 22:1 is misunderstood by the bystanders to imply that he is calling Elijah. According to a tradition in later Judaism, since Elijah did not die but was taken by God in a whirlwind (2 Kings 2:1–12), he would return in an equally instantaneous way to help those in distress (*b. Ned.* 50a).[445]

He filled it with wine vinegar, put it on a stick, and offered it to Jesus to drink (27:48). The drink offered Jesus is *oxos*, from the word for "sharp, sharpness," which was used to refer to a sour wine used by common people and soldiers as a daily drink with meals. The same drink was given to Jesus by the soldiers in mockery (cf. Luke 23:36), and nothing indicates that the earlier mockery of the crowds has ceased.[446]

The Immediate Impact of the Death (27:51–56)

The curtain of the temple was torn in two from top to bottom (27:51). The word for curtain (*katapetasma*) is used in the LXX sometimes of the curtain between the Holy Place and the Most Holy Place,[447] and sometimes of the curtain over the entrance to the Holy Place.[448] The former is more likely meant here. The curtain was an elaborately woven fabric of seventy-two twisted plaits of twenty-four threads each and the veil was sixty feet long and thirty wide (cf. *m. Šeqal.* 8:5).[449] Being split from top to bottom is a sign that God has done this, signifying that the new and living way is now open into the presence of God through the sacrifice of Christ.[450]

The tombs broke open and the bodies of many holy people who had died were raised to life (27:52). The expression "holy people" probably refers to pious Old Testament figures selected to bear testimony to the resurrection of Jesus. We might think of the way in which Moses and Elijah were selected to appear with Jesus on the Mount of Transfiguration (17:1–8). But in this case it is a resurrection of their bodies. The best implication of the text is that they are not raised until after Jesus is raised, which anticipates Paul's teaching on Jesus being the firstfruits of the dead (1 Cor. 15:20–23).

▶The Women Followers of Jesus

Women and men were originally created by God as equal human beings, who were complementary coworkers in ruling God's creation for him (Gen. 1:26–28). But in some circles within Judaism, because of misinterpretation of Scripture and cultural bias, women had lost their dignity, value, and worth.

Josephus states, "The woman, says the Law, is in all things inferior to the man,"[A-117] apparently interpreting Genesis 3:16 to indicate that women are not only under the authority of men, but also have a lower personal status. Women are categorized in the repeated rabbinic formula, "women, slaves and minors,"[A-118] demonstrating that a woman, like a Gentile slave and a minor child, is under the authority of a man and has limited participation in religious activity. One of the most widely cited rabbinic sayings from the days after the formation of the Mishnah, but prior to the formation of the Talmud, reflects at least among some of the rabbis an inferior position of women. This attitude was echoed in a threefold daily prayer: "Praised be God that he has not created me a gentile! Praised be God that he has not created me a woman! Praised be God that he has not created me an ignoramus!"[A-119]

Nevertheless, the rabbinic literature in other places reiterates the Old Testament directive that honor is to be given equally to the mother and father. One passage indicates that since the father is listed first in Exodus 20:12 and the mother is listed first in Leviticus 19:3, Scripture teaches that "both are equal."[A-120] One saying attributed to R. Joseph indicates his attitude toward the spiritual status of his mother. When he heard his mother's footsteps coming he said, "Let me arise before the approach of the Shekinah (Divine presence)."[A-121] The wife and mother were considered to be of substantial spiritual value.

One direct result of Jesus' ministry has been the restoration and affirmation of women that God intended from the beginning of creation, which we can see demonstrated in the following ways.

- Women were equally worthy of Jesus' saving activity (e.g., John 4:1–42).
- Women were called to be Jesus' disciples (Matt. 12:48–50).
- Women received instruction and nurture as Jesus' disciples (Luke 10:38–42).
- Women were part of his ministry team (Luke 8:1–3).
- Because of their courageous presence at the cross and the empty tomb, women were designated as the first to testify to the reality of Jesus' resurrection (Matt. 28:10; Mark 16:7; John 20:17).

For women to be disciples of a great master was certainly an unusual circumstance in Palestine in the first century. Yet here we find another instance of the unique form of discipleship Jesus instituted. While women were not part of the Twelve, several women disciples traveled with Jesus and had a significant part in his earthly ministry. Jesus restores and reaffirms to women their dignity and worth as persons fully equal to men as humans created in the image of God. He also preserves the male-female distinction of humans, so that they are restored and affirmed in the different roles that God intended from the beginning. Distinctions among Jesus' disciples relate to function, not spiritual standing or commitment or essential personal worth. Jesus restores and affirms to women the status of being coworkers with men in God's plan for working out his will on earth.[A-122]

Many women were there, watching from a distance. They had followed Jesus from Galilee (27:55). All of the evangelists mention a group of women who followed and served Jesus in Galilee and who also followed him to Jerusalem, witnessing the events of the final week, including the crucifixion[451] and the resurrection.[452] Their following means that they had been accompanying Jesus as his disciples.

To care for his needs (27:55). According to Luke 8:1–3 a group of women joined Jesus and the Twelve as a part of the mission team. The term behind the expression "care for his needs" (*diakoneō*) is better rendered "serve." Besides providing financial support for the missionary outreach (Luke 8:1–3), the women joined the Twelve as Jesus' companions and as witnesses of his ministry.

Among them were Mary Magdalene, Mary the mother of James and Joses, and the mother of Zebedee's sons (27:56). "Magdalene" implies that Mary was from Magdala (see comments on 15:39). The only information about Mary's personal life is that she is the woman "from whom seven demons had come out" (Luke 8:2).

Her being listed first demonstrates her prominence in the days of Jesus' ministry, as she was likely a leader among the women. The other Mary may be the mother of James who is identified with one of the Twelve called James, the son of Alphaeus (cf. Matt. 10:3). The mother of Zebedee's sons is likely Salome, Jesus' mother's sister, or Jesus' aunt on his mother's side. This would mean that James and John, the sons of Zebedee, are Jesus' cousins on his mother's side (see comments on 20:20).

The Burial of Jesus by Faithful Followers (27:57–61)

As evening approached (27:57). Jewish custom dictated that bodies should be taken down before evening, especially with the Sabbath beginning at sundown (approx. 6:00 P.M.).[453]

A rich man from Arimathea, named Joseph (27:57). Joseph, one of the most common names for Jewish men, was from Arimathea. The location is in doubt, identified by some as Ramathaim, the birthplace of Samuel (1 Sam. 1:1, 19), and by others as Rathamein (1 Macc. 11:34) or Ramathain.[454] Extensive apoc-

ryphal legends later circulated about Joseph of Arimathea, which have no scholarly historical support.

A disciple of Jesus (27:57). Joseph was a fellow member of the Sanhedrin with Nicodemus, both of whom appear as exemplary Jews anticipating the arrival of the kingdom of God (Mark 15:43; Luke 23:50–51; John 3:1–15; 19:38–42). Joseph is an example of a person who apparently did not follow Jesus around in his earthly ministry, but who was still considered a disciple, even as he continued to serve within the religious establishment of Israel.[455] Now is the turn for these two men to step forward and show their true colors.

Going to Pilate, he asked for Jesus' body (27:58). Because he is a rich man, Joseph's tomb becomes the fulfillment of the proper place for a burial for Jesus (Isa. 53:9). Not only is the Sabbath approaching, but Deuteronomy 21:22–23 instructs that a person hanged on a tree should be buried the same day so that the land will not be defiled, for the person hanged on a tree is under God's curse. Rabbinic interpretation insisted that burial should be completed if possible on the day of death: "Every one that suffers his dead to remain overnight transgresses a negative command."[456]

Joseph took the body, wrapped it in a clean linen cloth (27:59). The Jews did not practice cremation or embalming.[457] Coffins were not used; rather, the body was dressed in linen cloths.[458] Contact with corpses caused ritual impurity, so tombs were marked with whitewash (cf. 23:27) to warn passersby. Corpses were left in tombs until the flesh decayed (from one to three years), when the bones were collected and placed in ossuaries (see comments on 23:29).[459]

Placed it in his own new tomb that he had cut out of the rock (27:60). On the location of this tomb, see "Golgotha" at 27:33. Burial was generally in a cave, to which the body was carried on a bier in a funeral procession (*m. Ber.* 3:1). Family tombs predominated in first-century Judaism, which could be reused over several generations. The tomb was a rectangular underground chamber cut into rock, sometimes in abandoned quarries. It was accessed through a low entry chamber, normally closed with a stone. The dead were laid out on benches cut parallel into the rock and/or placed in perpendicular burial slots or recesses cut into the sides of the tomb chambers. Large family tombs were quite expensive, sometimes with several chambers connected together with tunnels.[460]

He rolled a big stone in front of the entrance to the tomb (27:60). Stones of various types were used to lodge against the entryway, which permitted repeated use of the tomb. Some were rolling disc-shaped stones, while others were more like plugs that were dislodged from the entry. The word for "rolled" (*proskyliō*) can be used of either "rolling away" or "dislodging."[461] The burial of bodies with some personal effects such as pottery, tools, or weapons was common, but the entrance to the tomb was not primarily to protect from grave robbers. Rather, it was used to protect the body from wild animals that would feed on carcasses.

Mary Magdalene and the other Mary (27:61). Prior to burial, out of respect and honor the corpse was watched over and washed.

Arrangements for a Guard at the Tomb (27:62–66)

The next day, the one after Preparation Day (27:62). The expression "Preparation Day" was a common expression for the day preceding the Sabbath (cf. Mark 15:42), that is, Friday, when the people made their preparations for the Sabbath. Therefore, the events Matthew now narrates occur on the day after the Preparation Day, another expression for "the Sabbath."

The chief priests and the Pharisees went to Pilate (27:62). As long as they did not travel more than a day's journey or enter the residence of the governor (John 18:28), the Jewish leaders would not defile the Sabbath (cf. Acts 1:12). Exodus 16:29 set a standard for travel on the Sabbath, admonishing people not to go out so that they would observe the Sabbath rest. The Qumran community interpreted the admonition to mean that a person "could not walk more than one thousand cubits outside the city" (CD 10:21), while the rabbis allowed a combination of a thousand cubits to travel a distance of two thousand cubits (*m. Soṭah* 5:3; see comments on 12:1).

Take a guard. . . . Go, make the tomb as secure as you know how" (27:65). An earlier contingent of Roman military had been assigned to the temple authorities for security, which had been used for the arrest of Jesus (cf. 27:47). This is the same guard troop Pilate indicates the Jewish officials are to use to make the tomb secure. The expression rendered as a charge, "Take a guard," may be a statement, "You have a guard" (NASB, NRSV), indicating that they are authorized to use the troops for this security assignment. The Jewish officials were not authorized to use the troops except for the purposes the Roman governor authorized.

They . . . made the tomb secure by putting a seal on the stone and posting the guard (27:66). After a family placed the body of one of its members in a burial recess in the tomb, a stone was placed over the entrance, and it was often sealed with clay.[462] However, the "seal" here seems to be more of an official security device, so it is more likely an apparatus such as a cord attached to both the stone that blocks the entrance and to the rock face of the tomb, with wax imprinted with the Roman seal anchoring both ends, so that any tampering can be detected (cf. Dan. 6:17). The military contingent standing guard also acts as a security seal.

The Women Followers Discover an Empty Tomb (28:1–7)

Matthew's concluding chapter climaxes the amazing story of Jesus Messiah. He was conceived in a miraculous manner as the Savior of his people. He lived a sensational life in the power of the Spirit, announcing the arrival of the kingdom of heaven. But he was tragically betrayed by his own people and crucified by the Roman government. Will that be the end of the story? Indeed not! On the third day after his crucifixion, Jesus Messiah is found missing from his grave! Various explanations have been set forth, but Matthew tells in convincing fashion that the only explanation for the empty tomb is that Jesus has been raised, just as he predicted. The angels announce the resurrection, his women followers are the first to witness both the empty tomb and the risen Jesus, and all of his followers now have the commission to proclaim the invitation to enter into a relationship with the risen Jesus as his disciples.

Mary Magdalene and the other Mary went to look at the tomb (28:1). The same women who courageously witnessed Jesus' gruesome crucifixion and burial observe the Sabbath from sundown Friday until Saturday evening, after which they purchase materials to continue preparing Jesus' body for burial (cf. Mark 16:1). At sunrise they intend to visit the tomb. Although there was a practice in the ancient world for family members to visit a tomb three days after the funeral to make certain that the person was dead (*b. Sem.* 8:1), no mention is made of this expectation. The military had made certain of Jesus' death on the cross (John 19:32). Instead, consistent with Jewish burial practices, the women have come to assist the surviving family as they finalize preparing the body for burial.

Mary Magdalene once again takes a prominent role, but also accompanying her is "the other Mary," the mother of James the younger and Joses (cf. Mark 16:2). A comparison of the various Gospel accounts points to the following women who attended Jesus at the cross and those who visit the tomb: (1) Mary Magdalene, (2) the "other Mary" (the mother of James the younger and Joses), (3) Salome (the mother of James and John the sons of Zebedee), (4) Jesus' mother, Mary, (5) Joanna, wife of Chuza, (6) Susanna, and several other unnamed women.[463]

A violent earthquake (28:2). One of the chief geological characteristics of Palestine has been its proneness to earthquakes, especially because the Jordan Rift Valley is part of a large fault zone that stretches northward from the entrance of the Gulf of Aqaba for over 683 miles to the foot of the Taurus range.[464]

Rolled back the stone and sat on it (28:2). The entrances to burial tombs were sealed in a variety of ways, including a plug-like stone inserted into the tomb opening,[465] but also as here, a cylindrical stone rolled up a trough, which was wedged open while a body was being attended inside the tomb.

His appearance was like lightning, and his clothes were white as snow (28:3). The brilliance of the angel of the Lord is often associated with descriptions of lightning.[466] The white clothing is typical to indicate angelic brilliant purity. The appearance of a fiery angel often terrified people (Judg. 13:19–20; *4 Ezra* 10:25–27).

He is not here; he has risen, just as he said. Come and see the place where he lay (28:6). Judaism hoped for the bodily resurrection of all people; now Jesus is the dramatic firstfruits of that expectation (1 Cor. 15:20, 23).

Go quickly and tell his disciples (28:7). Several of the women witnessed the sealing of the tomb[467]; they are among the first witnesses of the empty tomb and the resurrected Jesus.[468] They are designated by both the angel and Jesus to be the

CHAMBER INSIDE THE CHURCH OF THE HOLY SEPULCHRE

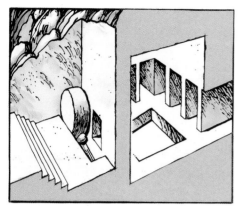

ORIGINAL TOMB CUT INTO SOLID BEDROCK

TOTAL DESTRUCTION BY THE ROMAN EMPEROR HADRIAN (After A.D. 135)
After suppressing the second Jewish Revolt Hadrian demolished the rock hillside down to about the level of the bench and built a temple to Venus over the area. Jerome stated that the sacred resurrection spot was occupied by a statue of Jupiter.

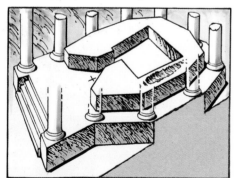

CONSTANTINE'S MONUMENTS
(After A.D. 326 when Christianity was official)
Following the Roman custom of building an "above ground" tomb for an important person, Constantine carved out all around the bench, lowered the floor and built a "small building" or "edicule". Around and above it he later erected a rotunda and dome. As reported by the traveler Egeria, by 395 pilgrims had chipped away pieces of the burial bench for souvenirs and it "began to resemble a trough". Marble slabs later covered it, as they do to this day.

Hadrian's Destruction and Constantine's Monuments

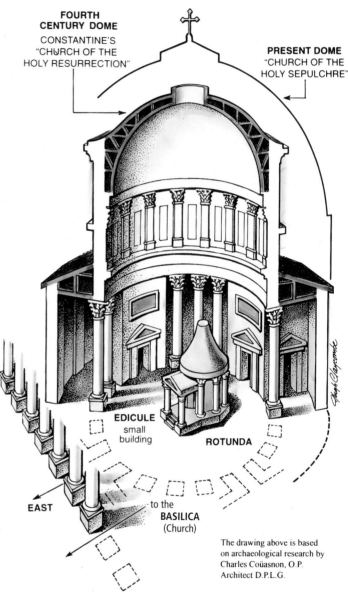

FOURTH CENTURY DOME
CONSTANTINE'S "CHURCH OF THE HOLY RESURRECTION"

PRESENT DOME "CHURCH OF THE HOLY SEPULCHRE"

EDICULE small building

ROTUNDA

EAST

to the **BASILICA** (Church)

The drawing above is based on archaeological research by Charles Coüasnon, O.P. Architect D.P.L.G.

Constantine's architects did not erect the dome exactly over the burial bench where Jesus' body had lain, but rather 48" to the South and 20" to the East. The focus point of the rotunda (the exact center) and centered under the dome was the outer edge of the entrance, precisely where the risen Christ first stepped out of the tomb into the world of the living. Thus the entire building complex commemorated the resurrection. Eastern churches still celebrate Easter at midnight, when closed doors are opened and pastors step out into the congregation proclaiming "Christ has Risen.

ones to carry their witness to the other disciples as the first to testify to the reality of the resurrection (28:10; Mark 16:7; John 20:17).

The Risen Jesus Appears to the Women (28:8–10)

They . . . clasped his feet and worshiped him (28:9). "Worship" can either indicate kneeling before an esteemed religious figure (e.g., 8:2) or, when linked with the action of grasping feet, indicate actual worship. By allowing this act of worship here and in 28:17, something that neither angels nor apostles allow,[469] Jesus accepts the acknowledgment of his deity. Only God is to be worshiped.

Go and tell my brothers to go to Galilee; there they will see me (28:10). Elsewhere Jesus' disciples are called his "brother, and sister, and mother" (12:49–50), indicating not only their relationship

to him but also their relationship to each other. They are now brothers and sisters of one family of faith. Galilee was the location of his boyhood, but even more important the central location of Jesus' earthly ministry (cf. 4:12ff.). Now Galilee continues as a central place of his earthly ministry, which will last forty days until his ascension (Acts 1:3).

The Conspiracy to Deny Jesus' Resurrection (28:11–15)

Some of the guards . . . reported to the chief priests everything that had happened (28:11). These Roman military personnel were assigned by Pilate to the temple authorities for security, which is why they report to them and not to Pilate (see 26:48; 27:65).

You are to say, "His disciples came during the night and stole him away while we were asleep" (28:13). It is unlikely

▶ The Resurrection of the Dead in Judaism and in Jesus

The expectation of a resurrection of the righteous to new life and the wicked to punishment is well attested in the Old Testament and Second Temple Jewish literature.[A-123] Resurrection in rabbinic Judaism refers to the concept of all the dead being brought back to life by God on the Day of Judgment, giving eternal life to the righteous and consigning the wicked to Gehenna. This was a central part of rabbinic belief from the first century after the destruction of the temple in A.D. 70, with the decline of the Sadducees, who rejected the notion of resurrection (Matt. 22:23; Acts 23:8) and the ascendance of Pharisaism, which placed resurrection as a central blessed hope.[A-124] Belief in the resurrection plays a prominent role in synagogue liturgy, including *Amidah* (Standing Prayer), with the *Shemoneh Esre* or *Tefillah* (Eighteen Benedictions, Prayers), which are recited in all worship services. The prayer of the second benediction praises God as one who resurrects the dead: "Who is like You, almighty, and who is compared to you, King, who kills and gives life and brings salvation to spring up? And You are reliable to give life to the dead. Praised are You, Lord, who gives life to the dead."[A-125]

But the resurrection of Jesus Messiah has even more far-reaching implications. With his resurrection Jesus is declared with power to be the Son of God (Rom. 1:2–6), through whom all peoples of the world now gain access to salvation through his sacrifice on the cross. With his resurrection, the age of the gospel of salvation is inaugurated with the sending of the Spirit of God at Pentecost. In his life, death, and resurrection, Jesus is the exemplar of the new people who will be regenerated and transformed into his image.[A-126]

that all of the guards would have been asleep on guard duty, because the penalty for falling asleep while on duty could be execution.[470] Further, rolling the stone away would surely have awakened at least some of the guards. And how did they know what had happened to the body if they were asleep? Besides these factors, the disciples had not had sufficient courage to attend the crucifixion and had even denied him, which makes it most unlikely that they would have mounted up a plot to steal Jesus' body from a well-guarded tomb. To concoct such a dubious story indicates the desperation of the religious leaders, but the religious leaders were desperate to hide what really happened.

The soldiers took the money and did as they were instructed (28:15). Military personnel are trained to do as ordered without asking questions of their superiors. These soldiers knew well enough the truth, but they could not have known the deep significance of the threat to the religious establishment, nor of the deep religious significance of the empty tomb.

This story has been widely circulated among the Jews to this very day (28:15). Matthew writes upwards of thirty years after these events, which indicates an active attempt to counteract the increasingly widespread declaration that Jesus had been raised from the dead in vindication of his claim to be the Messiah. Nearly a century later the rumor was still circulating among the Jews, as is evident in the writings of Justin Martyr (*Dialogue with Trypho* 108.2). The famous "Nazareth Decree," a stone slab with a decree from Caesar (Claudius?) warning of capital punishment for those violating tombs, points to the seriousness with which disturbing graves and moving dead bodies was held in the ancient world. It may also give some insight to the events in Matthew's narrative, if it was erected (as some propose) in A.D. 50 in Nazareth in response to the controversy between Jews and Christians about Jesus' empty tomb.[471]

The Galilean Appearance and Great Commission (28:16–20)

The eleven disciples went to Galilee, to the mountain where Jesus had told them to go (28:16). Jesus' and the disciples'

R E F L E C T I O N S

MANY SCHOLARS CONSIDER GOD'S CHOICE OF WOMEN as the first witnesses of Jesus' resurrection to be one of the bedrock truths of the resurrection narratives and the historicity of the resurrection itself. It is unlikely that any Jew would have created such a story as fiction, for a variety of reasons.

(1) Because of the debated status of a woman in Judaism at the time, there was disagreement among some of the rabbis as to the acceptability of a woman giving testimony in a court of law. This would make it much less likely that a Jew would fictionalize a woman's testimony in the case of Jesus' resurrection.[A-127]

(2) The cowardly picture painted of the men hiding away in Jerusalem, while the women boldly carry out their responsibilities to prepare Jesus' body for burial, would certainly offend the sensibilities of Jewish readers and doubtless would not have been recorded unless it were true.

(3) The listing of the names of the women weighs against being fiction, because these women were known in early Christian fellowship and would not have easily been associated with a false account.

(4) Jesus' appearances to these women with debated status lend credibility to the account, because again, they would be unlikely selections for a fictionalized account trying to be understood as believable.

For these reasons and more, the selection of women as the first witnesses yields high credibility to the resurrection narratives and to the resurrection itself.[A-128] It is vitally important for us to build our faith on the solid foundation of the historically verifiable truth of the resurrection of Jesus Christ.

familiarity with Galilee and their regular retreat to the hills[472] to escape the press of the crowds implies that there had been a prearranged meeting place. Mount Tabor has been the traditional site associated with this appearance, but for the same reasons that it was likely not the site of the Transfiguration (see comments on 17:1ff.), it is likely not the scene of this resurrection appearance. Rather, Jesus has arranged to meet with the disciples at some spot known to them in the many hills surrounding the Sea of Galilee.

When they saw him, they worshiped him; but some doubted (28:17). The Eleven, who had received at least two or three appearances from the risen Jesus prior to this in Jerusalem, are prepared to worship him. However, those disciples in Galilee who have not yet seen the risen Jesus (cf. "brothers" in 28:10), much like Thomas prior to his experience with the risen Jesus (John 20:24–29), doubt until Jesus appears to them bodily. This historical reminiscence by Matthew stresses the historicity of Jesus' resurrection, which was not met by gullible enthusiasm, but by logical hesitancy until people were convinced by facts. This may well be an allusion to the group of more than five hundred persons to whom the apostle Paul states Jesus appeared, most of whom were still alive when he wrote (1 Cor. 15:6).

All authority in heaven and on earth has been given to me (28:18). In his earthly ministry Jesus had declared his authority as the Son of Man to forgive sin (9:6) and to reveal the Father (11:27). Now as the risen Messiah he has been given all authority, glory, and power, who is rightly worshiped by all peoples and nations and whose dominion and kingdom last forever (Dan. 7:13–14).

Therefore go and make disciples of all nations (28:19). Disciples of a significant master were a common phenomenon in the ancient world, but throughout his ministry Jesus had developed a unique form of discipleship for those who would follow him. He breaks through a variety of barriers—gender, ethnic, religious, social, economic, and so on—by calling all peoples into a personal discipleship relationship with himself. Being a disciple of Jesus is not primarily an academic endeavor like the Pharisees (e.g., 22:16), nor even a commitment to a great prophet like John the Baptist (e.g., 9:14). A disciple of Jesus has come to him for salvation and eternal life and will always be only a disciple.

Baptizing them (28:19). Purity washings were common among the various sects in Israel, whether for entrance to the temple or for daily rituals. Proselyte baptism increasingly indicated conversion from paganism to Judaism. But Jesus' form of baptism is unique. It is the symbol of conversion of discipleship, indicating a union and new identity with Jesus Messiah, who had died and been raised to new life (cf. Rom. 6:1–4).

In the name of the Father and of the Son and of the Holy Spirit (28:19). Jews were

MIQVEH

The pools were used for Jewish ritual purity washings. This miqveh was discovered in the excavations near Herod's palace in Roman Jericho.

not baptized in the name of a person. Baptism in the "name" (note the singular) of the Father, Son, and Holy Spirit associates the three as personal distinctions, an early indication of the Trinitarian Godhead and an overt proclamation of Jesus' deity.

Teaching them to obey everything I have commanded you (28:20). Access to education under an esteemed rabbi was normally reserved for privileged men in rabbinic Judaism. Some rabbis denied young girls even the basics of Torah instruction, such as Eliezer who said: "If any man gives his daughter a knowledge of the Law it is as though he taught her lechery" (*m. Soṭah* 3:4). But Jesus once again breaks down barriers to indicate that *all* of his disciples—women and men, Gentile and Jew, poor and rich—are to be taught to obey everything he has commanded. But the emphasis is not simply on acquisition of knowledge. The goal of instructing new disciples of Jesus is obedience to what he has commanded, so that their lives increasingly become like their Master (10:24–25). What Jesus has done

ANNOTATED BIBLIOGRAPHY

Blomberg, Craig L. *Matthew: An Exegetical and Theological Exposition of Holy Scripture, NIV Text*. NAC 22. Nashville: Broadman, 1992.

This commentary serves a valuable purpose for pastors and lay teachers because it is brief, yet based on sound scholarship.

Carson, Donald A. "Matthew." Pages. 3–599 in vol. 8, *EBC*. Grand Rapids: Zondervan, 1984.

For many years this was the best evangelical, exegetical commentary on Matthew. While it is somewhat dated, it deserves a prominent place of reference for study, teaching, and preaching on Matthew.

Davies, W. D., and Dale C. Allison Jr. *A Critical and Exegetical Commentary on the Gospel According to Saint Matthew*. ICC. 3 vols., rev. ed. Edinburgh: T. & T. Clark, 1988, 1991, 1997.

This 3-volume set surfaces all possible interpretations of the text from a historical-critical perspective. It discusses the Jewish cultural and historical issues, but one must weigh carefully its critical orientation.

Hagner, Donald A. *Matthew*. WBC 33 A-B. 2 vols. Dallas: Word, 1993, 1995.

Hagner has provided the most comprehensive exegetical commentary on Matthew from a professedly evangelical perspective. The commentary requires the basic use of Greek, but is not burdensome. His discussion of background issues is broadly informed.

Keener, Craig S. *A Commentary on the Gospel of Matthew*. Grand Rapids: Eerdmans, 1999.

This is a valuable commentary for discussing historical, social/cultural backgrounds to Matthew's Gospel. Keener comments on the text from a theological perspective, adding many helpful devotional insights. Additionally, he has many extensive excurses that go into depth on background issues.

Morris, Leon. *The Gospel According to Matthew*. Pillar Commentaries. Grand Rapids: Eerdmans, 1992.

Morris has a classic, genuine grasp of the meaning of the text and communicates in a warm, pastoral fashion. Recommended for pastors and teachers.

Rousseau, John J. K., and Rami Arav. *Jesus and His World: An Archaeological and Cultural Dictionary*. Minneapolis: Fortress, 1995.

The authors have compiled a wealth of valuable material, although at many points are unduly critical of conservative conclusions.

Wilkins, Michael J. *Matthew*. NIVAC. Grand Rapids: Zondervan, forthcoming.

This is a commentary for pastors and informed laypersons that combines analysis of the original meaning of the text with discussion of biblical theology and suggestions for contemporary application.

_____. *Following the Master: A Biblical Theology of Discipleship*. Grand Rapids: Zondervan, 1992.

This is an extensive discussion of the Hellenistic and Jewish backgrounds to discipleship, leading to a full discussion of a biblical theology of discipleship to Jesus.

in making disciples of his first followers, succeeding generations of the church will do in the making of new disciples of Jesus.

Surely I am with you always, to the very end of the age (28:20). Jesus' entrance into history is encapsulated in the name Immanuel, "God with us" (1:23), and his abiding presence with his disciples throughout history is pronounced in his concluding assurance, "I am with you always." A true Israelite would proclaim only God to be eternal and omnipresent, so here Matthew records a concluding claim by Jesus to his deity, as he is with his disciples forever.

CHAPTER NOTES

Main Text Notes

1. Tacitus, *Annals* 1.4.
2. Ibid.
3. A study that is still valuable for establishing this thesis is Édouard Massaux, *The Influence of the Gospel of Saint Matthew on Christian Literature before Saint Irenaeus, Book 1: The First Ecclesiastical Writers*, trans. Norman J. Belval and Suzanne Hecht; ed. Arthur J. Bellinzoni (New Gospel Studies 5/1; 1950; Macon, Ga.: Mercer, 1990).
4. E.g., 1:22–23; 2:4–5, 15, 17, 23; 5:17–20.
5. See 16:18; 18:15–20; cf. 28:20.
6. E.g., Luke 1:31; 3:21, 23; Matt. 1:21.
7. Heb. *māšiah*.; Aram. *mêšiham*, "anointed."
8. See Marshall D. Johnson, *The Purpose of Biblical Genealogies*, 2d. ed. (SNTSMS 8; Cambridge: Cambridge Univ. Press, 1988).
9. E.g., Ruth 4:12–22; 1 Chron. 1:34; 2:1–15; 3:1–24.
10. E.g., Josephus, *Life* 1 §6; idem, *Ag. Ap.* 1.6–10 §§28–56.
11. *Gen. Rab.* 98:8; *y. Taʿan.* 4:2.
12. Cf. 2 Sam. 5:14; Matt. 1:6; Luke 3:32.
13. Cf. 22:41–46; 2 Sam. 7:12–16; Ps. 89:19–29, 35–37; 110:1–7; 132:11–12.
14. E.g., 1 Chron. 1:39; 2:3–4, 16, 18, 24, 26, 29, 48–49; 3:9, etc.
15. See Moshe Idel, *Kabbalah: New Perspectives* (New Haven, Conn.: Yale Univ. Press, 1990).
16. Cf. Lev. 20:10; 22:23ff.; Deut. 22:13–21.
17. Gen. 21:17; 22:15–18; Ex. 3:2ff.; Judg. 6:11ff.
18. Cf. Zech. 1:8–17; Luke 1:26; *1 En.* 6:7; 8:3–4; 69:1.
19. See Larry W. Hurtado, *One God, One Lord: Early Christian Devotion and Ancient Jewish Monotheism* (Philadelphia: Fortress, 1988), 71–92; Carol A. Newsom, "Gabriel," *ABD*, 2:863; also Carol A. Newsom and Duane F. Watson, "Angel," *ABD*, 1:248–55.
20. Ovid, *Metam.* 9.685–701; Tacitus, *Annals* 2.14.
21. Natural (Eccl. 5:3), divine (Gen. 28:12; Dan. 2:19), evil (Deut. 13:1, 2; Jer. 23:32).
22. Gen. 37:5–11; Num. 12:6; Job 33:15–17; Dan. 7:1–28.
23. Cf. 1:20; 2:12, 13, 19, 22; 27:19.
24. Cf. Ps. 130:8; *Pss. Sol.* 18:3–5.
25. Gen. 24:43; Ex. 2:8; Ps. 68:25.
26. *Pseudo-Phocylides* 186 (c. 100 B.C.–A.D. 100).
27. Josephus, *Ag. Ap.* 2.25 §§202–203.
28. Josephus *Ant.* 18.9.2, 5, §§318–19, 340.
29. Suetonius, *Vesp.* 5.
30. Josephus (*J.W.* 3.8.9 §§399–408; 6.5.4 §§310–15) and Tacitus (*Hist.* 5:13) make similar mention of this widespread expectation (the debate includes whether these Roman historians read Josephus).
31. E.g., CD 7:18–26; 4QTest. 9–13.
32. 2 Peter 1:19; Rev. 22:16; cf. 2:28.
33. Suetonius, *Nero* 13; cf. Dio Cassius, *Rom. Hist.* 63.1.7.
34. See Josephus, *Ant.* 14.13.3–10 §§335–69; 17.2.1 §23.
35. *Nomikos*; cf. 23:4, Luke 11:45–46.
36. Ruth 4:11–21; 1 Sam. 17:12.
37. John S. Holladay, Jr., "House, Israelite," *ABD*, 3:313; Rousseau and Arav, "House," *Jesus and His World*, 128–31.
38. Gen. 43:11–15; 1 Sam. 9:7–8; 1 Kings 10:1–2.
39. *Libanos*; Lev. 2:1; 14:7; Neh. 13:9.
40. W. E. Shewell-Cooper, "Frankincense," *ZPEB*, 2:606–7.
41. Est. 2:13; Ps. 45:8; Prov. 7:17; Song 3:6.
42. Kjeld Nielsen, "Incense," *ABD*, 3:404–9; Victor H. Matthews, "Perfumes and Spices," *ABD*, 5:226–28; Joel Green, "Burial of Jesus," *DJG*, 88–92.
43. Gen. 12:10; 42:1–2; 1 Kings 11:40; 2 Kings 25:26; Zech. 10:10.
44. E.g., Ps. 78; 81; 105–106; Jer. 2:6; 7:22–25; Ezek. 20:1–20; Mic. 6:1–4.
45. Josephus, *Ant.* 17.8.1 §§188–89. Herod's grandson, Agrippa I (10 B.C.–A.D. 44; Acts 12, called Herod) and great-grandson Agrippa II (c. A.D. 28–93; Acts 25–26) continued Herod's influence in Palestine through much of the first century.

46. Josephus, *Ant.* 17.9.3 §§213–18; idem, *J.W.* 2.6.2 §§88–90.

47. Josephus, *J.W.* 2.7.3 §111.

48. The earliest extant reference is by Julius Africanus (A.D. 170–240), as cited by Eusebius (*Eccl. Hist.* 1.7.14).

49. James F. Strange, "Nazareth (Place)," *ABD*, 4.1050–51.

50. Cf. 21:11; 26:71. For a good general overview of the terms and various other interpretations, see A. F. Walls, "Nazarene," *Illustrated Bible Dictionary*, 2:1060–61, and J. W. Charley, "Nazareth," *Illustrated Bible Dictionary*, 2:1061–63.

51. E.g., Isa. 4:2; 53:2; Jer. 23:5; 33:15; Zech. 3:8; 6:12; 1QH 14:15; 15:19; 16:5–10 [=1QH 6:15; 7:19; 8:5–10]; 4QIsaᵃ 3:15–26 (some of these use *ṣemaḥ*, not *neṣer*, though the meaning is essentially the same). See Marinus de Jonge, "Messiah," *ABD*, 4:777–88.

52. 4QFlor 1:10–12.

53. Ps. 22:6–8, 13; 69:8, 20–21; Isa. 11:1; 49:7; 53:2–3, 8; Dan. 9:26; the theme especially culminates in Isa. 52–53.

54. E.g., Ex. 19:1ff.; 1 Kings 17:2–3; 19:3–18; 1 Macc. 5. See Joseph Patrich, "Hideouts in the Judean Wilderness," *BAR* 15.5 (Sept./Oct. 1989): 32–42. For an overview of these groups, see Richard A. Horsley and John S. Hanson, *Bandits, Prophets, and Messiahs: Popular Movements at the Time of Jesus* (Minneapolis: Winston, 1985).

55. See Ben Witherington III, "John the Baptist," *DJG*, 384; John P. Meier, *A Marginal Jew: Rethinking the Historical Jesus* (ABRL; New York: Doubleday, 1994), 2:49–52; Darrell L. Bock, *Luke* (BECNT; Grand Rapids: Baker, 1994), 1:198; Rousseau and Arav, *Jesus and His World*, 80–82, 262; Todd S. Beall, *Josephus' Description of the Essenes Illustrated by the Dead Sea Scrolls* (SNTSMS 58; Cambridge: Cambridge Univ. Press, 1988).

56. Cf. 12:28; 19:24; 21:31, 43; Mark 10:24–25; Luke 18:24–25.

57. E.g., *m. Ber.* 2:2, 5.

58. E.g., 1 Macc. 3:18–19; 4:10; 12:15; *m. ᵓAbot* 1:3, 11.

59. Cf. Josephus, *J.W.* 1.24.3 §480.

60. Cf. Gen. 37:34; 2 Sam. 3:31; 2 Kings 6:30; Heb. 11:37.

61. Cf. Neh. 9:1; Jer. 6:26.

62. CD 12:13–15.

63. See the interesting presentations by G. S. Cansdale, "Locust," *ZPEB*, 3.948–50; Edwin Firmage, "Zoology (Animal Profiles): Locusts; Bees," *ABD*, 6:1150.

64. For a discussion of the religious and social dynamic addressed to the general audience, see Robert L. Webb, *John the Baptizer and Prophet: A Socio-Historical Study* (JSNTSup 62; Sheffield: JSOT, 1991), 289–300.

65. Cf. Isa. 64:1; Ezek. 1:1; John 1:51; Acts 7:56; 10:11.

66. Cf. 4QFlor 1:10–13; 4QpsDanᵃ. See Ben Witherington III, *The Christology of Jesus* (Minneapolis: Fortress, 1990), 148–55.

67. BAGD, 646. This is true as well for the noun *peirasmos*, which can mean either "temptation" or "test."

68. Ex. 24:18; Deut. 9:25; 1 Kings 19:8; Ezek. 4:6. See Horst Balz, "τεσσεράκοντα," *TDNT*, 8:135–39; R. A. H. Gunner, "Number," *IBD*, 2:1098–1100.

69. Cf. Josephus, *Ant.* 15.11.5 §§411–13.

70. Josephus, *Ant.* 18.5.2 §§116–19.

71. Josephus, *J.W.* 3.10.8 §520.

72. For an excellent archaeological overview of the history of Capernaum, see John C. H. Laughlin, "Capernaum: From Jesus' Time and After," *BAR* 19.4 (May 1993): 55–61, 70; Bargil Pixner, *With Jesus Through Galilee According to the Fifth Gospel* (Israel: Corazin, 1992), 35.

73. Mendel Num, "Ports of Galilee: Modern Drought Reveals Harbors from Jesus' Time," *BAR* 25.4 (July/August 1999): 19–31, 64.

74. E.g., Pixner, *With Jesus Through Galilee*, 33–35.

75. For full description and illustrations, see Mendel Nun, *The Sea of Galilee and Its Fishermen in the New Testament* (Kibbutz Ein Gev: Kinneret Sailing Co., 1989), 23–37; idem, "Cast Your Net Upon the Waters: Fish and Fishermen in Jesus' Time," *BAR* 19.4 (July/August 1993): 52–53.

76. *m. ᵓAbot* 1:6, 16

77. See Martin Hengel, *The Charismatic Leader and His Followers* (1968; ET; New York: Crossroad, 1981), 42–57; Wilkins, *Following the Master*, 100–109, 124–25.

78. Josephus, *J.W.* 2.11.10 §645.

79. Accounts that Josephus gives of traversing the lake with soldiers confirm these numbers: Josephus, *Life* 9 §32; idem, *J.W.* 2.21.8–9 §§636–641.

80. For the fascinating story of the discovery and excavation of the boat by the lead excavator, see Shelley Wachsmann, *The Sea of Galilee Boat: An Extraordinary 2000 Year Old Discovery* (New York: Plenum, 1995).

81. *Sagēnē*; cf. 13:47–48.

82. This most likely was the kind that Peter and his men use in Luke 5:1–11 and John 21:1–14 (Nun, *The Sea of Gaililee and its Fishermen*, 16–44). The general term for net, *diktyon*, is used in all of the fishing accounts (Matt. 4:20, 21; Mark 1:18, 19; Luke 5:2, 4–6; John 21:6, 8, 11). Matthew used a different term (*sagemnem*) for the "dragnet" in 13:47.

83. See Carl G. Rasmussen, *Zondervan NIV Atlas of the Bible* (Grand Rapids: Zondervan, 1989), 166–67. Josephus' statistic of 15,000 people living in even the smallest of the 204 cities and villages (Josephus, *J.W.* 3.3.2 §43; cf. idem, *Life* 45 §235), implying that Galilee has three million people, is probably an exaggeration.

84. Matt. 4:23; 9:35; 24:14.

85. Josephus, *Ant.* 12.4.9 §222; idem, *J.W.* 3.3.3 §§46–47.

86. Pixner, *With Jesus Through Galilee*, 34. Pixner also equates the place with Magadan (see comments on 15:39).

87. Cf. 13:1–2; 15:29; 24:3–4; 26:55.

88. E.g., Eph. 1:18; Col. 1:12; Heb. 9:15.

89. Ps. 24:3–6; 73:1; Prov. 22:11.

90. Cf. Ps. 28:3; Eccl. 3:8; Isa. 26:3.

91. See the interesting discussion of this view by a soils professor, Eugene P. Deatrick, "Salt, Soil, Savior," *BA* 25 (1962): 41–48.

92. Pliny, *Nat. Hist.* 31.102.

93. See K. M. Campbell, "The New Jerusalem in Matt. 5:14," *SJT* 31 (1978): 335–63; Rousseau and Arav, *Jesus and His World*, 127–28.

94. Cf. Mark 4:21; Luke 11:33.

95. Cf. *m. Šabb.* 16:1. See John Rea, "Lamp," *ZPEB*, 3:865–66, for pictures of excavated lamps from patriarchal times to the New Testament era; cf. Carol Meyers, "Lampstand," *ABD*, 4:141–43.

96. Cf. Matt. 7:12; 11:13; 22:40; Luke 24:27, 44; Rom. 3:21.

97. *m. ʾAbot* 2:1; 4:2.

98. *b. Mak.* 23b.

99. 2 Kings 16:3; 21:6; Jer. 32:35; cf. 7:31–32; 19:1–13.

100. For a fine discussion and numerous illustrations of various coinage see D. H. Wheaton, "Money," *IBD*, 2:1018–23; John W. Betlyon, "Coinage," *ABD*, 1:1076–89; Rousseau and Arav, *Jesus and His World*, 55–61.

101. Lev. 20:10; cf. Deut. 22:22–24.

102. See the attitude of the Essenes toward oaths recorded in Josephus, *J.W.* 28.6 §135; see also Sir. 23:9, 11; Philo, *Decalogue* 84–95.

103. See Ex. 21:24; Lev. 24:20; Deut. 19:21.

104. Cf. *m. B. Qam.* 8:6.

105. Ex. 22:26–7; Deut. 24:12; Ezek. 18:7; Amos 2:8. For a good overview of ancient wardrobes, see Douglas R. Edwards, "Dress and Ornamentation," *ABD*, 2:232–38.

106. BAGD. For a helpful chart showing equivalent distances, see H. Wayne House, *Chronological and Background Charts of the New Testament* (Grand Rapids: Zondervan, 1981), 26.

107. See "Lend, Lending," *DBI*, 506–7.

108. See Ps. 5:4–5; cf. 45:7; Deut. 7:2; 30:7.

109. Using the translation of Geza Vermes, *The Dead Sea Scrolls in English* (2d ed.; New York: Penguin, 1975), 72. Note also 1QS 1.3–4.

110. Gen. 6:9; 17:1; Deut. 18:13; 2 Sam. 22:24–27.

111. E.g., 1 Cor. 14:20; Eph. 4:13; Heb. 5:14; 6:1.

112. See Acts 9:36; 10:2; 24:17; cf. Tobit 1:3, 16; 4:7–8; Sir. 7:10.

113. *m. Šeqal.* 2:1.

114. E.g., Diogenes Laertius, *Lives of Eminent Philosophers* 7.160.

115. Josephus, *Ant.* 14.4.3 §65.

116. Deut. 14:1; 32:6; Ps. 103:13; Jer. 3:4; 31:9; Hos. 11:1.

117. E.g., *Jub.* 1:24, 28; 19:29; *Jos. Asen.* 12:14; Sir. 23:1, 4; Wisd. Sol. 2:16–20; 14:3; Tobit 13:4; 4Q372; 1QH 9:35 [17:35]. See Geza Vermes, *The Religion of Jesus the Jew* (Minneapolis: Fortress, 1993), 152–83; see "Father, God as," *DJBP*, 224.

118. Cited in James H. Charlesworth, "A Caveat on Textual Transmission and the Meaning of *Abba*: A Study of the Lord's Prayer," in *The Lord's Prayer and other Prayer Texts from the Greco-Roman Era*, ed. James H. Charlesworth with Mark Harding and Mark Kiley (Valley Forge, Pa.: Trinity, 1994), 7.

119. Cf. 5:16, 45, 48; 6:26, 33; 7:11.

120. Cited in James D. G. Dunn, "Prayer," *DJG*, 617.

121. 1 Cor. 16:22; *Did.* 10.6; cf. Rev. 22:20.

122. See Grant R. Osborne, *The Hermeneutical Spiral: A Comprehensive Introduction to Biblical Interpretation* (Downers Grove, Ill.: InterVarsity, 1991), 100–101, 108.

123. Ex. 16:4; Deut. 8:16; 1 Peter 1:7.

124. *b. Ber.* 60b, cited in Joachim Jeremias, *New Testament Theology: The Proclamation of Jesus* (New York: Scribner's, 1971), 202.

125. The ending that many Christians are accustomed to pray—"For yours is the kingdom, and the power, and the glory forever, Amen"—is not included in the oldest manuscripts, but it is found in many old ones. The earliest probably dates back to the late second century. Although it was not originally included in Matthew's Gospel, it is in line with many other scriptural concepts (e.g., 1 Chron. 29:11).

126. Lev. 16:29–34; 23:26–32.

127. BDB, 776, 847; see John E. Hartley, *Leviticus* (WBC 4; Dallas: Word, 1992), 242; R. Laird Harris, "Leviticus," *EBC*, 2:591.

128. E.g., 1QS 10:18–19; Sir. 31:8–11.

129. E.g., eyes become dimmed; Gen. 27:1; 48:18. See D. C. Allison Jr., "The Eye Is the Lamp of the Body (Matthew 6.22–23 = Luke 11.34–36)," *NTS* 33 (1987), 61–83.

130. This expression occurs similarly in Matt. 20:15, where the literal expression "evil eye"

indicates envy (cf. NIV; see G. Harder, "πονηρός," *TDNT*, 6:555–56. So also Donald A. Hagner, *Matthew* (WBC 33; Dallas: Word, 1993), 1:158.

131. Marvin A. Powell, "Weights and Measures," *ABD*, 4:899.

132. Irene and Walter Jacob, "Flora," *ABD*, 2:813; Pixner, *With Jesus Through Galilee*, 37.

133. See 1 Kings 10:1–29; 2 Chron. 9:1–28.

134. Ps. 37:2; 102:4, 11; 129:6; Isa. 40:6–8, quoted in 1 Peter 1:24–25; James 1:10; see "Grass," *DBI*, 348–49.

135. But for similar sayings, see Prov. 27:1; *b. Sanh.* 100b; *b. Ber.* 9a; Hagner, *Matthew*, 166.

136. See Michael J. Wilkins, "Prayer," *DLNT*, 941–48.

137. For discussion, see Firmage, "Zoology (Animal Profiles: D. Fish," *ABD*, 6:1146–47.

138. Jer. 6:13–15; 8:10–12; Ezek. 13:1–23; 22:27–29; Zeph. 3:1–4.

139. Josephus, *J.W.* 2.13.4 §259.

140. Josephus recounts stories of each of these: Theudas (*Ant.* 20.5.5 §§97–98), the Egyptian false prophet (*Ant.* 20.9.6 §§169–71; *J.W.* 2.14.5 §§261–63), and Jesus son of Hananiah (*J.W.* 6.5.3 §§300–309). For an overview of these groups, see Horsley and Hanson, *Bandits, Prophets and Messiahs*, 160–89.

141. Attributed to Elisha ben Abuyah in *Abot de-Rabbi Nathan* A, 24, 77; cited in Vermes, *Religion of Jesus the Jew*, 102.

142. Gordon Franz, "The Parable of the Two Builders," *Archaeology in the Biblical World* 3.1 (1995): 6–11.

143. A. N. Sherwin-White, *Roman Society and Roman Law in the New Testament* (Oxford: Clarendon, 1963), 123–24.

144. E.g., Luke 16:8 refers to "sons of light," and 1QM 17.8 refers to "sons of his truth" and "sons of his covenant."

145. Matt. 22:13; 5:29; cf. *4 Ezra* 7:93; *1 En.* 63:10.

146. See comments on 2:23.

147. E.g., Morna D. Hooker, "Did the Use of Isaiah 53 to Interpret His Mission Begin with Jesus?" in *Jesus and the Suffering Servant: Isaiah 53 and Christian Origins*, eds. William H. Bellinger Jr. and William R. Farmer (Harrisburg, Pa.: Trinity, 1998), 88–103.

148. David Hill, *The Gospel of Matthew* (NCBC; London: Marshall, Morgan and Scott, 1972), 161; e.g., *b. Sanh.* 98b: "Surely he hath borne our griefs and carried our sins, yet we did esteem him stricken with leprosy, and smitten of God and afflicted."

149. See Hengel, *Charismatic Leader*, 3–15.

150. See Wilkins, *Following the Master*, ch. 6.

151. Ex. 20:12; Deut. 5:16.

152. Cf. Tobit 4:3; 6:15.

153. See Freyne, *Galilee from Alexander the Great to Hadrian*; idem, "Galilee, Sea of," *ABD*, 2:900; Riesner, "Archeology and Geography," 37.

154. Nun, *The Sea of Galilee*, 16–44.

155. Wachsmann, *The Sea of Galilee Boat*, 326–28.

156. 2 Sam. 22:16; Ps. 18:15; 104:7; 106:9; Isa. 50:2; Nah. 1:4.

157. Josephus, *Life* 9 §42.

158. See Vassilios Tzaferis, "A Pilgrimage to the Site of the Swine Miracle," *BAR* 15.2 (March/April 1989): 44–51. This location best accounts for the variant readings in Mark and Luke.

159. Num. 19:11, 14, 16; Ezek. 39:11–15.

160. Lit. "diligent guards," a reference to the fallen angels (cf. *1 En.* 1–36).

161. Cf. Jude 6; Rev 20:10; *Jub.* 10:8–9; *T. Levi* 18:12; 1QS 3:24–24; 4:18–20.

162. Pixner, *With Jesus Through Galilee*, 35.

163. Josephus, *Ant.* 17.11.4 §319.

164. Cf. R. T. France, *Matthew: Evangelist and Teacher* (Grand Rapids: Zondervan, 1989), 70–74.

165. E.g., Philo, *Contempl. Life* 40–89; 1QSa 2.

166. Dennis E. Smith, "Table Fellowship," *ABD*, 6:302–4; see "Table Fellowship," *DJBP*, 613.

167. J. H. Harrop, "Tax Collector," *IBD*, 3:1520–21.

168. For background to the various uses of "sinner" in the Gospels, see Michael J. Wilkins, "Sinner," *DJG*, 757–60.

169. Ibid., 760.

170. Lee I. Levine, *The Ancient Synagogue: The First Thousand Years* (New Haven, Conn.: Yale Univ. Press, 2000), 402–3.

171. E.g., Gen. 22:5; Ex. 4:31; Deut. 26:10; Ps. 5:7.

172. 1 Sam. 24:9; 1 Kings 1:16, 23.

173. D. H. Trapnell, "Health, Disease and Healing," *IBD*, 2:619.

174. *m. Ketub.* 4:4; cf. *b. Moʾed Qat.* 22b–23a.

175. Gen. 50:10; 1 Sam. 31:13; Sir. 22:12.

176. "Sheep, Shepherd," *DBI*, 782–85.

177. Cf. Karl H. Rengstorf, "δώδεκα," *TDNT*, 2:326.

178. Cf. Gal. 1:17, 19; 1Cor. 9:1–5; 15:7; Eph. 2:19–22.

179. Barnabas in Acts 14:4, 14; Titus in 2 Cor. 8:23; Epaphroditus in Phil. 2:25; probably Timothy and Silas also in 1 Thess. 1:1 with 2:6; cf. Andronicus and Junias in Rom. 16:7. James the brother of Jesus seems to be included among the apostles in Jerusalem as a "pillar of the church" (Gal. 1:17; 2:9).

180. E.g., Gen. 12:2–3; 22:18.

181. Cf. John 15:21; 2 Tim. 3:12; 1 Peter 4:13–14.

182. *Baʿal zebub*, Heb. for "Lord of the flies."

183. βεελζεβούλ in most Greek MSS, βεεζεβούλ according to ℵ and B, βεελζεβούβ or βεελζεβυβ read by many non-Greek MSS.

184. Reflecting the Semitic *zbl* (lord/exalted one; or [exalted] abode, i.e., heaven).

185. See "Beelzebul," *DJBP*, 84.

186. E.g., Isa. 23:1–17; Jer. 25:22; 27:3–7; Ezek. 26:2–9; Joel 3:4–8; Zech. 9:2–4.

187. Gen. 18:16–19:29; Ezek. 16:48; cf. *m. Sanh.* 10.3.

188. A cubit was 17–18 inches, or the common length from elbow to tip of fingers. The formalized Jewish cubit was 17.5 inches.

189. Isa. 41:8–10; 44:1–3, 21; 45:4 [49:3?].

190. Isa. 42:1–4; 49:5–7.

191. See "Beelzebul," *DJBP*, 84.

192. Josephus, *Ant.* 8.2.5 §45–49; cf. "roots" in *J.W.* 7.6.3 §185.

193. Cf. *T. Moses* 10:1; Rev. 20:2.

194. James D. G. Dunn, "Sign," *IBD*, 3:1450.

195. The genitive "of Jonah" is an epexegetic genitive.

196. Cf. Gen. 42:17–18; 1 Sam. 30:12–13; 1 Kings 20:29; 2 Chron. 10:5, 12; Esth. 4:16; 5:1.

197. *b. Naz.* 5b; *m. Pesaḥ.* 4:2; cf. *y. Šabb.* 12a, 15, 17; cited in Gerhard Delling, "ἡμέρα," *TDNT*, 2:949–50.

198. Isa. 13:21; 34:14; Tobit 8:3; *1 En.* 10:4.

199. From earliest times the number seven also had sacred associations (Gen. 2:2; 4:24; 21:28; Ex. 20:10; Lev. 25:2–6, 8).

200. Charles R. Page, *Jesus and the Land* (Nashville: Abingdon, 1995), 85; Pixner, *With Jesus Through Galilee*, 40.

201. E.g., Matt. 5:14–15; 7:24–27; 9:16–17; 12:27–29, 43–45.

202. For an overview of the relationship to Jewish usage, see Vermes, *Religion of Jesus the Jew*, 90–97.

203. John W. Sider, *Interpreting the Parables: A Hermeneutical Guide to Their Meaning* (Grand Rapids: Zondervan, 1995), 88–89.

204. Judg. 6:11; Ruth 2:23; 2 Sam. 4:6.

205. Oded Borowski, "Agriculture," *ABD*, 1:97–98; idem, *Agriculture in Ancient Israel* (Winona Lake, Ind.: Eisenbrauns, 1987).

206. Some understand this to imply an extraordinary, superabundant, perhaps even miraculous crop, because typical Palestinian harvests yielded only about five to ten times the quantity sown; e.g., Joachim Jeremias, *The Parables of Jesus* (2d ed; New York: Scribner's, 1972), 149–51.

207. E.g., Job 15:8; Ps. 25:14; Prov. 3:32; Amos 3:7.

208. Cited in Vermes, *The Religion of Jesus the Jew*, 100.

209. "Yeast," *Encyclopædia Britannica Online*; J. D. Douglas, "Leaven," *IBD*, 2:891.

210. Nun, *The Sea of Galilee and its Fishermen*, 16–44.

211. The term is *mathēteuō*, which the NIV renders "has been instructed." The same verb occurs elsewhere in Matthew at 27:57; 28:19, and only in Acts 14:21 elsewhere in the New Testament. Each case should be translated, "become a disciple." See Michael J. Wilkins, *Discipleship in the Ancient World and Matthew's Gospel* (2d ed.; Grand Rapids: Zondervan, 1995), 160–63.

212. Josephus, *Ant.* 18.5.1 §109–115.

213. For a brief overview, see Harold W. Hoehner, "Herodian Dynasty," *DJG*, 322–25. For the most extensive treatment of the era, see idem, *Herod Antipas: A Contemporary of Jesus* (Grand Rapids: Zondervan, 1972; repr. 1980).

214. Cf. Josephus, *J.W.* 7.6.2 §§172–76.

215. Josephus, *Ant.* 18.5.1–2 §§112, 119.

216. For brief overviews, see F. F. Bruce, "Machaerus," *IBD*, 2:928–29; Stanislao Loffreda, "Machaerus," *ABD*, 4:457–58.

217. The term *korasion* in 14:11 is the diminutive "little girl."

218. Josephus, *Ant.* 18.6.10 §§225–39; cf. Acts 12.

219. Ibid., 13.14.2 §380.

220. Wilkins, *Following the Master*, 86–88, 253–56.

221. The Arabic *Et-Tabgha* is a corruption of the Greek *Heptapegon*.

222. Cited in Pixner, *With Jesus Through Galilee*, 36; cf. Bargil Pixner, "The Miracle Church at Tabgha on the Sea of Galilee," *BA* 48 (1985): 196–206.

223. Cf. Deut. 8:8; Ruth 2:17; Ezek. 4:9; cf. Philo, *Spec. Laws* 3.57.

224. See Dodo Joseph Shenhav, "Loaves and Fishes Mosaic Near Sea of Galilee Restored," *BAR* 10 (1984): 22–31.

225. Rudolf Bultmann/Dieter Lührmann, "φάντασμα," *TDNT*, 9:6.

226. For Matthew's portrait of Peter and his developing leadership role, see Wilkins, *Discipleship in the Ancient World*, 173–216, 264.

227. See Num. 34:11; Deut. 3:17; Josh. 12:3; 13:27.

228. Douglas R. Edwards, "Gennesaret," *ABD*, 2:963.

229. Samuel Sandmel, *Judaism and Christian Beginnings* (New York: Oxford, 1978), 103.

230. Danby, ed., *The Mishnah*, 446 n. 4.

231. Ibid., 446 n. 5.

232. Cf. Josephus, *Ant.* 13.10.6 §297.

233. Gen. 18:4; 19:2; 1 Sam. 25:41; cf. John 13:1–10.

234. *m. Yad.* 1:1.

235. Danby, *The Mishnah*, 778 n. 9.

236. See "Washing of Hands," *DJBP*, 667.

237. Danby, *The Mishnah*, 264 n. 1.

238. Ibid.

239. E.g., Isa. 23:1–17; Jer. 25:22; 27:3–7; Ezek. 26:2–9; Joel 3:4–8; Zech. 9:2–4.

240. E.g., *m. Qidd.* 1:3.

241. 1 Sam. 17:43; Ps. 22:16; Prov. 26:11. See "Dog," *DJBP*, 172; "Animals," "Dogs," *DBI*, 29, 213–14.

242. Gen. 12:3; see comments on Matt. 1:1; 8:5–13.

243. A. R. Millard, "Basket," *IBD*, 1:177–78; Pixner, *With Jesus Through Galilee*, 83.

244. Rainer Riesner, "Archaeology and Geography," *DJG*, 38.

245. See Pixner, *With Jesus Through Galilee*, 29, 73, 84.

246. So Robert H. Gundry, *Matthew: A Commentary on His Handbook for a Mixed Church Under Persecution* (2d ed.; Grand Rapids: Eerdmans, 1994), 322; Craig S. Keener, *A Commentary on the Gospel of Matthew* (Grand Rapids: Eerdmans, 1999), 420; Rousseau and Arav, *Jesus and His World*, 189–90.

247. Josephus, *J.W.* 2.21.8–10 §634–641; 3.9.7–3.10.5 §§443–503.

248. James F. Strange, "Magdala," *ABD*, 4:463–64.

249. See Shenhav, "Loaves and Fishes Mosaic Near Sea of Galilee Restored," 22–31.

250. James D. G. Dunn, "Sign," *IBD*, 3:1450.

251. Josephus records signs that warned of the destruction of Jerusalem. He believed God brought a star resembling a sword that stood over the city of Jerusalem, a comet that continued for a year, and a brilliant light that shone around the altar for half an hour (*J.W.* 6.5.1 §§288–292).

252. Josephus, *Ant.* 13.10.6 §298.

253. Cf. John 6:14; 7:40, 52; Acts 3:22; 7:37.

254. E.g., priests (1QRule of the Community [1QS] 9:11) and prophets (CD 2:12; 5:21–6:1; 1QM 11:7–8).

255. E.g., 1QRule of the Congregation (1QSa) 2:14, 20. See, e.g., Lawrence H. Schiffman, *The Eschatological Community of the Dead Sea Scrolls: A Study of the Rule of the Congregation* (SBLMS 38; Atlanta: Scholars, 1989).

256. *Pss. Sol.* 17:21.

257. 4QFlor 1:10–12. For an overview, see Marinus de Jonge, "Messiah," *ABD*, 4:777–88.

258. Joseph Fitzmyer, "Aramaic *Kepha'* and Peter's Name in the New Testament," in *To Advance the Gospel* (New York: Crossroad, 1981), 115.

259. Isa. 38:10; Wisd. Sol. 16:13; *3 Macc.* 5:51.

260. Job 38:17; Ps. 9:13; 107:18; cf. 1QH 6:24–26 [14:24–26].

261. See James D. Tabor, "Martyr, Martyrdom," *ABD*, 4:574–579; Arthur J. Droge and James D. Tabor, *A Noble Death: Suicide and Martyrdom Among Greeks and Romans, Jews and Christians in the Ancient World* (San Francisco: HarperSanFrancisco, 1992).

262. See comments on 8:19; cf. 12:38; 21:15. For an overview of these groups, see Brown, *The Death of the Messiah*, 1425–29.

263. Wilkins, *Discipleship in the Ancient World*, 116–24.

264. Cf. Matt. 13:41; 18:7; the cognate verb occurs in 11:6.

265. Plutarch, *Moralia* 554A/B; cf. 554D: "Every criminal condemned to death bears his cross on his back" (see comments on 27:26, 35). See also Martin Hengel, *Crucifixion in the Ancient World and the Folly of the Message of the Cross* (Philadelphia: Fortress, 1977), 77.

266. Ryken, et. al., "Cross," *DBI*, 184.

267. Ex. 34:29–35; cf. Dan. 12:3; 2 Esdras 7:97.

268. Cf. *As. Mos.*; *b. Soṭah* 13b.

269. Matt. 14:28–31; 15:15; 16:17–19; 17:24–27; 18:21.

270. Ex. 19:16; 20:18; 34:30; Deut. 4:33; 5:5, 23–27; Hab. 3:2–6, 16.

271. *m.ʿEd.* 8:7; cf. *m. B. Meṣiʿa* 3:5.

272. Mal. 4:5–6 (possibly a reference to Rev. 11:3–13?).

273. Cf. Josephus, *Ant.* 3.8.2 §§194–96.

274. John I. Durham, *Exodus* (WBC 3; Waco, Tex.: Word, 1987), 402–3; John W. Betlyon, "Coinage," *ABD*, 1:1076–89; Marvin A. Powell, "Weights and Measures," *ABD*, 6:897–908 (esp. 905–8).

275. See *m. Šeqal.* 1:3; 2:1; *y. Šeqal.* 6:1, 5; Josephus, *J.W.* 5.5.2 §200; idem, *Ant.* 18.9.1 §312–313.

276. Cf. Josephus, *Life* 12 §§62–63. Betlyon, "Coinage," 1089; Powell, "Weights and Measures," 905–8; Rousseau and Arav, *Jesus and His World*, 309–11; see "Tax Collectors" and "Taxes," *DJBP*, 618–19.

277. The negative particle *ou* is used in a question when an affirmative answer is expected, while *mē* is used when a negative response is expected; BDF §427.2 (p. 220).

278. Strange and Shanks, "Has the House Where Jesus Stayed in Capernaum Been Found?" 196.

279. Nun, "Cast Your Net," 46–56, 70.

280. Rousseau and Arav, *Jesus and His World*, 56; Archer, "Coins," 906.

281. Cf. Albrecht Oepke, "παῖς, παιδίον," *TDNT*, 5:639–40.

282. Ps. 127:3–5; 128:3–4; *Pss. Sol.* 1:3.

283. Josephus, *Ant.* 4.8.24 §§260–265.

284. E.g., Tobit 12:13–22; *1 En.* 100:5; *Jub.* 35:1; *T. Levi* 5:3.

285. E.g., Ps. 23; Isa. 53:6; Jer. 13:17; Zech. 10:3; 13:7.

286. E.g., Ps. 119:176; Isa. 53:6; Jer. 23:1–4; 50:6; Ezek. 34:1–30.

287. Edwin Firmage, "Zoology (Animal Profiles): Sheep," *ABD*, 6:1126–27; Keener, *Matthew* (1999), 452.

288. See *Rule of the Community* (1QS 5:24–6:1); cf. also CD 9:2–4.

289. Cf. *m. Sanh.* 1:1; *b. Ber.* 6a.

290. BDF §248.2, 130.

291. Josephus, *Ant.* 17.11.4 §§317–320.

292. Ex. 21:2–6; 7–11; Deut. 15:12–18.

293. See Karel van der Toorn, "Prison," *ABD,* 5:468–69.

294. E.g., *m. Soṭah.* 5:1; *m. Yebam.* 2:8.

295. E.g., Josephus, *J.W.* 2.8.13 §§160–161; 2.8.2 §120; Pliny, *Nat. Hist.* 5.73. See James C. VanderKam, *The Dead Sea Scrolls Today* (Grand Rapids: Eerdmans, 1994), 90–91.

296. *m. Yebam.* 8:4–6; cf. Deut. 23:1.

297. *b. Ber.* 55b.

298. See "Vine and Vineyard," *DJBP,* 657–58.

299. See comments on 17:24–27; 18:24–28; 22:19. Using the current minimum wage of $5.15 an hour in the United States in 2000, a common laborer would receive the equivalent of $41.20 a day.

300. Cf. Luke 8:3; Gal. 4:2.

301. Josephus, *Ant.* 6.11.9 §235.

302. Plato, *Gorgias,* 491e; cf. 492b; cited in H. W. Beyer, "διακονέω, διακονία, διάκονος," *TDNT,* 2:82.

303. E.g., *diakonos:* 2 Cor. 3:6; Eph. 3:7; Col. 1:23; *doulos:* Rom. 1:1; Gal. 1:10.

304. E.g., *diakonos:* Phoebe, Rom. 16:1; Tychicus, Eph. 6:21; Epaphras, Col. 1:23; *doulos:* Epaphras, Col. 4:12.

305. Cf. BAGD.

306. Cf. Sydney Page, "Ransom Saying," *DJG,* 660–62.

307. Matt. 21:17; cf. John 12:1–10.

308. See Scott T. Carroll, "Bethphage," *ABD,* 1:715.

309. Cf. *m. Menaḥ.* 7:3 [n. 11 in Danby]; 11:2.

310. Cf. D. A. Carson, "Matthew" (*EBC* 8; Grand Rapids: Zondervan, 1984), 437; Gundry, *Matthew,* 593.

311. Cf. Gundry, *Matthew,* 409–10.

312. See 2 Sam. 14:4; 2 Kings 6:26.

313. Cf. John 6:14; 7:40, 52; Acts 3:22; 7:37.

314. See *m. Mid.* 1:3; Josephus, *Ant.* 15.11.5 §§410–11. For discussion, see Rousseau and Arav, *Jesus and His World,* 304–9; Kathleen and Leen Ritmeyer, "Reconstructing the Triple Gate," *BAR* 15.6 (Nov./Dec. 1989): 49–53.

315. See Kathleen Ritmeyer, "A Pilgrim's Journey," *BAR* 15.6 (Nov./Dec. 1989): 43–45, for an informative insight to a journey into the temple. Also in the same issue, see Kathleen and Leen Ritmeyer, "Reconstructing Herod's Temple Mount in Jerusalem," *BAR* 15.6 (Nov./Dec. 1989): 23–42, for a painstaking overview of the specifics of the temple architecture.

316. The term "robber" (*lēstēs*) was not used for a common thief, but for one who was an insurrectionist, such as Barabbas and the two robbers between whom Jesus was crucified, who fought against the Roman occupation; cf. Michael J. Wilkins, "Barabbas," *ABD,* 1:607. This may be a subtle use of the term to indicate that the Temple authorities were insurrectionists against God's intended plan for the Temple.

317. For a discussion of the symbolism of the fig tree and Israel, see "Fig, Fig Tree," *DBI,* 283–84.

318. See Keener, *Matthew,* 506, for background and literature.

319. See "Vine and Vineyard," *DJBP,* 657–58.

320. See Rousseau and Arav, *Jesus and His World,* 328–32.

321. See "ḥatunnâ," *DJBP,* 275.

322. See Gundry, *Matthew,* 436–37.

323. E.g., Judg. 1; 8; Isa. 5:24; 1 Macc. 5:28; *T. Jud.* 5:1–5.

324. Gundry, *Matthew,* 439; W. D. Davies and Dale C. Allison Jr., *A Critical and Exegetical Commentary on the Gospel According to Saint Matthew* (ICC; Edinburgh: T. & T. Clark, 1997), 3:204 n. 53; Keener, *Matthew,* 522 n. 189.

325. See Keener, *Matthew,* 523.

326. Joachim Jeremias, "πολλοί," *TDNT,* 6:536–45.

327. Cf. Mark 12:13–17; Luke 20:20–26.

328. See Matt. 9:11; 12:38; 17:24; 19:16; 22:16, 24, 36.

329. Colin Brown, Norman Hillyer, "Tax, Tax Collector," *NIDNTT,* 3:751–59.

330. See Rousseau and Arav, *Jesus and His World,* 278.

331. Rousseau and Arav, *Jesus and His World,* 55–61.

332. E.g., 2 Macc. 7; *1 En.* 102; *2 Bar.* 49–51.

333. E.g., *m. Sanh.* 10:1; *b. Roš Haš.* 16b–17a.

334. The patriarchs are assumed to continue to enjoy the blessings of the covenant, even though they had been long deceased; cf. Gen. 24:12, 27, 48; 26:24; 28:13; 32:9; 46:1, 3–4; 48:15–16; 49:25; Carson, "Matthew," 462.

335. See Abraham Malamat, "Love Your Neighbor As Yourself," *BAR* 16.4 (July/Aug. 1990): 50–51.

336. See comments on 1:1; cf. 2 Sam. 7:12–14; Ps. 89:4; Isa. 11:1, 10; Jer. 23:5; cf. *Pss. Sol.* 17:21.

337. See comments on 1:1, 20; 9:27; 12:23; 15:22; 20:30–31; 29:9.

338. See Hagner, *Matthew,* 651.

339. For more on meal customs and seating, see comments on 26:20.

340. Levine, *The Ancient Synagogue,* 313–17.

341. Neusner and Green, "Rabbi," *DJBP,* 516; Levine, "The Sages and the Synagogue," in *The Ancient Synagogue,* 440–70.

342. For discussion of this distinction, see Levine, *The Ancient Synagogue,* 449–51.

343. See Wilkins, *Discipleship in the Ancient World,* 116–24.

344. E.g., R. Abba Benjamin (*b. Ber.* 6a); R. Abba bar Ahda (*y. Ber.* 1.6.3d); R. Hdiyya bar Abba (*y. Ta‘an.* 4.5.68b). See other examples in *DJBP*, 2–3.

345. See Levine, *The Ancient Synagogue*, 404–6.

346. Deut. 14:1; 32:6; Ps. 103:13; Hos. 11:1; Jer. 3:4; 31:9.

347. E.g., *Jub.* 1:24, 28; 19:29; *Jos. Asen.* 12:14; Sir. 23:1, 4; Wisd. Sol. 2:16–20; 14:3; Tobit 13:4; 4Q372 1:16; 1QH 9:35 [17:35]. See in "Father, God as," *DJBP*, 224.

348. A direct allusion to the original leader of the Qumran community was first suggested by C. Spicq, "Une allusion au docteur de justice dans Matthieu, XXIII, 10?," *RB* 66 (1959): 387–96, but followed recently by several others, including M. Eugene Boring, "The Gospel of Matthew: Introduction, Commentary, Reflections," *The New Interpreter's Bible* (Nashville: Abingdon, 1995), 3:432.

349. Most commentators doubt a direct allusion, including Davies and Allison, *Matthew*, 3:278; Carson, "Matthew," 476 n. 10.

350. E.g., Dionysius of Halicarnassus, *Jud. De Thuc.* 3, 4; Plutarch, *Moralia* 327; Vettius Valens 115, 18; PGiess. 80, 7; 11; POxy. 930, 6; 20 (BAGD). See Bruce W. Winter, "The Messiah as the Tutor: The Meaning of καθηγητής in Matthew 23:10," *TynBul* 42 (1991): 152–57.

351. E.g., Robertson, *Grammar*, 138.

352. E.g., six "woes" in Isa. 5:8–22; five in Hab. 2:6–20; cf. the two series of three in Rev. 8:13; 9:12; 11:14; 12:12; and 18:10, 16, 19.

353. See Werblowsky and Wigoder, "Proselytes," *EJR*, 312–13.

354. Josephus, *J.W.* 2.20.2 §§560–561.

355. Josephus, *Ant.* 20.2.2–4 §§24–48.

356. Especially suggested by the work of Scot McKnight, *A Light Among the Gentiles: Jewish Missionary Activity in the Second Temple Period* (Minneapolis: Fortress, 1991), esp, 106–8; followed by, among others, Blomberg, *Matthew*, 344; Hagner, *Matthew*, 669; Donald Senior, *Matthew* (ANTC; Nashville: Abingdon, 1998), 261.

357. E.g., Tacitus, *Hist.* 5.5.

358. See Louis H. Feldman, *Jew and Gentile in the Ancient World: Attitudes and Interactions from Alexander to Justinian* (Princeton, N.J.: Princeton Univ. Press, 1993); Werblowsky and Wigoder, "Proselytes," 312–13; Keener, *Matthew*, 548.

359. Lev. 27:30–33; Num. 18:21, 24; Deut. 12:5–19; etc.

360. Colin J. Hemer, "Bury, Grave, Tomb," *NIDNTT*, 1:265.

361. See Rachel Hachlili, "Burials," *ABD*, 1:789–94.

362. Hagner, *Matthew*, 677; Davies and Allison, *Matthew*, 3:319; Keener, *Matthew*, 556.

363. Morris, *Matthew*, 589 n. 45.

364. *b. B. Bat.* 4a.

365. Josephus, *J.W.* 5.5.6 §§222–223. The Mishnah tractate *Middot* ("Measurements") renders a description of the temple as it was before its destruction in A.D. 70. The tractate is traditionally assigned to Rabbi Eliezer ben Jacob, who was a young boy at the time of the first Jewish revolt in the A.D. 60s (cf. *m. Mid.* 1:2, 9; 2:6; 5:3).

366. For an overview, see Michael O. Wise, "Temple," *DJG*, 811–17.

367. Neusner and Green, "Bar Kosiba, Simon," *DJBP*, 77–78.

368. Isa. 13:8; 21:3; 42:14; Jer. 30:7–10; Hos. 13:13.

369. Isa. 26:17–19; 66:7–11; Jer. 22:23; Mic. 4:9–10.

370. See Dan. 9:27 NIV; cf. 12:11, which is similar to the expressions in 8:13; 11:31.

371. 1 Macc. 1:54; cf. 2 Macc. 6:2.

372. See Josephus, *Ant.* 18.3.1 §§55–59. For discussion see Paul Barnett, *Jesus and the Rise of Early Christianity: A History of New Testament Times* (Downers Grove, Ill.: InterVarsity, 1999), 144–48.

373. Philo, *Embassy* 200–203; Josephus, *Ant.* 18.8.1–9 §§257–309. See F. F. Bruce, *New Testament History* (New York: Doubleday, 1969), 253–57.

374. For discussion of related issues, see Gleason L. Archer Jr., "Daniel" (*EBC* 7; Grand Rapids: Zondervan, 1985), 111–21.

375. Eusebius, *Eccl. Hist.* 3.5.3.

376. See Joseph Patrich, "Hideouts in the Judean Wilderness," *BAR* 15.5 (Sept./Oct. 1989): 32–42. For an overview of these groups, see Horsley and Hanson, *Bandits, Prophets, and Messiahs.*

377. Josephus, *J.W.* 4.9.3–5, 7 §§508–515.

378. Ibid., 5.6.1 §§250–51.

379. Cf. Ezek. 32:7; Joel 2:31; 3:15; Amos 8:9; 2 Esd. 5:4–5; 7:39; *T. Mos.* 10:5.

380. Isa. 18:3; 27:13; Jer. 4:21; 6:1; 51:27; 1QM 3–4, 8, 16, 17–18; cf. 1 Cor. 15:51–52; 1 Thess. 4:16.

381. Ex. 32:6; Isa. 28:7; 56:12; 1 Cor. 10:7; Gal. 5:21.

382. See J. S. Wright and J. A. Thompson, "Marriage," *IBD*, 2:955–56; Victor P. Hamilton, "Marriage (OT and ANE)," *ABD*, 4:559–69; Jeremias, *Parables of Jesus*, 173–74.

383. Isa. 54:4–6; 62:4–5; Ezek. 16:7–34; Hos. 2:19.

384. For a good discussion of the different types of lamps, see R. E. Nixon, "Lamp, Lampstand, Lantern," *IBD*, 2:871–73.

385. Ex. 22:25; Lev. 25:35–37; Deut. 23:19.

386. For discussion, see "Interest," *DJBP*, 319.

387. Matt. 9:36; 10:6; 15:24; cf. Ezek. 34.

388. Matt. 10:16; cf. 26:31 quoting Zech. 13:7; John 10.

389. In the New Testament the form *eriphos* occurs only here and the diminutive *eriphion* in 10:33; Luke 15:29 has a textual variant between the two essentially synonymous forms.

390. George S. Cansdale, "Goats," *ZPEB*, 2:739–41.

391. Cf. *m. Pesaḥ* 5:1. This is the modern practice.

392. Nisan 15–21; cf. Ex. 12:1–20; 23:15; 34:18; Deut. 16:1–8; Luke 22:1, 7. See discussion of the original Passover in Walter C. Kaiser Jr., "Exodus" (*EBC* 1; Grand Rapids: Zondervan, 1990), 371–76.

393. See the helpful overview of the Sanhedrin in Keener, *Matthew*, 614–16.

394. E.g., Josephus, *Ant.* 18.4.3 §95.

395. Josephus, *Ant.* 17.9.3 §§213–18; *J.W.* 2.6.2 §§88–90.

396. Rousseau and Arav, *Jesus and His World*, 216–20.

397. Josephus *Ant.* 14.2.1 §21; 17.9.1 §213; 18.2.2 §29; idem, *J.W.* 2.1.3 §10. See Robert H. Stein, *Jesus the Messiah: A Survey of the Life of Christ* (Downers Grove, Ill.: InterVarsity, 1996), 200–201.

398. Bargil Pixner, "Church of the Apostles Found on Mt. Zion," *BAR* 16.3 (May/June 1990): 16–35, 60. Pixner contends that the reconstructed building was intended as a Judeo-Christian synagogue.

399. See the striking illustrations at "Pompeii," *Encyclopædia Britannica* Online.

400. For various customs, see Gene Schramm, "Meal Customs (Jewish)," and Dennis E. Smith, "Meal Customs (Greco-Roman)," *ABD*, 4:648–53.

401. For an overview of Second Temple Jewish practices, see "Haggadah of Passover," *DJBP*, 266–67; Joachim Jeremias, *The Eurcharistic Words of Jesus* (trans Norman Perrin; London: SCM, 1966), 84–88. For an overview of contemporary Passover rituals, see Werblowsky and Wigoder, "Haggadah, Passover," *EJR*, 166–67.

402. See Werblowsky and Wigoder, "Haggadah, Passover," for modern expressions of the cups.

403. Werblowsky and Wigoder, "Cups," *EJR*, 104; idem, "Haggadah, Passover," 166–67.

404. Walter C. Kaiser Jr., *The Messiah in the Old Testament* (Grand Rapids: Zondervan, 1995), 226–27.

405. Cf. Luke 13:19; John 19:41.

406. Joan E. Taylor, "The Garden of Gethsemane: NOT the Place of Jesus' Arrest," *BAR* 21.4 (July/Aug. 1995): 26–35, 62. See also Rousseau and Arav, *Jesus and His World*, 110–11.

407. Josephus, *J.W.* 5.12.4 §523.

408. Taylor, "The Garden of Gethsemane," 35.

409. Cf. John 18:3, 12; see comments on Matt. 27:65; 28:11.

410. Matt. 10:4; 26:25; 27:3; Mark 8:19; Luke 6:15–16; John 6:71; 12:4; 13:2; 18:2, 5. See Wilkins, *Following the Master*, 164ff.

411. Josephus, *J.W.* 2.8.4 §§125–26.

412. For an extensive discussion, see Brown, *Death of the Messiah*, 340–57.

413. Matt. 16:16; cf. 2 Sam. 7:14; Ps. 89:26–27.

414. Cf. "Blaspheme," *DJBP*, 97–98.

415. Keener, *Matthew*, 655, citing Martin Dibelius, *Jesus* (trans. C. B. Hedrick and F. C. Grant; Philadelphia: Westminster, 1949), 40. See also Morris, *Matthew*, 689 n. 123; Richard A. Horsley, *Archaeology, History, and Society in Galilee: The Social Context of Jesus and the Rabbis* (Valley Forge, Pa: Trinity, 1996), 162–71.

416. See Flusser, *Jesus*, 205–6.

417. 11QTemple Scroll 64:7–8; cf. also *t. Ter.* 7:20 and *y. Ter.* 7:46b.

418. See the extended discussion in Leen and Kathleen Ritmeyer, "Akeldama: Potter's Field or High Priest's Tomb?" *BAR* 20 (Nov./Dec. 1994): 22–35, 76–78; also in the same issue, Gideon Avni and Zvi Greenhut, "Akeldama: Resting Place of the Rich and Famous," *BAR* 20 (Nov./Dec. 1994): 36–46.

419. Bruce M. Metzger, *A Textual Commentary on the Greek New Testament* (2d ed.; New York: United Bible Societies, 1994), 56.

420. W. F. Albright and C. S. Mann, *Matthew* (AB 26; Garden City, N.Y.: Doubleday, 1971), 343–44.

421. Josephus, *J.W.* 5.4.4 §177ff.

422. Rousseau and Arav, *Jesus and His World*, 12–14.

423. Cf. Josephus, *Ant.* 20.8.11 §§1223–24; idem, *J.W.* 6.7.1 §358. See Rainer Riesner, "Archaeology and Geography," *DJG*, 42–43.

424. Dio Cassius 44.17.1; cited in Davies and Allison, *Matthew*, 3:587 n. 38.

425. Deut. 21:6–9; Ps. 26:6; 73:13.

426. Herodotus, *Hist.* 1:35; Virgil, *Aen.* 2.719; Sophocles, *Ajax* 654.

427. *Let. Aris.* 305–6.

428. E.g., Matt. 1:21; 2:6; 4:16; 15:8.

429. E.g., Lev. 20:9; Josh. 2:19; 2 Sam. 1:16; Ezek. 18:13; Acts 5:28; 18:6.

430. *m. Sanh.*; *m. Mak.*

431. Rousseau and Arav, *Jesus and His World*, 151–52.

432. Josephus, *J.W.* 5.5.8 §244.

433. For background to the Roman military contingents, see Ferguson, *Backgrounds of Early Christianity*, 46–52.

434. Page, *Jesus and the Land*, 149–51.

435. Plutarch, *Moralia* 554A/B; cf. 554D; *De sera numinis vindicta* (*On the Delays of Divine Vengeance*) 9.

436. *b. Sanh.* 43a, citing Prov. 31:6.

437. The most important study as it helps clarify Jesus' fate is Hengel, *Crucifixion*, 77.

438. Joe Zias and James H. Charlesworth, "Crucifixion: Archaeology, Jesus, and the Dead Sea Scrolls," in *Jesus and the Dead Sea Scrolls*, ed. J. H. Charlesworth (New York: Doubleday, 1992), 273–89; Joe Zias and E. Sekeles, "The Crucified Man from Giv'at ha-Mivtar—A Reappraisal," *IEJ* 35 (1985): 22–27; V. Tzaferis, "Jewish Tombs at and near Giv'at ha-Mivtar, Jerusalem," *IEJ* 20 (1970): 18–32; idem, "Crucifixion—the Archeological Evidence," *BAR* 11.1 (Jan./Feb. 1985): 44–53; N. Haas, "Anthropological Observations on the Skeletal Remains from Giv'at ha-Mivtar," *IEJ* 20 (1970): 38–59.

439. See Frederick T. Zugibe, "Two Questions About Crucifixion: Does the Victim Die of Asphyxiation? Would Nails in the Hands Hold the Weight of the Body?" *BRev* 5.2 (1989): 34–43.

440. Quintilian, *Declamationes* 274 (cited in Hengel, *Crucifixion*, 50 n. 14).

441. Ex. 10:21; Ps. 88:13; Prov. 2:13–14; Matt. 25:30; 1 Thess. 5:4–7.

442. Joel 2:2; Amos 5:18, 20; Zeph. 1:15; Matt. 24:29; Rev. 6:12–17.

443. Michael J. Wilkins, "Darkness," *EDBT*, 142–43; Hans Conzelmann, "σκότος, κτλ." *TDNT*, 7:423–45; H.-C Hahn, "Darkness," *NIDNTT*, 1:420–25.

444. The saying in Matthew's Gospel may be a transliteration that is partly from the Hebrew (*ēli ēli*) and partly from the Aramaic (*lema sebachthani*) (Metzger, *Textual Commentary*, 58–59, 99–100). The best MSS have "Eli, Eli, Lema Sabachthani?" although it is more likely that the entire saying is a variation of Aramaic, since the Aramaic Targum to Psalm 22:1 has *ēli ēli*. (See Davies and Allison, *Matthew*, 3:624.)

445. Joachim Jeremias, "Ἠλ(ε)ίας," *TDNT*, 2:930–31.

446. See Hans W. Heidland, "ὄξος," *TDNT*, 5:288–89.

447. E.g., Ex. 26:31–35; 27:21; 30:6; 2 Chron. 3:14; Heb. 6:19; 9:3; 10:20.

448. E.g., Ex. 27:37; Num. 3:26.

449. Josephus gives a detailed description of the curtain in *J.W.* 5.5.4 §212–13. (See comments on Mark 15:38.)

450. Eph. 2:11–22; Heb. 10:20.

451. Matt. 27:55–56, 61; cf. Mark 15:40–41; Luke 23:49, 55–56; John 19:25–27.

452. Matt. 28:1; cf. Mark 16:1; Luke 24:1, 10–11; John 20:1–18.

453. 11QTemple Scroll 64:11–12.

454. Cf. Josephus, *Ant.* 13.5.9 §127.

455. Michael J. Wilkins, "Named and Unnamed Disciples in Matthew: A Literary/ Theological Study" (*SBLSP* 30; Atlanta: Scholars, 1991), 418–39.

456. *m. Sanh.* 6:5; cf. *b. Sanh.* 46b; 11QTemple Scroll 64:11–12. See Colin J. Hemer, "Bury, Grave, Tomb," *NIDNTT*, 1:263–66.

457. Joseph and Jacob were embalmed using Egyptian practice; cf. Gen. 50:2, 26.

458. Shemuel Safrai and Menahem Stern, eds., *The Jewish People in the First Century* (Philadelphia: Fortress, 1974–76), 2:776–77.

459. See "Burial," *DJBP*, 103–4.

460. For background, see Rousseau and Arav, *Jesus and His World*, 164–69.

461. See Amos Kloner, "Did a Rolling Stone Close Jesus' Tomb?" *BAR* 25.5 (Sept./Oct. 1999): 23–29, 76.

462. See citation of examples in "Burial Sites," *DJBP*, 104.

463. Cf. Matt. 27:56, 61; 28:1; Mark 15:40–41; 16:1; Luke 8:1–3; 23:55; 24:1, 10–11; John 19:25; 20:1ff.

464. See the drawings showing the primary faults in D. R. Bowes, "Earthquake," *ZPEB*, 2:178–80.

465. See Kloner, "Did a Rolling Stone Close Jesus' Tomb?" 22–29, 76.

466. Cf. Rev. 4:5; 16:17–18.

467. Cf. 27:60–61; Mark 15:46–47; Luke 23:55.

468. Matt. 28:1–6; Mark 16:1–6; Luke 24:1–8; John 20:1–16.

469. Matt. 4:9–10; 14:33; Acts 10:25–26; 14:11–15; Rev. 22:8–9.

470. Cf. Petronius, *Satyricon* 112; Acts 12:19.

471. Favoring a reconstruction that understands the Decree being given in response to Christian and Jewish disputes over the empty tomb is E. M. Blaiklock, "Nazareth Decree," *ZPEB*, 391–92; see also idem, *The Archaeology of the New Testament* (Nashville: Nelson, 1984). Doubting any association with the Christian-Jewish controversy is Raymond E. Brown, *The Death of the Messiah*, 2:1294.

472. See 4:8; 5:1–2; 14:23; 15:29; 17:1; 24:3; 26:30. The phrase used here (*eis to oros*) often carries a looser connotation of "hills" as opposed to a specific mountain.

Sidebar and Chart Notes

A-1. Irenaeus, *Against Heresies*, 5.33.4.

A-2. Ibid., 3.1.1.

A-3. See Joachim Jeremias, *Jerusalem in the Time of Jesus: An Investigation into Economic and Social Conditions During the New Testament Period* (1962; ET; Philadelphia: Fortress, 1969), 363–68; J. S. Wright and J. A. Thompson, "Marriage," *IBD*, 2:955–56;

Victor P. Hamilton, "Marriage (OT and ANE)," *ABD*, 4:559–69.

A-4. Heb. ʾērûsîn and qiddûšâ.

A-5. *m. ʾAbot.* 5:21; *b. Qidd.* 29b–30a.

A-6. See *m. Ketub.* 1:2; 4:2.

A-7. *m. Ketub.* 1:5; *b. Ketub.* 9b, 12a.

A-8. Cf. Josephus, *Ant.* 7.8.1 §168.

A-9. *m. Ketub.* 5:2; *m. Ned.* 10:5.

A-10. Heb. keٰtûbâ.

A-11. ḥuppâ ("canopy"); cf. Ps. 19:5; Tobit 7:16.

A-12. See the work of the astronomer David Hughes, *The Star of Bethlehem: An Astronomer's Confirmation* (New York: Walker, 1979). Another astronomer discusses an alternative conjunction of Jupiter and Venus on June 17, 2 B.C. (John Mosley, *The Christmas Star* [Los Angeles: Griffith Observatory, 1988]), but that date is rejected by most because it is after the accepted dating of King Herod's death in 4 B.C.

A-13. Mark Kidger, *The Star of Bethlehem: An Astronomer's View* (Princeton, N.J.: Princeton Univ. Press, 1999).

A-14. E.g., Rev. 1:16, 20; 2:1; 3:1. See also Job 38:7; Dan. 8:10; *1 En.* 43:1–4, 90:20–27; *2 En.* 29; *3 En.* 46; *Pseudo Philo* 32:13–15; *Jos. Asen.* 14:1–14; *T. Sol.* 20:14–17; *b. ʿAbod. Zar.* 43a-b. Jesus is referred to as the "morning star" (Rev. 22:16; cf. 2:28; also 2 Peter 1:9).

A-15. Rev. 8:10, 11; 9:1. Cf. *1 En.* 86:1–6; 90:20–27; *2 En.* 29. Satan is referred to as a fallen morning star (Isa. 14:12–13).

A-16. E.g., *1 En.* 1:2 ff.; *T. Levi* 2–5; *History of the Rechabites* 1:3 and throughout.

A-17. Dale C. Allison, "What Was the Star that Guided the Magi?" *BRev* 9.6 (1993): 24.

A-18. For a thorough overview of Herod's life, see Harold W. Hoehner, "Herodian Dynasty," *DJG*, 317–26; Lee I. Levine, "Herod the Great," *ABD*, 3:161–69; Stewart Henry Perowne, "Herod," *Encyclopædia Britannica*. For the most extensive recent study, see Peter Richardson, *Herod: King of the Jews and Friend of the Romans* (rev. ed; Philadelphia: Fortress, 1999).

A-19. Josephus, *Ant.* 14.8.1–5 §§127–55.

A-20. Strabo, *Geog.* 16.2.46.

A-21. *b. B. Bat.* 4a.

A-22. Josephus, *Ant.* 17.1.3 §§19–22.

A-23. Ibid., 16.10.5–16.11.8 §§324–404.

A-24. Ibid., 17.10.1 §253.

A-25. Macrobius, *Saturnalia* 2.f.11.

A-26. Josephus calculates the length of Herod's reign as thirty-seven years from his accession or thirty-four from the time of his effective reign (Josephus, *Ant.* 17.8.1 §191; idem, *J.W.* 1.1.8 §665), and those years indicate that he died in 4 B.C. Therefore, Herod's death is placed by most scholars at the latter part of March, 4 B.C. For extensive discussion, see Harold W. Hoehner, *Chronological Aspects of the Life of Christ* (Grand Rapids: Zondervan, 1977), 11–27.

A-27. Josephus gives a most graphic description of Herod's terminal disease (*Ant.* 17.6.5 §§168–69), which some think was syphilis or arteriosclerosis (Richardson, *Herod*, 18).

A-28. Josephus, *Ant.* 17.6.5 §§174–79; 17.8.2 §193.

A-29. Ibid., 17.8.3 §§196–199.

A-30. Ibid., 17.8.1 §191.

A-31. E.g., the diseased person (Lev. 14:1–8); men with bodily discharges and menstruating women (ch. 15); the high priest before and after rites of atonement (16:4, 24).

A-32. Matt. 15:1–2; the later Mishnah has an entire tractate, *Miqwaʾot*, devoted to ritual washings.

A-33. 1QS 3:4–12.

A-34. Josephus, *Ant.* 13.5.9 §171.

A-35. The composition of the "Sanhedrin" is debated by modern scholars because the ancient sources (e.g., Josephus, New Testament, and the rabbinic literature) demonstrate a changing nature of this body. See comments on 26:59; cf. Anthony J. Saldarini, *Pharisees, Scribes, and Sadducees* (Wilmington, Del.: Michael Glazier, 1988).

A-36. 2 Cor. 4:4; Eph. 2:1–2; Rev. 13:1–2.

A-37. Num. 34:11; Deut. 3:17; Josh. 12:3; 13:27.

A-38. John 6:1; 21:1.

A-39. Luke 5:1, 2; 8:22, 23, 33. "Lake Gennesaret" is a grecized version of the Hebrew "Lake of Kinneret."

A-40. Josephus, *J.W.*, 2.20.6 §573; 3.10.1 §463; 3.10.7 §506; 3.10.7–8 §§515–16; idem, *Ant.* 5.1.22 §84; 13.5.7 §158; 18.2.1, 3 §28, 36; cf. 1 Macc. 11:67. Pliny assumes that the usual name is the "lake of Gennesaret" (*Nat. Hist.* 5.15, 71).

A-41. Strabo, *Geog.* 16.2; Pliny, *Nat. Hist.* 5.15, 71; Josephus, *J.W.* 3.10.7 §506.

A-42. E.g., Matt. 15:32; Mark 8:2.

A-43. Matt. 8:24; 14:19, 24; Mark 4:37; Luke 8:23; John 6: 1–4, 18. See Seán Freyne, *Galilee from Alexander the Great to Hadrian* (Wilmington, Del.: Michael Glazier, 1980); idem, "Galilee, Sea of," *ABD*, 2:900; Rainer Riesner, "Archeology and Geography," *DJG*, 37.

A-44. 1 Thess. 4:11–12; 2 Thess. 3:6–15; 1 Tim. 5:8.

A-45. Prov. 19:17; Acts 11:27–30; Rom. 15:25–27; 2 Cor. 8:1–15; Gal. 6:7–10; Eph. 4:28; 1 Tim. 5:3–7.

A-46. 1 Cor. 9:3–14; Phil. 4:14–19; 1 Tim. 5:17–18.

A-47. 1 Sam. 17:43; Ps. 22:16; Prov. 26:11.

A-48. See "Dog," "Pork," *DJBP*, 172; "Animals," "Dogs," "Swine," *DBI*, 29, 213–14; Edwin Firmage, "Zoology," *ABD*, 6:1130–35, 1143–44.

A-49. For other examples, see Hans Dieter Betz, *The Sermon on the Mount: A Commentary on the Sermon on the Mount, Including the Sermon on the Plain (Matthew 5:3—7:27 and Luke 6:20–49)* (Hermeneia; Minneapolis: Fortress, 1995), 509–16.

A-50. See P. S. Alexander, "Jesus and the Golden Rule," in *Hillel and Jesus: Comparative Studies of Two Major Religious Leaders*, ed. James H. Charlesworth and Loren L. Johns (Minneapolis: Fortress, 1997), 363–88.

A-51. Everett Ferguson, *Backgrounds of Early Christianity* (2d ed.; Grand Rapids: Eerdmans, 1993), 47–48.

A-52. For a popular recounting, see James F. Strange and Hershel Shanks, "Has the House Where Jesus Stayed in Capernaum Been Found?: Italian Archaeologists Believe They Have Uncovered St. Peter's Home," vol. 2 of *Archaeology in the World of Herod, Jesus and Paul, Archaeology and the Bible: The Best of BAR*; (Washington D.C.: Biblical Archaeological Society, 1990), 188–99.

A-53. James H. Charlesworth, *Jesus Within Judaism: New Light from Exciting Archaeological Discoveries* (ABRL; New York: Doubleday, 1988), 109–15.

A-54. E.g., Ezek. 2:1, 3, 6, 8, etc.; cf. Dan. 8:17.

A-55. Although the dating of this portion of *1 Enoch* is debated, current scholarly opinion dates it around the time of Herod the Great. Cf. E. Isaac, "1 (Ethiopic Apocalypse of) Enoch," in *The Old Testament Pseudepigrapha*, ed. James H. Charlesworth (Garden City, N.Y.: Doubleday, 1983), 1:7.

A-56. Matt. 8:20; 9:6; 11:19; 12:8; 12:32, 40.

A-57. Matt. 16:13, 27–28; 17:9, 12, 22; 20:18, 28; 26:2, 24, 45.

A-58. Matt. 10:23; 13:37, 41; 19:28; 24:27, 30, 37, 39, 44; 25:31; 26:64.

A-59. See, respectively, Deut. 22:13–19, Lev. 20:17–21, Num. 5:1–4. See also *m. Mak.* 3.1–2.

A-60. Levine, *The Ancient Synagogue*, 131–32, 417; Carl Schneider, "μαστιγόω, μάστιξ," *TDNT*, 4:515–19.

A-61. For brief overviews, see F. F. Bruce, "Machaerus," *IBD*, 2:928–29; Stanislao Loffreda, "Machaerus," *ABD*, 4:457–58.

A-62. Josephus, *J.W.* 7.6.2 §171.

A-63. Ibid., 7.6.2 §172.

A-64. Pliny, *Nat. Hist.* 5.15.72.

A-65. Cf. Josephus, *J.W.* 7.6.1 §§163–70.

A-66. Josephus, *Ant.* 18.5.1–2 §§112, 119.

A-67. Josephus, *J.W.* 7.6.1 §§163–64; 7.6.4 §§190–209.

A-68. *t. Mak.* 3:8; *b. Menah.* 85a, 85b.

A-69. See "Chorazin," *DJBP*, 118–19; Rousseau and Arav, *Jesus and His World*, 52–54.

A-70. Most archaeologists today consider the site of ancient Bethsaida to be et-Tell. A minority position held by Mendel Nun contends for el-Araj to be the real Bethsaida. See Mendel Nun, "Has Bethsaida Finally Been Found?" *Jerusalem Perspective* (July/Aug. 1998).

A-71. Rami Arav, Richard A. Freund, and John F. Shroder, "Bethsaida Rediscovered: Long-Lost City Found North of Galilee Shore," *BAR* 26.1 (Jan./Feb. 2000): 45–56. See also "Bethsaida," *DJBP*, 89.

A-72. Josephus, *J.W.* 3.10.7–8 §§515–18.

A-73. Trachonitis, Gaulanitis, Auranitis, Batanaea, and Ituraea (cf. Luke 3:1; Josephus, *Ant.* 18.4.6 §106).

A-74. Josephus, *Ant.* 18.4.6 §106.

A-75. Cf. 14:6–11; Josephus, *Ant.* 18.5.4 §136–37.

A-76. Josh. 11:17; Judg. 3:3; 1 Chron. 5:23.

A-77. Josephus, *Ant.* 15.10.3 §360–64

A-78. Ibid., 18.2.1 §28; idem, *J.W.* 2.9.1 §168. Both names reflect Philip's Roman backing.

A-79. See Seán Freyne, *Galilee From Alexander the Great to Hadrian*, 13–14, 32, 43, 52 n. 28, 136–37, 272. Also, John Kutsko, "Caesarea Philippi," *ABD*, 1:803.

A-80. Nun, "Cast Your Net," 48–51.

A-81. Cf. Gleason L. Archer, "Coins," *ZPEB*, 1:902–11; Rousseau and Arav, *Jesus and His World*, 57.

A-82. A denarius was the equivalent of a day's wage for a common laborer (see comments on 17:24-27; 22:19). Using the minimum wage of $5.15 an hour in the United States in 2000, a common laborer would receive $41.20 a day. A talent, therefore, would be worth approximately $247,200 (cf. 25:15) by modern U.S. standards. The figure would be much lower in many areas of the world. The comparisons are only suggestive.

A-83. T. A. Holland, "Jericho," *ABD*, 3:737.

A-84. Cf. Ehud Netzer, "Jericho: Roman Period," *ABD*, 3:737–39; Rousseau and Arav, *Jesus and His World*, 132–36.

A-85. Cf. Matt. 21–28; Mark 11–16; Luke 19–24; John 12–21. See comments on 26:1 for a discussion of the chronological problems.

A-86. For background, dating and discussion, see Ferguson, *Backgrounds of Early Christianity*, 24-38. A convenient collection of charts of Roman (and other) organizational entities is found in House, *Chronological and Background Charts*, 64-65, etc.

A-87. For thorough discussion, see Levine, "Cathedra of Moses," *The Ancient Synagogue*, 323–27.

A-88. Levine, *The Ancient Synagogue*, 326.

A-89. See Neusner and Green, "Tefillin" and "Tefillin, Archaeology of," *DJBP*, 621.

A-90. Josephus, *Ant.* 18.2.2 §35.

A-91. Ibid., 18.4.3 §95.

A-92. Ibid., 20.10 §§224–251. See David Flusser, *Jesus* (2d ed.; Jerusalem: Magnes, 1998), 195–205; Bruce Chilton, "Caiaphas," *ABD*, 1:803–6.

A-93. Cf. 1QHabakkuk Pesher 1:13; 9:4–5.

A-94. Flusser, *Jesus*, 195.

A-95. For narrative on the discovery and the ancient burial practices, as well as drawings and pictures, see Hershel Shanks, *In the Temple of Solomon and the Tomb of Caiaphas* (Washington, D.C.: BAS, 1993), 35–45.

A-96. See also Matt. 27:62; Mark 15:42; Luke 23:54; John 19:14, 31, 42.

A-97. Matt. 27:62; Mark 15:42; Luke 23:54; John 19:14, 31, 42.

A-98. Cf. John 13:1–2; 13:27–29; 18:28; 19:14, 31.

A-99. Annie Jaubert, *The Date of the Last Supper*, trans. Isaac Rafferty (Staten Island, N.Y.: Alba, 1965).

A-100. Harold Hoehner, "Chronology," *DJG*, 121; so also Robert L. Thomas and Stanley N. Gundry, eds., *The NIV Harmony of the Gospels* (San Francisco: Harper & Row, 1988), 312–13.

A-101. D. A. Carson, *The Gospel According to John* (Grand Rapids: Eerdmans, 1991), 455–58; so also Blomberg, *Historical Reliability of the Gospels*, 175–78.

A-102. E.g., Josephus, *J.W.* 2.17.5 §422; 2.17.6 §§426–27, 429.

A-103. These accounts include the journal of the Bordeaux Pilgrim (c. A.D. 333), the account of Theodosius (A.D. 530), and the Madaba mosaic map, the earliest known map of Jerusalem (c. A.D. 560).

A-104. For a recounting of the excavation and the possible relationship to the Gospel accounts, see Arthur Rupprecht, "The House of Annas-Caiaphas," *Archaeology in the Biblical World* 1.1 (Spring 1991): 4–17. See also Rousseau and Arav, *Jesus and His World*, 136–39.

A-105. Pilate is called Pontius Pilate in the New Testament in Luke 3:1; 4:27; 1 Tim. 6:13.

A-106. Josephus, *Ant.* 18.2.2 §35; 18.3.1–2 §§55–62; 18.4.1–2 §§85–89; idem, *J.W.* 2.9.2–4 §§169–77.

A-107. Philo, *Embassy* 299–305.

A-108. Tacitus, *Annals* 15.44.

A-109. Barnett, *Jesus and the Rise of Early Christianity*, 144–49; cf. Daniel R. Schwartz,

"Pontius Pilate," *ABD*, 5:395–401; Rousseau and Arav, *Jesus and His Times*, 225–27.

A-110. Mark 15:7; Luke 23:19; cf. Acts 3:14.

A-111. Horsley and Hanson, *Bandits, Prophets, and Messiahs*, 48–87.

A-112. See comments on 27:38; Mark 15:27.

A-113. Excerpt from Michael J. Wilkins, "Barabbas," *ABD*, 1:607.

A-114. "Despite the Christian use of Matthew for anti-Semitic attacks, the harsh polemics in the gospel do not attack Jews as a group but the leaders of the Jews (scribes, Pharisees, Sadducees, chief priest, elders) and those people who have been misled into hostility toward Jesus" ("Matthew, Jews in the Gospel of," *DJBP*, 416).

A-115. Gabriel Barkay, "The Garden Tomb: Was Jesus Buried Here?" *BAR* 12.2 (March/April 1986): 40–57; John McRay, "Tomb Typology and the Tomb of Jesus," *Archaeology in the Biblical World* 2.2 (Spring 1994): 34–44.

A-116. Dan Bahat, "Does the Holy Sepulchre Church Mark the Burial of Jesus?" *BAR* 12.3 (May/June 1986): 26–45; Joan E. Taylor, "Golgotha: A Reconsideration of the Evidence for the Sites of Jesus' Crucifixion and Burial," *NTS* 44 (1998): 180–203.

A-117. Josephus, *Ag. Ap.* 2.25 §201.

A-118. *m. Ber.* 3:3; *m. Sukkah* 2:8.

A-119. *t. Ber.* 7:18.

A-120. *m. Ker.* 6:9; cf. *m. Ned.* 9:1.

A-121. *b. Qidd.* 31b.

A-122. This material is developed more fully in Michael J. Wilkins, "Women in the Teaching and Example of Jesus," in *Complementarity in Church Ministry*, Robert L. Saucy and Judy TenElshof, eds. (Chicago: Moody, forthcoming).

A-123. E.g., Isa. 26:19; Dan. 12:2; 2 Macc. 7; *1 En.* 102; *2 Bar.* 49–51.

A-124. E.g., *m. Sanh.* 10:1; *b. Roš Haš.* 16b–17a.

A-125. See "Amidah," "Resurrection," *DJBP*, 30–31, 526–27.

A-126. Rom. 8:29; 1 Cor. 15; 2 Cor. 3:18.

A-127. E.g., Rabbi Akiba; *m. Yebam.* 16:7. See also *m. Šeb.* 4:1; Josephus, *Ant.* 4.8.15 §219. See Witherington, *Women in the Ministry of Jesus*, 9–10, for a discussion of the mixed rabbinic attitudes toward women's ability to give witness.

A-128. For discussion of the broader issues, see William L. Craig, "Did Jesus Rise From the Dead?" in *Jesus Under Fire: Modern Scholarship Reinvents the Historical Jesus*, Michael J. Wilkins and J. P. Moreland, eds. (Grand Rapids: Zondervan, 1995), 151, 155.

CREDITS FOR PHOTOS AND MAPS

ALSO AVAILABLE

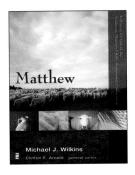

Matthew

Michael J. Wilkins

Clinton E. Arnold *general editor*

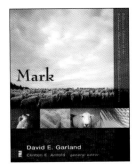

Mark

David E. Garland

Clinton E. Arnold *general editor*

Luke

Mark L. Strauss

Clinton E. Arnold *general editor*

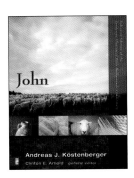

John

Andreas J. Köstenberger

Clinton E. Arnold *general editor*

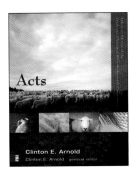

Acts

Clinton E. Arnold

Clinton E. Arnold *general editor*

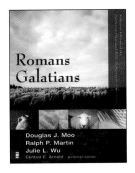

**Romans
Galatians**

Douglas J. Moo
Ralph P. Martin
Julie L. Wu

Clinton E. Arnold *general editor*

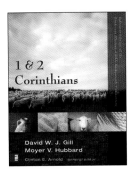

**1 & 2
Corinthians**

David W. J. Gill
Moyer V. Hubbard

Clinton E. Arnold *general editor*

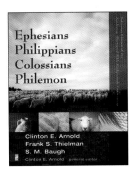

**Ephesians
Philippians
Colossians
Philemon**

Clinton E. Arnold
Frank S. Thielman
S. M. Baugh

Clinton E. Arnold *general editor*

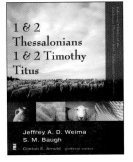

**1 & 2
Thessalonians
1 & 2 Timothy
Titus**

Jeffrey A. D. Weima
S. M. Baugh

Clinton E. Arnold *general editor*

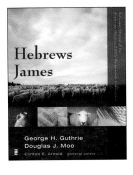

**Hebrews
James**

George H. Guthrie
Douglas J. Moo

Clinton E. Arnold *general editor*

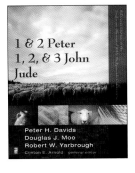

**1 & 2 Peter
1, 2, & 3 John
Jude**

Peter H. Davids
Douglas J. Moo
Robert W. Yarbrough

Clinton E. Arnold *general editor*

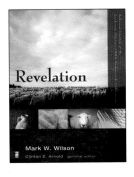

Revelation

Mark W. Wilson

Clinton E. Arnold *general editor*

We want to hear from you. Please send your comments about this book to us in care of zreview@zondervan.com. Thank you.

ZONDERVAN.com/
AUTHORTRACKER
follow your favorite authors